METAPHYSICAL
POETRY

EDWARD ARNOLD

© EDWARD ARNOLD (PUBLISHERS) LTD 1970

First published 1970 by
Edward Arnold (Publishers) Ltd
41 Maddox Street, London W 1

Boards edition SBN: 7131 5473 X
Paper edition SBN: 7131 5492 6

Printed in Great Britain by
Butler & Tanner Ltd, Frome and London

STRATFORD-UPON-AVON STUDIES 11

General Editors

MALCOLM BRADBURY
& DAVID PALMER

Already published in this series:

* *Under the general editorship of John Russell Brown and Bernard Harris*

Contents

Preface

SINCE Dr. Johnson's definitive statement in his 'Life of Cowley' that 'about the beginning of the seventeenth century appeared a race of writers that may be termed the *metaphysical poets*', it is not only the term itself which has endured, but also the notion that the poets so described formed a distinct 'race', or 'school' even, founded, as Johnson observes, 'by the example of Donne'. If Johnson's list of Donne's 'immediate successors', which includes Suckling, Waller, Denham, Cowley, and Cleveland, also omits most of the names that the modern reader would associate with 'metaphysical poetry', such as the religious poets Herbert, Vaughan, and Crashaw, with Andrew Marvell coming last but not least, the reason is that the modern reader's conception of who the 'metaphysical poets' are derives mainly from H. J. C. Grierson's anthology of 1921, *Metaphysical Lyrics and Poems of the Seventeenth Century*, and from the critical work of T. S. Eliot and F. R. Leavis. Eliot's influential essay of 1921 on 'The Metaphysical Poets' was actually a review of Grierson's selection, and this, with Grierson's fine edition of Donne in 1912, is a memorable example of the fruitful intercourse between scholarship and criticism, which some say, like Marvell's 'loves oblique', 'though infinite can never meet'.

The critical interest in early seventeenth-century poetry fostered by Eliot and Leavis in particular during the nineteen twenties and thirties, in addition to making this poetry more widely known, has produced during subsequent years some of the best work in contemporary literary studies. Inevitably, the orthodoxies of interpretation current a generation ago no longer pass unchallenged today, and an important aim in the design of this volume has been to reflect the shifts of emphasis that have taken place since the revival of modern interest in 'metaphysical poetry'. It is striking that in most of the essays here the inadequacy or arbitrariness of the term 'metaphysical' itself is more or less ignored, as though, after the numerous attempts that have been made to arrive at an appropriate definition or even to substitute a more satisfactory name, we are now resigned to accept what is merely a conventional appellation, not to be taken too seriously. On the other hand, there is a strong dissatisfaction with the idea that the 'metaphysical poets' constitute a school or race apart. There is an evident desire to see these poets in new contexts, and to relate them to a more varied and extensive awareness of the different kinds of poetic activity that belong to this period.

We therefore open the volume with Patrick Cruttwell's vigorous protest against some recent approaches to Donne, which, he argues, seem to diminish the stature and originality of the poet, as seen through the eyes of one who recalls the excitement of discovering Donne in the thirties. Whether or not these new attitudes to 'metaphysical poetry' are less exciting the rest of the volume must show; certainly, while Donne is in no danger of falling from favour (as Milton, supposedly, fell 'with remarkably little fuss' when Eliot and Leavis rearranged the map of the seventeenth century), his traditional position as the source and fountainhead of 'metaphysical poetry' is now called into question. Louis Martz, whose studies in the meditational framework of religious poetry during the period are among the most important contributions to our present understanding of these poets, warns us here against over-estimating Donne's influence. The chapters by D. J. Palmer and Brian Morris remind us that Donne's achievements in reviving the classical forms of the verse epistle and satire, however central to the poetic concerns he shared with his own generation, left little impression upon the subsequent development of these forms. And in the concluding chapter, F. J. Warnke, illustrating the similarities between the wit of the English 'metaphysical' and their European contemporaries, finds other reasons for qualifying the conventional estimate of Donne as the progenitor of a 'school'.

However, the volume was not conceived tendentiously to support any particular view of 'metaphysical poetry'. As the chapters by Molly Mahood and Joseph Summers suggest, there is much to commend the study of a single poet for his own particular qualities, regardless of the labels that might be attached to them, especially when, as in the case of Marvell, it enables us to see more clearly than usual the identifying features that belong to his work as a whole. Like Joseph Summers, who relates the art of Marvell's 'private' lyrics to that of his later and less familiar 'public' poetry, A. J. Smith and Robert Hinman break down any rigid preconceptions of 'metaphysical poetry' as a narrowly self-contained and enclosed tradition. Clearly, if we are to continue to use the term, it must be with a sense of the diverse and multiple cross-currents that link so many different kinds of poetic achievement in the seventeenth century. From this point of view, therefore, J. W. Saunders discusses the continuity and the change in a social environment that was common to 'metaphysicals' and non-metaphysicals alike. For what emerges from this collection of studies is not merely a negative rejection of traditional orthodoxy, but rather an enriched apprehension of the patterns formed by the poetry of the period as a whole, and also, we believe, a proof of the lively and rewarding interest which it continues to arouse in modern scholarship and criticism.

This volume is the first to appear in Stratford-upon-Avon Studies under our editorship. We take this opportunity of warmly acknowledging the work of our predecessors, John Russell Brown and Bernard Harris, who by establishing such a high reputation for the series have eased our task of attracting distinguished contributors, while leaving us with the charge of maintaining the editorial standards they have set.

D. J. PALMER
MALCOLM BRADBURY

March 1969

Bibliographical Note

IN references to books throughout the volume the place of publication is London unless otherwise stated.

Note

Modern Editions

The great edition of H. J. C. Grierson, *The Poems of John Donne* (2 vols., Oxford, 1912), preceded and, together with his anthology, *Metaphysical Lyrics & Poems of the Seventeenth Century* (Oxford, 1921,) made possible the renewed critical interest in Donne which was associated in particular with T. S. Eliot.

Helen Gardner's recent edition of the love poetry, *John Donne: Elegies and the Songs and Sonnets* (Oxford, 1965), re-examines the manuscript sources and offers some new readings, as well as departing from the 'traditional' arrangement of the poems as they were first published in 1633 and as preserved by Grierson.

Critical Studies. For more extensive bibliographies the reader should consult Sir Geoffrey Keynes' *Bibliography of Donne* (Second edition 1932), and the references given by Douglas Bush in *English Literature in the Earlier Seventeenth Century* (Oxford, 1945; second edition 1962) and by Robert Ellrodt, *Les Poètes Métaphysiques Anglais* (3 vols., Paris, 1960). Among the studies that have shaped modern approaches to 'metaphysical' poetry are: S. Johnson, 'Life of Cowley', *Lives of the Poets*, edited by G. Birkbeck Hill (Oxford, 1905); T. S. Eliot, 'The Metaphysical Poets' (1921) in *Selected Essays* (1932); G. Williamson, *The Donne Tradition* (1930); J. Smith, 'On Metaphysical Poetry', *Scrutiny*, 11 (1933); F. R. Leavis, *Revaluation* (1936); J. B. Leishman, *The Monarch of Wit* (1951).

Patrick Cruttwell's *The Shakespearean Moment* (1954) sets the poetry of Donne in the context of an interpretation of the English cultural situation at the end of the sixteenth century, and relates the characteristics of his style to the dramatic verse of his contemporaries, especially Shakespeare. The present chapter is in part a reconsideration of the main thesis presented there. C. S. Lewis's provocative disparagement of Donne's love poetry, 'Donne and Love Poetry in the Seventeenth Century', was published in *Seventeenth-Century Studies, presented to Sir Herbert Grierson* (Oxford, 1938). Rosemond Tuve's study, *Elizabethan and Metaphysical Imagery* (Chicago, 1947), challenges much previous criticism of Donne, and argues that as far as the rhetorical theory of poetic imagery is concerned there was no radical break between the poetry of Donne and that of earlier Elizabethan poets.

References to other studies are contained in the footnotes.

I

The Love Poetry of John Donne: Pedantique Weedes or Fresh Invention?

PATRICK CRUTTWELL

★

LITERARY criticism in the nineteen sixties, especially if its author is an academic, does not favour the unashamedly autobiographical; it prefers passive verbs, abstract nouns, and the impersonal mood. But all criticism is in truth autobiographical; the differences are in the degrees of awareness and of concealment. I propose to begin this essay by going counter to the current preference; I shall relate my personal experience, over the last forty years, of the love poetry of Donne. It has been, I suspect, thoroughly typical: which may, perhaps, give it a little more value than such egoism might promise.

It began as the experience of a thoroughly bookish, middle-class boy who went from school to Cambridge in 1929. I had read a vast amount of poetry, virtually all of it romantic. The anthologies which had moulded my taste were the *Golden Treasury* and the *Oxford Book of English Verse*. My favourite modern poet was Housman. My reading of love poetry (though I didn't know this then) was to a large extent a substitute for my total ignorance of its subject-matter. I had read nothing of Donne.

Cambridge very quickly instructed me that Donne was not only a poet who must be read but, almost, *the* poet who must be read now. The first encounter with the *Songs and Sonets* and the *Elegies* had much of the pleasures of pornography; from the *Elegies* especially—such as 'To His Mistris, going to bed'. 'Loves Progresse', and 'Loves Warre'— I derived the liberating knowledge that pornography and poetry need not be separate or mutually hostile: they might be one and the same. This was a notable enlargement of the possibilities of both. I was, of course, as far as education was concerned, simply a belated Victorian; not till many years later did I find that Donne had performed exactly the same function for many readers much nearer the Victorian age—readers such as Arthur Symons, Lytton Strachey, and Rupert Brooke. In 1969, this will seem a very naïve beginning: so it was. But it was also a beginning appropriate to the poems; for it is surely clear that the main intention of those *Elegies* is precisely to *shock*. Their assumed speaker and reader are both deliciously aware of other persons who would be much displeased by such verses, if they came across them. This, of course, was a very ancient stance for love poets. It lies behind all Ovid's *Art of Love* and *Amores*, and is made specific in the lines of Catullus:

> rumoresque senum severiorum
> omnes unius aestimemus assis

('and as for all the tittle-tattle of our Puritanical elders—well, let us not reckon it worth a farthing').

Simultaneously with this naïve yet necessary enlightenment, the reading of Donne brought some other revelations. It convinced me that a great deal of intense cerebration and intellectuality—even some tongue-in-cheek show-off displays of erudition—could be quite compatible, in the same poem, with expressions of intense passion and devout adoration: could even seem to reinforce these, in a manner I was not quite capable of analysing but was certainly capable of feeling. It was not true that poetry had to be 'simple' in order to be 'sensuous and passionate'; the 'true voice of feeling' didn't have to sound like this:

> I arise from dreams of thee
> In the first sweet sleep of night,
> When the winds are breathing low,
> And the stars are shining bright . . .

It could just as well sound like this:

> Deare love, for nothing lesse than thee
> Would I have broke this happy dreame,
>   It was a theme
> For reason, much too strong for phantasie,
> Therefore thou wak'd'st me wisely; yet
> My Dreame thou brok'st not, but continued'st it . . .

It could even consort with sardonic humour and bawdy suggestiveness.
True 'feeling' didn't have to express itself, in poetry, through a trem-
bling tone of reverential purity, like this:

> I fear thy kisses, gentle maiden,
> Thou need'st not fear mine;
> My spirit is too deeply laden
> Ever to burthen thine . . .

It might sound just as convincing—indeed, I began to suspect, a great
deal more so—when expressed with a randy bedroom directness, like
this:

> Enter these armes, for since thou thought'st it best
> Not to dreame all my dreame, let's act the rest.

Simultaneous also was a retraining of my ear for verse. The verse it
had hitherto been trained on was that which obeyed almost unvary-
ingly those precepts, first formulated in the eighteenth century, of
'smoothness' and 'harmony', which are admirably expounded by Dr.
Johnson in the eighty-eighth *Rambler*:

> That verse may be melodious and pleasing, it is necessary, not only
> that the words be so ranged as that the accent may fall in its proper
> place, but that the syllables themselves be so chosen as to flow
> smoothly into one another. This is to be effected by a proportionate
> mixture of vowels and consonants, and by tempering the mute con-
> sonants with liquids and semi-vowels.

'A regular series of proportionate sounds'—as Johnson defines it in
another *Rambler* (the eighty-sixth)—this was the governing metrical
principal of all English verse at least from Milton to Bridges, disregarded only by a handful of eccentrics (Smart, Blake, Hopkins) who
were disregarded themselves. For myself, who came to Donne after a
metrical diet of Shelley, Swinburne, Housman and Brooke, this was a
novelty almost as stimulating as the bawdy and the erudition. What it
really was (as I can see now, but could not then) was a matter linked
more essentially with syntax than with metrics. For Donne is reason-
ably observant of syllable-count, his basic beat is thoroughly iambic,
and he always rhymes; but his stanzas are often crossed against an
intricate syntactical structure, and the apparently metrical difficulty
('harshness', Johnson would call it) is in truth the difficulty of seeing

how the stanza and the sentence are to be harmonized. If one prints as prose the first two stanzas of 'The Legacie', it is only the rhymes that tell one how the stanza is shaped:

> When I dyed last, and, Deare, I dye as often as from thee I goe, though it be but an hour ago, (and Lovers houres be full eternity), I can remember yet, that I something did say, and something did bestow; though I be dead, which sent me, I should be mine own executor and Legacie. I heard mee say, Tell her anon, that my selfe, (that is you, not I), did kill me, and when I felt mee dye, I bid mee send my heart, when I was gone, but I alas could there finde none, when I had ripp'd me, and search'd where hearts did lye; it killed mee againe, that I who still was true, in life, in my last will should cozen you.

To harmonize syntax with stanza is the whole secret of reading Donne's lyrics. It is not a secret one has to learn in order to read the lyrics of the Romantics, in which the syntactical units coincide almost invariably with the metrical:

> Bright Star, would I were steadfast as thou art!/Not in lone splendour hung aloft the night,/and watching, with eternal lids apart,/like Nature's patient sleepless eremite,/the moving waters at their priestlike task/of pure ablution round earth's human shores . . .

This last revelation will seem very odd indeed (as 'revelation', that is) to the ear of the sixties, which now needs retraining in the opposite direction. It needs to be taught the techniques and qualities of *regular* verse; for the average young reader of 1969 is liable not to understand, metrically, the simplest iambic line, and is quite capable of speaking Marlowe's 'And ride in triumph through Persepolis' with an accent on the last syllable but one. This, of course, is simply proof of how thoroughly successful that revolution was. It was successful because it coincided (or seemed to coincide) with a revolution in contemporary verse. I cannot now remember whether it was before or after my discovery of Donne and the other metaphysical poets that I discovered Eliot, Hopkins and Pound. They seem now, through the telescoping effect of nearly forty years, to have reached me all in a mass, as a single experience: and my point is that in essence that is just how they did reach me. Donne, therefore, came to me in the company of contemporary and revolutionary poets and as if he too were one of them. This may have been a delusion, as the learned scholarship and criticism of the fifties and sixties is arguing it was (but I propose to quarrel with those arguments in a moment); it may have been based, that is, on a misunderstanding of Donne. But no amount of erudition is going to persuade me that the personal experience I have been describing did not happen to me, and happen more or less as described.

The critical formulation and justification for it did not come to me till a little later. And that, I am sure, is the right order, if it can be managed—experience first, explanation second. When it did come, it came through Eliot and Leavis: the former in those essays which are too well known to need specifying, the latter in these words from *Revaluation*:

> At this [Leavis has just quoted the opening stanza of 'The Good-morrow'] we cease reading as students, or as connoisseurs of anthology-pieces, and read on as we read the living. The extraordinary force of originality that made Donne so potent an influence in the seventeenth century makes him now at once for us, without his being the less felt as of his period, contemporary—obviously a living poet in the most important sense.

This passage—especially its last sentence—has been much frowned on by later critics, on the ground of its being 'unhistorical' in seeing Donne as having had 'an extraordinary force of originality'. Whether or not Leavis was 'unhistorical' with reference to Donne in the fifteen nineties is a matter I propose to discuss later in this essay; what I am quite sure about is that he was completely 'historical' about myself in the nineteen thirties.

From this beginning, Donne's poetry became, as it were, lodged in the tissue of my life, from which it has never been displaced. (I have never encountered any critical observation which seemed to me so totally at variance with my own experience as C. S. Lewis's remark to the effect that the 'interest' of Donne's poetry, 'save for a mind specially predisposed in its favour, must be short-lived and superficial, though intense'.) It accommodated itself to my own experience of love, and seemed to illuminate it more profoundly than almost any other poetry. Not until many years later—after war and teaching and other things had intervened—did I try to formulate on paper my version of Donne; and when I did so, in *The Shakespearean Moment*, I had two main objectives.

The first was to clarify and justify a conviction that a major clue to the understanding of Donne was to be found through Shakespeare (and of Shakespeare through Donne, incidentally): for these two had a great deal in common, and what they had in common was that the basic stance of both was a *dramatic* stance. This, as it seemed to me, was the true difference between their poetry, as it developed from the fifteen nineties onwards, and the earlier Elizabethan poetry of Sidney and Spenser.

My second objective was to see Donne's poetry in the context of the society it was written in and for—the well-born, highly educated, predominantly Catholic (Anglo or Roman) society which flourished in the period after the years of bitterest strife between the government and the English Roman Catholics but before the next great struggle, between monarchy and Parliament. This society, I thought—though it was far from being an ideological 'group', whether in politics or in theology—did have something approximating to a common philosophy. It was hierarchical, ritualistic, ceremonial—in a word, dramatic: in another word, anti-Puritan.

Of the general truth of my first proposition, I remain convinced; I am not so sure of the second, in which I now detect a degree of oversimplification. I have become more suspicious than I used to be of accepting any writer as 'representative' of his class, community, nation, ideology, or anything whatsoever except himself. I have become even more suspicious of making any deductions, based on the state of imaginative literature at any given period, concerning the general state of that period's culture and civilization. Those reviewers who detected a whiff of nostalgia for a golden past in some passages of *The Shakespearean Moment* were not, I now feel, entirely wrong; there is always a danger—and I did not entirely escape it—of letting one's real passion for certain works of art spill over into an imaginary passion for the society in which and for which they were made.

★   ★   ★

For the writing of this essay, I decided, a quick re-reading was called for: a swift survey, as nearly as possible at one go, of all the *Songs and Sonets* and the *Elegies*. And for this it seemed appropriate to use what may now be claimed to be the 'standard' edition, displacing Grierson's, Miss Helen Gardner's Oxford edition of *The Elegies and the Songs and Sonnets*, first published in 1965. I found the reading of this—especially of the *Songs and Sonnets*—a thoroughly disconcerting experience, and in fact I abandoned it fairly soon and returned to Grierson. But it was also a useful experience, for as I searched for the reasons that had made me unhappy with Miss Gardner's edition, I found that I was searching also for what I really felt about this body of poetry. The big change Miss Gardner makes is in the order of the *Songs and Sonnets*. She abandons the traditional order, which is that of the first printed editions, and puts in its place an order based on her own subjective impressions. She divides the poems into two groups. These groups depend partly on criteria of metre and stanza-forms, partly on the mood of the poems; thus, all the 'cynical, promiscuous' poems go into the first section, and all those with philosophical, mystical or idealistic elements into the second section. This she attempts to justify by some biographical speculation which, as far as I know, has no firm basis in known fact; it is really a piece of circular reasoning which goes from the poems to the 'life' and then back again. Miss Gardner argues that the cynical, Ovidian, epigrammatic poems (her first group) were written in the fifteen nineties; the others after 1600, as a result of Donne's reading of mystical writings, his runaway marriage, and the 'enforced retirement' which was the consequence of his having 'lost the world for love'. Thus Donne's love poetry, in this arrangement, is presented as something near to a *sequence*: as poems which can be arranged in groups or stages, corresponding to stages, if not actual events, in their author's life.

Whatever one may think of this argument, there is no doubt of the effect which a change in the order of the poems produces on one's reading of them as an entity, as a body of love poetry. The effect is a total reversal, an alteration in the experience. In their original order, the short poems—and the *Elegies* also, which differ in genre, not in material—come to one as a body of verse which says in effect that *every* aspect of love is liable to be present, in reality or in imagination, at any time, on any occasion: promiscuity, misogyny, hopeless adoration, intimate tenderness, bitter hate, Platonic adoration, frivolous cynicism, brothel-lust, monogamous devotion, all of them. What Swift wrote in *Cadenus and Vanessa* might serve as these poems' epigraph:

> Love why do we one passion call,
> When 'tis a compound of them all?
> Where hot and cold, where sharp and sweet,
> In all their equipages meet;

> Where pleasures mix'd with pains appear,
> Sorrow with joy, and hope with fear . . .

If this be the true total meaning of Donne's love poetry, then the order of the first editions, whether deliberate or haphazard, serves that meaning admirably. Miss Gardner complains that 'the order, being wholly irrational, cannot be memorized . . .' But why should anyone *want* to memorize it? (We're not all editors.) And what if the author was saying that love itself is 'irrational'? Suppose one extends to the unknown original editor (Donne's scapegrace son, possibly) the courtesy of the English law. Imagine him innocent till proved guilty; imagine his order was intended to demonstrate what I have suggested is the total meaning of this poetry, and then see if it is 'wholly irrational'.

The first poem[1] is 'The Good-morrow', a poem which expresses tenderness and passion for one woman, and a vivid feeling of discovery: now, at last, after many false starts, they have found what real love is. Next comes the 'Song', 'Goe, and catche a falling starre . . .': a cynical, but not very serious, denial that any woman can be both 'true and faire'. Third is 'Womans Constancy', another piece of cheerful cynicism, which adds to the former the proposition that he himself is no better. Fourth is 'The Undertaking', a celebration of Platonic adoration, which declares that such love is a higher thing than 'the Hee and Shee' and claims moreover that the poet himself has experienced it. After that, 'The Sunne Rising': a joyfully pagan, Ovidian hymn to a completely satisfactory love. Married? adulterous? mercenary?—one isn't told, and it doesn't matter (as far as the poem is concerned). Then, 'The Indifferent': back to cynicism, reinforced, in this, by an explicit mocking of the Petrarchan doctrine of eternal faithfulness, putting in its place the anti-morality which argues that constancy is a 'heresy' and that 'Love's sweetest part' is 'variety'. Seventh, 'Loves Usury', another Ovidian poem, addressed to the 'God of Love', asking him to give to the lover a freedom from all cerebration, all moral twinges, all emotional involvements, allowing his body alone to 'reign'. And if one adds, eighth, 'The Canonization', which is a quasi-serious, quasi-self-mocking poem on the theme directly opposite to that of 'The Indifferent', arguing that he and his lady are the ideal

[1] In Grierson and in the first printed edition, 1633. In the second edition (1635) *The Flea* is printed first. This change makes little difference to the over-all effect of the first half-dozen or so poems.

Petrarchan lovers, fit to be 'canonized' as saints in the religion of love and worshipped accordingly, then one has pretty well all the themes and moods this poetry plays with. And the collection continues in this style: indeed, the pack has been shuffled so thoroughly, the absence of any order which can be 'memorized' is so striking, that one begins to wonder if the original editor was quite such a fool as Miss Gardner thinks him—if he didn't, perhaps, know what he was up to.

This question of the order of the *Songs and Sonets* is not just a question of scholarly pedantry—or of some long-standing reader, like myself, who has become incurably 'fixated' on Grierson. It does really touch on one's response to the poems. There is an interesting, though to my mind totally wrong-headed, attack on them by C. S. Lewis, which is relevant here. Lewis's response is very personal (a reference back to the beginning of this chapter will show that I do not intend this as criticism); he obviously disliked intensely the sexual personality which he deduced from the poems, and did so because the concept of love which he thought that personality held conflicted with his own.

In one way, indeed, Donne's love poetry is less true than that of the Petrarchans, in so far as it largely omits the very thing that all the pother is about. Donne shows us a variety of sorrows, scorns, angers, disgusts, and the like which arise out of love. But if anyone asked 'What is all this about . . . ?', I do not know how we could reply except by pointing to some ordinary love-poetry. . . . He shows us amazing shadows cast by love upon the intellect, the passions, and the appetite; to learn of the substance which cast them we must go to other poets, more balanced, more magnanimous, and more humane. . . . In the main, his love poetry is *Hamlet* without the prince.

Lewis's objection is really theological (all his criticism was in essence theology); he is objecting because he believes that there *is* 'a thing called Love'—an ultimate reality of which all these symptoms or phenomena are mere 'imitations'. But suppose the whole point of Donne's love poetry is, not exactly to deny this proposition (I would have said that he has many poems which affirm it, for all readers except Lewis), but rather to suggest that if one's business is to make poems—and essentially dramatic poems—out of the 'amazing shadows cast by love', then each 'shadow' must be treated as if it were just as valid as all the others. Love, for this poetry, is not an entity above, apart from, distinct from, all these phenomena. Love is the sum of them, and no one can say that any item in the sum is worth more than any other.

Donne's love poetry, then, is a body of verse whose effect (rather than intention; I suspect it had no intention) is to present as total a knowledge of the experience of love as one imagination could compass. If we look at it like this, the question of 'personality' and 'sincerity' becomes irrelevant; Leishman's phrase, 'the dialectical expression of personal drama', puts very well the manner in which this poetry fuses three ingredients—the analytical, the autobiographical, and the dramatic—and does so with such completeness that it is vain and foolish to try to separate them. Of this experience of love there are only two limiting conditions. It is entirely human, not divine, however much it may play with philosophical and theological concepts. And it is entirely, even aggressively, masculine and hetero-sexual. There is no trace of that ambi-sexual strand which is in Shakespeare's sonnets and in so much more of the poetry and art of the earlier Renaissance.

This love-experience takes place in a definite setting, which is quite clearly registered though not self-consciously described. It is a setting of cultivated, sophisticated people. It is thoroughly urban. All round the lovers is the manifold variegated life of a great city: its furtive adulteries in domestic interiors; its music-making, play-going, whoring; its church-going, funerals, marriages; its plagues; its fashions; its traders, merchants, town-criers, porters at house-doors, lawyers, alchemists, schoolboys. And nearby is the court, with its royal hunts and 'progresses', its intriguing flattering courtiers, and its ladies of easy virtue.

Beyond the city and court are hints of wider horizons. Excursions into the countryside; travel abroad by the lover, with the lady left behind; a vivid awareness of the countries and peoples of the continent, of foreign customs and foreign politics; an awareness too of war, and of that as something which the lover himself may be engaged in. And a powerful picturesque interest in the voyages of the discoverers, in the new things—spices or precious metals or jewels—they had brought back with them.

The man by whom the poems are 'spoken'—and they are virtually all composed as if 'spoken', and that by a man[2]—is well-born,

[2] 'Confined Love' is an exception. It is apparently spoken by a woman, who protests against the morality which enforces her sex to have only one lover. Another exception is 'Breake of Day', an aubade in which a woman pleads with her lover not to leave her.

highly educated, able (and very ready) to refer casually to a wide range of reading and general intellectual knowledge, including theology, law and science; well informed, indeed, about things in general, such as the characteristics of foreigners, theological squabbles, and the behaviour of courtiers, and taking towards them all an attitude of sophisticated cynicism. He thinks of himself as a thorough 'modern', living in a complex, sceptical, immoral, revolutionary age. He lives, of course, in a society in which monogamy is the sexual norm and which pronounces adultery and extra-marital copulation to be sins; but he takes it for granted that these rules are perpetually broken, for all men (and most women), he is sure, have their affairs, and all that society, in practice, demands is a modicum of concealment and a degree of theoretical deference to the concepts of feminine 'honour' or chastity. But he is very far from being a radical protester against the church-and-court society he belongs to: on the contrary, he regards protesters and outsiders (Puritans, for example, and city merchants) with great scorn. What he demands—and gets—is licence within a society to break its laws and yet stay within it.

He assumes that basically all love is one topic, whether the woman be wife, mistress, whore, or Platonic ideal 'She', and that therefore there is no need always to inform us which, at the moment, she happens to be. He assumes that the man is always the initiator, the attempter to seduce and conquer, whether successful or not, and that women may respond to his attempts either by an impregnable chastity or a wanton yielding, but that in either case they will understand the rules of the game and will play it properly: that is, if they decide to be chaste they will be so in the high Petrarchan fashion (even though they, and he, may privately know this is nonsense), and if they decide to be wanton they will be that with a full-blooded libertinism. He assumes (I consider him now as writer) that the poems he makes will be read by people largely of his own kind and, many of them, his own friends; he has no intention of getting them printed, and would regard that way of 'publishing' them as ill-bred and in the worst of taste; indeed, he professes to be somewhat annoyed if they are set to music and sung. This audience of friends and equals will understand not only the allusions and witticisms, but (what is harder) just when he is serious and when not, and just what kind of seriousness is being displayed; they will understand also where the poems are 'personal' and where not, and again just what kind of 'personality' is involved. What he writes are not exactly 'sugared sonnets', but they are certainly written 'among his private friends', and he would feel very sympathetic towards Mr. Shakespeare if he happened to know that the latter's sonnets had been piratically printed.

So much for the man: what of the woman? There is less to be said of her, since, as remarked above, all this poetry is composed exclusively, even domineeringly, from the viewpoint of the man. The woman is the partner in the sexual dance, and that is all she is. But because the dance is very varied, there are many alternative responses available to her, and there is at least a pretence that she has a free choice among them. The man calls the tunes, but it is up to her which of them she will elect to dance to. She may decide to strip and go to bed with him—for one occasion only, or for a long affair, or for a lifetime—or she may decide to 'kill' him with her icy 'cruelty'. Whatever she does is done in response to him—to his urging, pleading, arguing, bullying, weeping—and the typical verbal mood of these poems is the imperative: 'come, madam, come . . .', 'enter these armes . . .', 'stand still, and I . . .', 'send me some token . . .', 'send home my long strayd eyes to me', 'marke but this flea . . .', 'oh doe not die . . .', 'for godsake hold your tongue . . .', 'here take my picture . . .', 'O stay here . . .'.

Man and woman alike are members of a mature, complex, in some ways corrupt society. Therefore they don't behave in the least 'naturally'; they behave, as we all do, according to patterns characteristic of their age and situation—which means, for them, in the manner of educated English gentry during the last years of Queen Elizabeth and first years of King James. What, then, were these patterns, in the domain of sexual love?

There were three main patterns. The first was that made by Christian marriage, sacramental and monogamous. The surprising thing here—surprising, at least, to an unprepared modern reader—is its complete absence from the poetry. It never occurs, specifically. Some of the poems, such as 'The Good-morrow', the song 'Sweetest love, I doe not goe', 'Lovers Infinitenesse', or 'A Feaver', express feelings of tenderness, constancy and devotion with such power and beauty that one would 'like to think' they had something to do with Mrs. Anne Donne; and one of them, 'A Valediction forbidding Mourning', was said by Izaak Walton, Donne's first and almost contemporary biographer, to have been written for her before Donne's departure for the continent in 1611.[3] But nothing in any poem identifies the status of the woman except those few (Elegie I, 'Jealosie', Elegie XII, 'His Parting from Her') which identify her as the wife of another man.[4] This exclusion of married love, specified as such, from the domain of love poetry was of course a commonplace of the medieval-Renaissance tradition;[5] but it would be totally wrong to make any deductions from this about the poet's personal life or opinions. It was no more than a social-aesthetic convention; but it is worth remembering—since we tend to forget it—that because this major area of men's, and women's, real experience was excluded, the love poetry had almost always a certain element of fictional expression: which does *not* mean that it was untrue, still less that it was insincere, but does mean that because of this social-aesthetic convention, which was thoroughly understood by everyone, there existed this area where art and life did not meet. Life, for one thing, in that area at that time, included many things somewhat resistant to poetry—dowries, jointures, family negotiations about matters of status and money, incessant pregnancies and almost equally incessant deaths of infants and children—and Donne's own life, which included a marriage that wrecked his worldly career for years and resulted in twelve children of whom five died in childhood, taught him better than most men's the difference between the love one wrote poems about and the love one lived.

[3] Miss Gardner denies this; she adduces some factual arguments which, she says, make it impossible that the poem could have been written for that occasion. Her critical attitude seems inconsistent on this matter of autobiographical content and possibility of 'identifying' the woman addressed: thus, she says that the woman of Elegie XIX ('Going to bed') is a London prostitute, on the grounds that Donne addresses her as 'Madam' and that she is 'richly dressed'. These seem inadequate reasons for pronouncing her to be a whore. 'Madam' is surely spoken in a tone of facetious imperiousness which any man might use to a wife or mistress (and when used with brothel-associations, it doesn't usually refer to one of the girls). And I doubt if it was only the London whores who, like Regan, were 'gorgeous' in their attire.

[4] When the woman is addressed, it is always in terms which do not specify her status: 'deare Love' ('Valediction of the Book', 'Dreame'); 'deare' ('Legacie', 'Lovers Infinitenesse'); 'sweetest love' ('Song'); 'love' ('Lecture upon the Shadow'); 'faire love' (Elegie XVI); 'madam' (Elegie XIX).

[5] Very few poems of the seventeenth century are admittedly addressed to the writer's wife. Bishop King's 'Exequy' and Milton's sonnet to his 'late espoused saint' are perhaps the only well-known examples. Cynics might remark that in each of these poems the wife is dead.

The second pattern was that of pagan libertinism. The literary ancestry of this was Roman, and its most powerful preacher was Ovid. Its basic dogma was that in some past Golden Age sexual love had been free, as it still is among the animals ('Confined Love') and still could be among us if only we lived as Nature meant ('Communitie'). But Shame and Honour (i.e., the modesty and chastity expected of Christian women) and the possessive exclusiveness which went with these idols, had destroyed that happy and natural freedom. Women had become 'cold' and 'proud', and men, therefore, were engaged in an endless war against what 'The Dampe' calls 'th' enormous Gyant, your Disdaine' and 'th' enchantresse Honor'. In this war they used all the weapons they could find—tears, flattery, rhetoric, casuistical arguments. And it was a war not only against the individual women whom the men desired, but also against society, which 'officially' disapproved of the men's assaults as an attack on sound morality—not to mention a frivolous waste of time. For the true lover was far too busy for 'business' ('Breake of Day') or for any sort of career ('The Canonization'); he was contemptuous of the demands of the state, and proclaimed his intention (though for reasons hardly ideological) of 'making love, not war' in the best twentieth-century manner (Elegie XX, 'Loves Warre'). In many of the poems which show this lover successful, there is a vivid sense of the pair *excluding* the rest of the world, shutting themselves away from a society conceived as hostile or simply busy with affairs which it regards as more important than love ('The Good-morrow', 'The Sunne Rising', 'The Canonization').

This lost freedom of love—however much society and morality may disapprove of it—is claimed to be what virtually all men (and quite a few women) would really like to return to. It has its mock morality, its anti-morality, whereby faithfulness and chastity and the rest are *vices*, and 'love's sweetest part' is 'variety' ('Womans Constancy', 'The Indifferent'); it proclaims too that many of the women who pretend to chastity do so only because respectability demands it: they would change sides if they dared, and after suitable treatment some of them do ('The Flea', 'The Exstasie'). Because of these cross-currents and oppositions, 'modern love' has become immensely more difficult than love used to be; it has become complex and agonized and all-demanding, for

> . . . every moderne god will now extend
> His vast prerogative, as far as Jove.

To rage, to lust, to write to, to commend,
    All is the purlewe of the God of Love . . .
                                    ('Loves Deity')

And from this comes a bitter doubt if what one gains from it is worth
the effort and agony, a suspicion that ''tis imposture all', 'a vaine
Bubles shadow' ('Loves Alchimie'), which only a fool would devote
his life and art to ('The Triple Foole'); and out of that doubt, again,
comes a fierce contempt for the women whom all the agony is about.
They are silly creatures, after all: you needn't hope for 'mind' in them
('Loves Alchimie'); their love is always less 'pure', less intellectual, than
men's ('Aire and Angels'); for all their talk about Honour and sentiment, they are not really interested in a 'naked thinking heart', only
in 'some other part' of a man ('The Blossome'); and they are quite
capable of bedding with one man after pretending impregnable
chastity to another ('The Apparition').

The third, and last, pattern of love was that formed by the Platonic-
Petrarchan adoration of a woman accepted as eternally chaste, through
whose cruelty the lover must die. This, of course, was the old tradition
of courtly love, now in its dotage. By Donne's time, at least for some-
one of his intelligence and temperament, this ancient convention could
no longer be taken quite straight; it had to be refreshed, either with
some irony or with a new range of intellectual reference and imagery.
Donne gives it both. But he is not at all inclined to abandon it. He uses
it in many poems: 'The Undertaking', 'The Legacie', 'Twicknam
Garden', 'The Nocturnall', 'The Funerall', 'The Relique'. . . . There
are variations within the convention. In some poems the lady, though
still denying, is still alive and the poet is still besieging her; in others,
she is dead and the poet is left alone to grieve; in others again, both she
and poet are imagined as dead. Where the presence of death is felt,
these poems take on a very strong theological colouring, and one
which is specifically Catholic;[6] I suspect, in fact, that the attraction of
this convention for Donne was that it enabled him to make a poetry
which bridged the passage between his two main subjects, sexual love
and religion. These poems tend to be the most ambiguous in effect of
all Donne's works, and also perhaps the most quintessentially Donne,
since they include all his manners and are liable to change keys with
bewildering rapidity. Take the first stanza of 'The Relique'. It begins

[6] Anglo-catholic or Roman: in this context, it makes little difference.

with a down-to-earth allusion to the fact that in the crowded church-yards of Donne's London the bodies were dug up after ten years or so, the bones thrown into a common pit, and the graves used again. This leads first to a cynical joke about women's fickleness, next to that famous line ('a bracelet of bright haire about the bone') which fuses with tremendous intensity images of beauty and death, after that to a Hamlet-like evocation of a simple-minded, superstitious gravedigger, then to the image of a pair of lovers still lying together in the grave, and finally to a picture of the Day of Judgement, seen in the literal medieval manner, with all the resurrected bodies standing beside their opened graves.

★   ★   ★

Such is the material of Donne's love poetry. It was, of course, completely characteristic of its age, of that 'moment' when Elizabethan was moving to Jacobean and medieval to modern, and when English society stood just on the edge of that long slow shift by which monarchical, Catholic and aristocratic were to yield the dominance to parliamentary, Puritan and bourgeois. C. S. Lewis takes a gloomy view of the effects of that 'moment' on Donne's love poetry, which displays, he thinks, 'the torments of a mind which has been baffled in its relation to sexual love by certain temporary and highly special conditions'. I cannot see, for my own part, any evidence that Donne's mind was more 'baffled' in that respect than a great many minds of other ages: but Lewis's comment—together with another remark he makes in the same essay, to the effect that Donne's originality has been over-stated and over-praised—forms a useful lead-in to a discussion of the changed responses to Donne's poetry which have developed over the last twenty years. For these responses, at least in academic criticism, have changed considerably, and they have changed in two directions: there is now a reluctance to see Donne as 'modern' in the way that Leavis saw him nearly forty years ago, and together with this, a reluc-tance to see him as a revolutionary, as possessing what Leavis again called 'an extraordinary force of originality'. The attitude sketched in the autobiographical beginning of this chapter looks thoroughly dated in 1969.

If one had to name one book more responsible than any others for this change, it would probably be Rosemond Tuve's *Elizabethan and*

Metaphysical Imagery, which was first published in 1947. Tuve's argument may be summarized like this: Eliot's famous and enormously influential remarks that in metaphysical poetry there is 'a direct sensuous apprehension of thought' and that 'a thought to Donne was an experience; it modified his sensibility', are not in truth more applicable to Donne and the metaphysicals than to earlier Elizabethan poetry; metaphysical imagery was *not* determined by the modern demand for 'sensuous particularity', but rather by decorum, that is, appropriateness to the argument of the poem. Metaphysical poetry did *not* represent a revolutionary break from, and reaction against, the poetry written immediately before; both were written according to the principles of Renaissance poetic and rhetorical theory. And the metaphysical poets were not trying to be complex, cryptic, obscure (it is we moderns who make them so); on the contrary, they were aiming at a 'more sharply lit clarity'.

This line has been developed by later writers into a more specific polemic against the criticism of the generation before them. S. L. Bethell, for example, recommends us to consider certain Spanish and Italian rhetoricians of the seventeenth century, whose works, he thinks, would be

more likely to assist our approach to seventeenth-century wit than are those modern writers, however brilliant, who rely on critical methods divorced from historical learning.[7]

In the same style, A. J. Smith advises us to discard

our determinedly inward-focused modern spectacles, to establish a full technical context, and to trace material sources. . . .[8]

—and talks about 'critics of the thirties school' (he is referring specifically to Empson), who 'have never shown themselves much concerned' with what metaphysical poetry was 'consciously driving at'[9].

It is clear (as Bethell recognized) that this, like so many critical quarrels, is largely a dispute between those who see themselves primarily

[7] 'The Nature of Metaphysical Wit' (1953): reprinted in *Discussions of John Donne*, edited by F. Kermode (Boston, 1962).
[8] 'The Metaphysic of Love' (1958): reprinted in Kermode, *op. cit.*
[9] 'New Bearings in Donne' (1960): reprinted in *John Donne, Twentieth Century Views*, edited by Helen Gardner (New Jersey, 1962).

as historians, concerned to discover, as far as can be decided from the evidence, what a particular poem 'meant' for its author and his contemporary readers, and those who see themselves simply as readers of poetry, concerned with recording what the poem 'means', here and now, for themselves. (I follow Mr. Smith's cautious example in putting the verb inside quotation marks. 'Ultimately', he writes, 'however it offends our pieties, we have to ask what "Air and Angels" "means".' My 'pieties', whatever *that* means, are not offended, and I can't imagine what other object any critical examination could possibly have.) This, of course, is to over-simplify the problem. It is in truth impossible to read poetry except as oneself, which means as a member of one's own age and society: no amount of erudition can turn us into anything at all like John Donne or one of his readers in the year 1600. Mr. Smith's metaphor of 'modern spectacles' which can be put on and discarded is betrayingly inexact. For behind spectacles are eyes; and it is eyes, not spectacles, we see with; and our eyes, incurably, are eyes of the twentieth century. Indeed, when Mr. Smith talks of 'the thirties school', I can't help wondering what quality of spectacles *he* is wearing; for it is news to me, as it would be, I suspect, to Messrs. Auden, Brooks, Leavis, Empson, Ransom and Richards, that there ever was such a school. There was certainly a 'thirties generation', of which I was a humble member, but its disagreements were quite as extensive as its agreements. Mr. Smith himself, I would guess (following his own critical principle), is a humble member of 'the fifties school', and I suspect that his critical stance is just as much conditioned by his school as mine by my school. He is, in fact, proving what I am arguing for: that you cannot, essentially, read poetry except as yourself—your time-limited, prejudice-limited self. What historical knowledge can do—and should certainly be called in to do—is simply this. Given that there has been, already, the genuine, individual response to the poem (and I don't see how such a response can have occurred at all unless the poem, in some sense, has been felt as 'contemporary'), then historical knowledge can enrich the response by revealing other facets, other 'meanings'; it can also act as a check or control by showing that certain meanings are demonstrably impossible. The latter function is undoubtedly valuable, and by some of the excesses of modern criticism is constantly called for: Shakespearean criticism, for example, abounds with interpretations which are simply ludicrous when presented as interpretations of the work of a professional Bankside playwright.

I would be quite prepared, then, to accept the verdict, if I were convinced that historical learning had proved beyond question the impossibility of my view of Donne. But I am not convinced of it. Take the question of Donne's originality and the degree to which his poetry was a real revolution, a genuine shock to established habits, when it first appeared in the fifteen nineties. The first point I would make is that if this view of it is an error, at least it is not an error confined to those who wear 'modern spectacles'. It is an error shared by many of Donne's own contemporaries. When Ben Jonson remarked that Donne 'for not keeping of accent deserved hanging', he was clearly registering his awareness of a rhythmical surprise: Donne's verse did not follow the beat that his ear had been used to. When he observed that Donne had written a certain poem 'to match Sir Edward Herbert in obscurenesse', and added the comment that 'Donne himself for not being understood would perish', it is plain that even if Rosemond Tuve in 1947 did not think that metaphysical poetry aimed at and attained obscurity, Ben Jonson in 1619 was of a different opinion. When Thomas Carew, after Donne's death, wrote his elegy in praise of him, he described with some exactness his estimate of what Donne's poetic achievement had been; and at many points in this estimate Carew is clearly saying that Donne was a revolutionary—had done things which were both new and shocking. What else is Carew saying in these lines?

> The Muses garden with Pedantique weedes
> O'rspred, was purg'd by thee; The lazie seeds
> Of servile imitation thrown away;
> And fresh invention planted, Thou didst pay
> The debts of our penurious bankrupt age . . .

Or in these?

> The subtle cheat
> Of slie Exchanges, and the jugling feat
> Of two-edg'd words, or whatsoever wrong
> By ours was done the Greeke, or Latine tongue,
> Thou hast redeem'd, and open'd Us a Mine
> Of rich and pregnant phansie, drawne a line
> Of masculine expression . . .

And in these lines, what else is he saying than that Donne had led a revolution in poetry, from which now, after his death, there would be a reaction?

> But thou art gone, and thy strict lawes will be
> Too hard for Libertines in Poetrie . . .

Carew was a poet of a younger generation than Donne, who had studied his work with an intensity which, perhaps, can only be bestowed by one poet on another poet of whom he regards himself as disciple. It is of course possible that a number of academics, none of whom has written any poetry and all of whom live more than three hundred years later, may understand the true contribution of a poet better than a contemporary poet who wrote in the same manner: possible, I suppose, but I shall need more evidence than I have so far been vouchsafed before I am sure of it.

Moreover, the case does not depend on the witness of one or two individuals. There is a mass of other evidence that Donne was regarded by contemporaries as the leader of a new school of verse, of which a deliberate obscurity or complexity was one of the most characteristic features. This was so clearly recognized as a school, that is, a group of poets having certain traits which both united them with each other and separated them from the rest, that it was given the clearest possible indication of such recognition, the bestowing of a 'label'. This kind of poetry was called, in the seventeenth century, the poetry of 'strong lines'. The evidence is conveniently assembled in George Williamson's article of that title[10]—an article which, to my mind, proves beyond question the *historical fact* that not only did Donne's contemporaries recognize him as an innovator and a revolutionary, but that they did so in terms very little different from those in which 'the thirties school' formulated it: they saw a distinction, in Williamson's words, between 'the close and strenuous style' and 'the soft, melting and diffuse style of the Spenserians'. And the poetry defined as 'strong lines', as Williamson also observes, was virtually identical with 'what we have come to know as "metaphysical poetry".'

But the real criticism of the Tuve–Bethell–Smith argument is that it has minimal relevance to the actual quality of the poetry. No amount of evidence that Donne took over from his predecessors many themes,

---

[10] 'Strong Lines' (1936): reprinted in *Seventeenth-Century Contexts* (1962).

poses, conventions, etc., and that he, like everyone then, had been well grounded in the poetic and rhetorical theories of the Renaissance, makes a poem by Spenser in the smallest degree less unlike a poem by Donne. Quotation is the way to demonstrate this. It would be clearly absurd if I picked out a passage from Donne when he is being cynical or bawdy, since that is a mode which Spenser does not use: but here they are both on the same theme, and that the theme of Petrarchan adoration—Spenser's home ground, one might say.

> For love is Lord of truth and loialtie,
> Lifting himselfe out of the lowly dust
> On golden plumes up to the purest skie,
> Above the reach of loathly sinfull lust,
> Whose base affect through cowardly distrust
> Of his weake wings dare not to heaven fly,
> But like a moldwarpe in the earth doth ly.

> His dunghill thoughts, which do themselves enure
> To dirtie drosse, no higher dare aspyre,
> Ne can his feeble earthly eyes endure
> The flaming light of that celestiall fyre
> Which kindleth love in generous desyre,
> And makes him mount above the native might
> Of heavy earth, up to the heavens hight.
>   (Spenser, 'Hymne in Honour of Love')

>   . . . But he who lovelinesse within
> Hath found, all outward loathes,
> For he who colour loves, and skinne,
> Loves but their oldest clothes.

> If, as I have, you also doe
> Vertue attir'd in woman see,
> And dare love that, and say so too,
> And forget the Hee and Shee;

> And if this love, though placed so,
> From prophane men you hide,
> Which will no faith on this bestow,
> Or, if they doe, deride:

> Then you have done a braver thing
> Then all the *Worthies* did;
> And a braver thence will spring,
> Which is, to keepe that hid.
>   (Donne, 'The Undertaking')

The differences are so striking that they need no detailed demonstration. What they amount to is a change so total that it renders irrelevant all particular resemblances. The change is from a concept of poetry as something chanting, bardic and pulpit-rhetorical, to something talking, man-to-man, and dramatic. To decide whether or not this change was sufficient to entitle Donne to be called poetic revolutionary is a matter of verbal quibbling (a recent work calls him a 'conservative revolutionary', which is perhaps as good a way as any of sitting on that particular fence); what does seem to me beyond dispute is that this is how his contemporaries saw him, and that if, in order to reach this perception, they were able to overlook certain minor conformities in Donne's verse, they were perfectly right to do so. But it does not follow, of course, that we of 'the thirties school' were right in seeing Donne's poetry and his whole intellectual and aesthetic situation as in some ways parallel to our own, and the poetry, for that reason, peculiarly 'contemporary'. This view, though it necessarily derived from a view of Donne as revolutionary in his own time, was in itself another proposition, which demands another justification.

It originated, effectively, with Eliot—although he had had many predecessors, now mostly forgotten.[11] Eliot put it in these terms:

> We can only say that it appears likely that poets in our civilization, as it exists at present, must be *difficult*. Our civilization comprehends great variety and complexity, and this variety and complexity, playing upon a refined sensibility, must produce various and complex results. . . . Hence we get . . . a method curiously similar to that of the 'metaphysical poets' . . .[12]

[11] See Joseph E. Duncan's 'Revival of Metaphysical Poetry, 1872–1912' (1953): reprinted in a book of the same title (Minnesota University Press, 1960) and also in Kermode, *op. cit.* This article demonstrates not only that there were many Victorian and Edwardian admirers of Donne, but also that the terms of their admiration anticipated those of Eliot's: e.g. they saw Donne as combining thought and passion in one, and they saw him as complex and difficult in a manner which seemed peculiarly 'modern'.

[12] 'The Metaphysical Poets' (1921): reprinted in *Selected Essays* (1932) and n Kermode, *op. cit.*

The term not precisely stated in Eliot's argument—though certainly implied—is that Donne's age also had 'great variety and complexity' and that this too was responsible for and justified the difficulty of his poetry. I agree that there was a degree of over-simplification in this. It is always dangerous to draw parallels between one historical epoch and another; it becomes even more dangerous when one of the epochs happens to be one's own; and the danger is compounded still further when the parallels are seen through the subjective gaze of poet and literary critic. But in spite of all these cautions, I am not inclined to regard the parallel as totally illusory; I would rather see it, now, as more precisely literary than I used to, not to be so easily equated with social and religious factors, and as more a matter of Donne's individual response to his age than of the 'age itself' (if that phrase has any real meaning).

The literary parallel lay in the kind of public Donne's poetry was written for and the manner in which the poetry reached them. J. B. Leishman has described this in these terms, which I believe to be accurate:

> Ben Jonson and John Donne . . . were both, in a sense, coterie-poets, poets who made their initial impact not upon the common reader, but upon comparatively small circles of intellectuals and literary amateurs . . . Donne's poems were always and Jonson's often intended to be handed round in manuscript and admired by connoisseurs.[13]

If one compares this with Clive Bell's account of the way in which Eliot's *Prufrock* was first distributed, the parallel is exact:

> If I met Eliot in 1916, it must have been in '17 that I went to Garsington for an Easter party taking with me some ten or dozen copies of the last, and perhaps the first, publication of the Egoist Press: *The Love Song of J. Alfred Prufrock*. Anyone with a taste for research can fix the date, for the book, or brochure rather, had just appeared and I distributed my copies hot from the press like so many Good Friday buns. Who were the recipients? Our host and hostess, Philip and Lady Ottoline Morrell, of course; Mrs. St. John Hutchinson,

---

[13] *The Monarch of Wit*. This is from chapter I, 'Donne and Seventeenth Century Poetry', which is reprinted in Gardner, *op. cit.*

B

Katherine Mansfield, Aldous Huxley, Middleton Murry, Lytton Strachey perhaps, and, I think, Gertler. Were there others? Maria Balthus, for instance (later Mrs. Aldous Huxley). I cannot tell: but of this I am sure, it was Katherine Mansfield who read the poem aloud.[14]

And so it is with Pound's poem in *Lustra*:

> I join these words for four people,
> Some others may overhear them,
> O world, I am sorry for you,
> You do not know these four people.

The poetry of Eliot and Pound, when it first appeared—and indeed until the nineteen forties at least—was admired by a very self-conscious minority, who thoroughly despised such recent poetry as had been popular (Housman, Noyes, Rupert Brooke, etc.) and who might have been described exactly in the terms Leishman used for Donne's readers—'intellectuals and literary amateurs . . . connoisseurs'. This situation no longer obtains. Poetry in the nineteen sixties has become more 'popular' in one sense (Pop might be more accurate), with the development of its spoken performance together with music; in another sense, it has become academic, in a way it was not in the nineteen thirties, with the poets-in-residence on the campuses, poetry-writing taught as an academic subject, and poetry-reading circuits by poets who make the rounds from campus to campus.[15] But the Bloomsbury-Garsington milieu which Clive Bell describes, and anything in the least resembling it, is now extinct; and this, I believe, is the end, as Donne's coterie of readers might be called the beginning, of that particular way of writing and reading poetry. The 'amateur', the 'connoisseur', the 'dilettante', in poetry—with all the associations, social and educational, good and bad, of those words—have vanished.

I suspect that it was this which accounted for a great deal of the congruity felt between the poetry of Donne and those upholders of

---

[14] *T. S. Eliot: a Symposium*. Edited by March and Tambimuttu (1948).

[15] I realize that these phenomena are as yet more American than British. But I gather (I write as an expatriate) that they are developing in Britain also. This contemporary way of being academic is not to be confused with older ways, of which in certain respects it is the antithesis: for it is academic in academes which are far more democratic than any of the past, and it is almost entirely confined to the young—an affair of the students far more than of the professors.

'minority culture'[16] in the twenties and thirties who were that poetry's readers. But as for Donne's response to his own age, in this there was even greater danger of some too easy drawing of parallels. Any vague notions that Donne felt about the 'new philosophy' of Galileo and Copernicus more or less as twentieth-century intellectuals felt (or persuaded themselves they ought to feel) about Einsteinian physics, or that his difficulties and scruples in matters of religion corresponded to our conflicts of ideologies, or that his mind was stirred and unsettled by the discoveries in the New World as ours were by advances in anthropology and ethnology, will not survive for long an unprejudiced examination of what he actually wrote. For the truth is that if one looks at his speculative intellect by itself, divorced from his imagination and emotions, one sees that his mind was, if anything, old-fashioned—and rather obtusely conservative. He wasn't at all upset by the fact that the 'new philosophy' put 'all in doubt'; he merely recorded, in a tone of some amusement, that 'one Soule thinkes one, and another way Another thinkes, and 'tis an even lay'. He certainly agonized for a time (though for somewhat mixed motives) whether Rome or Canterbury were the true Church; but he seems never to have had the faintest doubt as to the truth of the Christian faith (his doubt was about his own salvation), and one can detect no trace in him of the new scientific humanism. He was not intrigued, as More and Montaigne had been, by the new polities which the 'savages' of the Americas had revealed to Europe; he was interested in the New World solely as a rich source of imagery and conceit—as a storehouse of new metaphors for lust and love: 'My Myne of precious stones, my Emperie, How blest am I in this discovering thee!'

If, then, we look for any 'contemporaneousness' in Donne through this way—through the way of perceiving philosophical or social or political parallels—we had better be careful. Such parallels are almost sure to be misleading, or at best irrelevant. But there is no need on that account to decide against Leavis's insight that Donne's poetry comes to us as 'contemporary' in a way which is not true of most of the lyrical poetry of the earlier Elizabethans.[17] The difference is not one of themes,

[16] This phrase, significantly, formed part of the title of a pamphlet by Leavis: *Mass Civilisation and Minority Culture*. And compare the wistful ending of *New Bearings in English Poetry* (1932): ' . . . So that poetry in the future, if there is poetry, seems likely to matter even less to the world. Those who care about it can only go on caring.'

[17] Sidney is sometimes an exception; and so, earlier still, is Wyatt.

or of subject-matter, or of ideas. The difference is in language. And that, in poetry, is the only difference that matters. What you have in Donne's love poetry is a quality of direct contact, of *intimacy*, both with the material and with the imagined hearer (woman addressed and/or friend supposedly listening). This sense of intimacy is produced through the absence of any intervening veil of 'poetic diction'. Whatever theme or mood Donne is expressing, he expresses it in a language which creates the illusion (all poetic language is engaged in creating an illusion) of natural speech—of the sort of speech suited to the topic and situation: erudite, pedantic even, if such is called for, as bawdy as Shakespeare when that is appropriate.

I can see no reason why this quality should not be felt just as strongly in 1969 as it was in 1929. I must admit, though, my own regretful agreement with what William Empson noted at a point midway between those dates:

> I get an impression that the young feel [Donne] much more remote now than the young did twenty years ago, and I wish they didn't.[18]

I would have to add also a feeling that this 'remoteness' has continued to increase; and it might be of interest to end this chapter with some attempt to speculate why this has happened.

One reason, I suspect, is that the Donne now presented by current academic criticism is a creature vastly less interesting to the common reader (if that individual still exists) than the Donne whom we of 'the thirties school' fondly imagined we were reading forty or thirty years ago. He has been brought back into the fold of rhetorical tradition; his affinities have been carefully documented, and heavily stressed, with everything that is most unreadable and most irreversibly dead in the medieval-Renaissance culture; his claims to have been an original and a revolutionary have been scornfully exploded as a delusion of said 'thirties school' (and perhaps, as I have suggested, of the fifteen nineties school also). All this has been done in the cause of historical truth. That is not a cause to which, as a rule, I find myself in opposition; all my prejudices are in fact on its side. But the historical truth that we are concerned with is that aspect of it which is relevant to the appreciation of great poetry; and when I read Mr. Smith's formulation of it —'to establish a full technical context, and to trace material sources'—

[18] *Kenyon Review*, Vol. XI (1949), p. 584.

well, I must admit, academic though I be myself, that my heart sinks at the dismal sound of it, and I cannot imagine how any young reader, who reads poetry simply to be moved and instructed in the 'context' of his own life, would not be immediately and finally deterred from the reading of *that* poet at least.

But in this case, as I have been arguing, I am not at all convinced that historical truth does have to be sacrificed: or rather, to put it more precisely, that the kinds of historical truth represented by the researches of Tuve, Bethell, etc., are as relevant to Donne's poetry as the other kind of historical truth represented by Ben Jonson's observations, Carew's elegy—and the lines in Shakespeare's 76th sonnet, which I have elsewhere argued may well refer to the beginnings of metaphysical poetry in the fifteen nineties (and if they do not refer to that, I cannot imagine what they do refer to):

> Why is my verse so barren of new pride?
> So far from variation or quicke change?
> Why with the time do I not glance aside
> To new found methods, and to compounds strange?

Such things are not in the least less historical than the discovery that Donne may have learned from the rhetorical precepts of Gracian and Tesauro; I suggest that they are more usefully relevant to us (the common readers of poetry) because they were comments made by poets about a poetry which was then contemporary.

But there are other reasons, for which academic criticism is not to be blamed, why Donne's poetry has lost some of the hold it had a generation or two ago. There seem, at the moment (1969), to be three dominant schools or kinds of poetry. The first one might call the 'Wallace Stevens school'. It sees a poem as a self-contained construction, a verbal artefact, hermetically sealed, to all appearances, from any autobiographical references.[19] For this, Donne's poetry is, or seems,

---

[19] This school has its corresponding school of criticism, the effects of which were amusingly described in a recent article by Angus Wilson. 'Like many students these days, she [one of his American pupils] believed that the teaching and the reading of English literature should be based rigidly on a system. . . . The idea was that you must study the text in front of you and nothing else. You mustn't talk about the author's life particularly; you mustn't concern yourself with other literature of the period, or other works written by that writer. In front of you is the text and this is enough. . . .' ('Sexual Revolution', *The Listener*, 10 October, 1968).

far too 'personal': the very strong sense of an individual character which it gives out—and the odd way in which this, sometimes, seems to *disturb* the poem, and therefore make it more moving—these qualities, which used to be assets, are now counted for liabilities.

Then there is the antithesis of the 'Wallace Stevens school', which might be called the 'school of Whitman'. This sees poetry as a free outpouring of ecstasy, a religious-emotional rhapsody. It is the culmination of the anti-rational aspect of romanticism, crossed with the American taste for diluted doses of Oriental cults. For this, Donne is far too cerebral, too ironic, too complex, too polylingual and scholastic—too Western, I would say, if it weren't that the home ground of this school happens to be in California.

And lastly, there is the school of poetry as confessional, the school of Lowell, Plath, Sexton, Jennings. 'To the psychiatrist's office and half way back' might be its motto, as it was (almost) the title of one of its members' books. For this, Donne fails through that elusive, many-layered, quasi-dramatic quality of his—the quality which reminds us that he was in his youth 'a great frequenter of plays'. You are never sure—you are meant not to be sure—when he is being confessional, and when it is really true of his love poetry what he said of it in later life, that he 'did best when [he] had least of truth to go by'.

So the poetry of Donne, it would seem, satisfies none of the criteria by which, at the moment, poetry is being written and judged. There may be, also, another point against him. There is no doubt (as the schools and names I have just been citing will show) that poetry in English is at present led from America. And Donne, from certain aspects, is among the most European, the most 'continental', of English poets. Some of his basic qualities—a baroque heaviness, a slow Latin *gravitas* at unexpected moments, a thorough enjoyment of the flesh combined with an Augustinian conviction of the flesh's inherent sinfulness—are qualities which have never successfully crossed the Atlantic.

Those who, like myself, continue unrepentantly to admire and enjoy him as much as ever, may perhaps defend him on this ground. Donne was not prepared to surrender or to suppress any part of himself when he made poetry: neither his personal experiences for the sake of art, nor his critical and logical faculties for the sake of ecstasy, nor his self-regarding, self-mocking irony for the sake of true confession. His is the poetry of a man who tried to keep himself whole and to express himself completely, and to do this in an age which was no less tortured, difficult and disintegrating than ours. If we ever 'learn' anything from poetry, we might learn this from Donne's: that just because the age one lives in is blinkered, fragmented, cruel, stupid and humourless, its poetry does not have to resemble it.

Note

Modern Editions
  The Poems of Thomas Carew, edited by R. Dunlap (Oxford, 1949).
  The Plays and Poems of William Cartwright, edited by G. B. Evans (Madison, 1951).
  The Poems of John Cleveland, edited by B. Morris and E. Withington (Oxford, 1967).
  The Poems of George Etherege, edited by J. Thorpe (Princeton, 1963).
  The Poems of Godolphin, edited by W. Dighton (Oxford, 1931).
  The Poems of William Habington, edited by K. Allott (1948).
  The Poetical Works of Herrick, edited by L. C. Martin (Oxford, 1956).
  The Poems of Richard Lovelace, edited by C. H. Wilkinson (Oxford, 1930).
  Poems by John Wilmot Earl of Rochester, edited by V. de S. Pinto (1964).
  Rochester's Poems on Several Occasions, edited by J. Thorpe (Princeton, 1950).
  The Works of Sir John Suckling, edited by A. H. Thompson (1910).
  The Poems of Edmund Waller, edited by G. Thorn Drury (1893).

There are several good anthologies representing the love poetry of the period, including *Seventeenth Century Lyrics*, edited by N. Ault (1928); *Minor Poets of the Seventeenth Century*, edited by R. G. Howarth (1953); and *Minor Poets of the Caroline Period*, edited by G. Saintsbury (Oxford, 1905-21).

Critical Studies. H. M. Richmond, *The School of Love* (Princeton, 1964); R. L. Sharp, *From Donne to Dryden* (Chapel Hill, 1940); K. A. McEwen, *Classical Influences upon the Tribe of Ben* (Cedar Rapids, 1939), and A. Alvarez, *The School of Donne* (1961) are studies generally concerned with Caroline poetry. Among books and articles on particular poets are C. H. Hartmann, *The Cavalier Spirit and its Influence on the Life and Work of Richard Lovelace* (1925); V. de S. Pinto, *Enthusiast in Wit, A Portrait of John Wilmot, Earl of Rochester* (1962); Anon., 'The Singing Cavalier: Suckling's Muse', *Times Literary Supplement* (9 May, 1942); F. O. Henderson, 'Traditions of *Précieux* and *Libertin* in Suckling's Poetry', *English Literary History*, IV (1937), 274-98; H. Levin, 'John Cleveland and the Conceit', *The Criterion*, XIV (1934-5), 40-53; and B. R. Morris, 'John Cleveland', *Times Literary Supplement* (13 January, 1956).

II

The Failure of Love:
Love Lyrics after Donne

A. J. SMITH

★

THE love poetry written in England after Donne's death falls in the decadence of a long European tradition of lyric verse which didn't survive the seventeenth century. So it's easy to picture the Caroline love poets cooing wittily round court and town while the serious business of literature, as of life, went on elsewhere: in Bemerton or Brecon or Horton as may be. Carew and Stanley seem pathetically small fry as the heirs of the great European masters from Cavalcanti to Tasso, or sporting in the wash of mighty causes. Yet this Stuart love poetry isn't negligible. It has its voice and quality and something of its own to say, a grasp of love different enough from earlier accounts to illuminate its times and a small area of general human experience. To place it in relation to other versions of love, and in particular to the mode of witty love poetry which developed in the Renaissance courts, may help us to see where we too stand.

By the sixteen thirties European rhetoricians who had never heard of Donne were analysing wit and categorizing witty poetry. A literary critic, had there been one, might have discriminated a rich diversity of attempts to organize experience wittily, going back at least a century and a half. Donne, indeed, changed things for good. An incidental interest of these poets who wrote of love after him is that they afford us a glimpse of what he really stood for in his own time.

The stamp of Caroline lyric poetry is its rhetoric, which has to do with the vivid articulation of a dramatic syntax:

> Go search the valleys; pluck up every rose,
> You'll find a scent, a blush of her in those;
> Fish, fish for pearl or coral, there you'll see

How oriental all her colours be;
Go, call the echoes to your aid, and cry
Chloris! Chloris! for that's her name for whom I die.
(Anon., 'Tell me, you wandering spirits of the air')

The fluent immediacy of that makes the movement of the Tudor madrigal look four-square, designed more to bring up the ceremonial pattern than to urge the slight witty hyperbole to excited life. There's an original impulse here whose outward means is the management of a long syntactical unit across the stanza pattern:

What though I spend my hapless days
In finding entertainments out,
Careless of what I go about,
Or seek my peace in skilful ways,
Applying to my eyes new rays
Of beauty, and another flame
Unto my heart, my heart is still the same.
(Godolphin, 'To Chloris')

One feels the formal virtuosity, but it's subdued to the easy flow, yet dramatically modulated tautness, that gives the stanza the aspect of a spontaneously developing idea.

The lithe subtle movement intimates how far lyric verse has relinquished its established rhetoric of celebration or lament to simulate the working mind. But the evidence of a real advance is an intellectual control, which even the poetic minnows manifest in a lucid exactness and restraint, the resolved grasp of a complex idea:

Though poorer in desert I make
My selfe whilst I admyre,
The fuell which from hope I take
I give to my desire.
(Godolphin, 'Song: Noe more unto my thoughts appeare')

Often a lyric more explicitly offers a process of sharp reasoning, and the appearance of metaphysical concern:

Love, like that angel that shall call
Our bodies from the silent grave,
Unto one age doth raise us all,
None too much, none too little, have;
Nay, that the difference may be none,

He makes two, not alike, but one.
        (Cartwright, 'To Chloe, Who wished
        herself young enough for me')

In particular these Caroline poets show a marked mental vivacity, an
incessant play of wit which itself bespeaks intelligence and enacts a
sceptical wariness of the prescribed professions of love. Rapture may
still break in but its expression is tempered by a guarded awareness of
the relativity of our commitments, and of human experience altogether.

The verse gets much of its life from the way it undermines the
accepted categories of love poetry and of love itself. A quite minor love
poet such as Stanley repeatedly sets up a challenging dialectic of love
which in some way vindicates his denial of the orthodox assumptions:

> Though when I lov'd thee thou wert fair,
>   Thou art no longer so;
> Those glories all the pride they wear
>   Unto opinion owe;
>   ('The Deposition')

The play of ironic wit keeps his poetic resplendencies cool:

> Beauties, like stars, in borrow'd lustre shine;
> And 'twas my love that gave thee thine.

Without fuss the figure reverses the old hyperbolic comparison of
beauty to a star, setting up a different relationship between the two
terms that pulls the mind back to ponder its implications. There's a
pungent economy of wit in the way a qualifying aside will transform
the sense:

> The flames that dwelt within thine eye
> Do now, with mine, expire;

The slight parenthesis demolishes the old troubadour account of the
physiology of enamourment, as it makes plangent the assumption of
the brittle relativeness of sexual attraction. Stanley's diction arrests one
with its sense of a mind coolly at work in the heat of the conception—

> Since by thy scorn thou dost restore
> The wealth my love bestow'd;

—that unexpected 'wealth' quietly suggesting a more basic sense in
which his desire lends her attractive power.

Stanley's poems move by a riddling logic and with contentious independence. 'The Idolater' seems to lean on a stock scepticism, that the worship of a mistress is idolatry; but then it rejects this for a tighter and more ingenious argument which makes the lover an idolater because he now worships disdain in the shrine of love. The Petrarchan texture is ironic for the poem isn't a familiar complaint but a patronizing display of solicitude which shows the lover his fate and warns him off it by disparaging the lady:

> Since thou (Love's votary before
> Whilst He was kind) dost him no more,
> But, in his shrine, Disdain adore.
> Nor will this fire (the gods prepare
> To punish scorn) that cruel Fair,
> (Though now from flames exempted) spare;

Evidently the dialectical manner isn't spurious. The qualifications do point and sharpen; they have place in a structure of argument as well as incidental witty force. The elaborate syntax suggests a terse syllogistic movement, processes of consecutive reasoning so delicately articulated that the pattern itself appears to be the witty element.

The substance of Stanley's logic may be another matter. But its processes are in any case subordinate to the graceful resolving of the syntax, which these witty dislocations hardly disturb. The wit is not like Donne's. Stanley moves with graceful point and neat antithesis; and he is not radically disruptive. Donne's wit looks outward to life and savages people; this looks inward to itself and the ingenious neatness of the performance. Yet Caroline love lyrics aren't mere self-sufficient jewels. They resonate with impulses that suggest an imaginative engagement beyond the play of complimentary figures. A simple evocation of natural life will involve the senses in the properties of a conceit with a fresh immediacy that is unlike the bright enamel work of Elizabethan pastoral poems:

> The Lark now leaves his watry Nest
>   And climbing, shakes his dewy Wings; . . .
> Awake, awake, the Morn will never rise,
> Till she can dress her Beauty at your Eies.
>   (Davenant, 'Song')

Their conceits persistently relate amorous motives to natural vitality and decay. Habington's 'To Roses in the bosome of Castara' makes

Castara's breasts a nunnery in which the flowers are virgin nuns who
prosper there in saintly odour, exempt from the world's contagion,
until they at last have a hallowed death and find an appropriate monu-
ment in that marble place:

> In those white cloysters live secure
> From the rude blasts of wanton breath,
> Each houre more innocent and pure,
> Till you shall wither into death.

The piece is slight yet Habington turns the conceited compliment to
enact a myth of innocence. He shows himself uneasily conscious where
sexual love stands in a corrupted creation whose vitalizing force is,
specifically, whatever can keep itself free from the 'blasts of wanton
breath': she sustains the flowers because she is impervious to a lover's
persuasions. There's an ambiguity in the impulse itself, caught as it is
between its own involvement in the contagion that rages everywhere in
the world and the wish to preserve a sequestered enclave of purity and
innocence where death can at least be hallowed.

Townshend finds a different way of playing off amorous desire
against innocence, making his mistress's breasts at once a saving distrac-
tion that might have averted the Fall, and a temptation that would
have served Satan's purpose better than the apple:

> Yett had hee ledd mee to thy brest,
>   That waye was best
> To have seduct mee from thy lipp.
> Those apples tempt mee most; They bee
>   Fruit of that Tree,
> That made our first forefathers slipp.
> I dare not touch them least I dye
> The death thou threatnest with thyne Eye.
>   ('Pure Simple Love')

These love lyrics keep coming back to our frailty, as it focuses sexual
guilt. Stanley's 'On a Violet in her Breast' shows a sensuous involvement in the drooping and revival of a flower that suggests an imitation,
through this figure, of some vital organic process in which human
beings and plants and all created existences are caught up, and whose
issue is our vitality or its loss. The curious plaintiveness of the praise

comes straight out of the poem's simultaneous evocation of squandered life and self-deceiving pride:

> this violet, which before
> Hung sullenly her drooping head,
> As angry at the ground that bore
> The purple treasure which she spread,

This Vaughan-like sense of human implication in the motives of a flower—'She swells with pride', 'Yet weeps that dew which kissed her last'—gives pertinent erotic force to the imitative movement of the stanza from a dropping syntax to a sudden rearing up, the 'swell and turn' Saintsbury noted:[1]

> Doth smilingly erected grow,
> Transplanted to those hills of snow.

Nothing better shows this distinctive quality of mid-century English poetry than to put Stanley's poem by Marino's 'Fiori, stelle d'Aprile', which Professor Praz says 'supplied both *motif* and conceits for "On a Violet in her Breast" ';[2] Marino's elegant antithesis between sustaining snows and destructive fire says something quite different and belongs to another world.

    Their concern with organic processes leads these poets to locate love in a prospect of natural flux, which disturbs their intimacies with a sense of lust turned to dust:

> *Castara*, see that dust, the sportive wind
> So wantons with. 'Tis happ'ly all you'le finde
> Left of some beauty: and how still it flies,
> To trouble, as it did in life, our eyes.
>   (Habington, 'To *Castara*: Upon Beautie')

Carew sets a woman's beauty off against a whole cosmos in constant evanescence, momentary splendours forever lost, typically seizing the metaphysical circumstances in sensuous instances:

> Aske me no more whether doth stray,
> The golden Atomes of the day:
>   ('A Song')

---

[1] *Minor Poets of the Caroline Period* (Oxford, 1905), Vol. III, p. 105 *n*.
[2] 'Stanley, Sherburne and Ayres as Translators and Imitators of Italian, Spanish and French Poets', *Modern Language Review*, XX (1925), pp. 280–93.

The haunted repetitions insistently question our own standing as well as that of our world and what seems fine in it; fine because of and in its momentariness or its fall, as the stars 'That downewards fall in dead of night'. The vivid cosmic figure, casually thrown off, delicately hints that when she has accumulated all these transitory splendours she herself is only another such. But the apprehension no more poses a metaphysical issue than it stands as mere hyperbolic compliment; nor does it offer the old invitation to use one's youth while one has it: 'Collige, virgo, rosas. . . .' Carew's precise artistry, delicate above all in the exact placing of syntax and diction, holds the movement throughout in a pattern of tranquil acceptance:

> where Jove bestowes,
> When June is past, the fading rose: . . .
> These flowers as in their causes, sleepe.

The parenthetical falling cadence picks out and lingers on the last word to leave a sense of a dissolution transformed into occult splendour, of a beauty forever fading and disappearing yet preserved in a tranquil dormancy—as the nightingale after May winters in the lady's throat and keeps warm his note there.

The Christian metaphysic of death and burial is implicit, but it's not the point of the poem. What one remarks is the openness of the consciousness that feels this sense in a girl's beauty and allows it to vibrate behind the rich lyric celebration; which constantly tries the standing of beauty while appraising it. The distinction is the inherent double impulse, to celebrate this life, and to see all our worldly attachments in a final context of impermanence without disquiet.

There's a readiness to entertain a radical uncertainty, even the prospect of a random universe. Hall's 'An Epicurean Ode' lightly poises the possibility of a chance world of flux against an assured experience of love, challenging the transcendental assumptions of earlier writers without subsiding into hedonism or despair:

> Since that this thing we call the world
> By chance on Atomes is begot,
> Which though in dayly motions hurld
>   Yet weary not,
>   How doth it prove
> Thou art so fair and I in Love?

The acclaim doesn't play down the possibility of our being 'but pasted up of Earth' and not 'cradled in the skies' at all; and this is the Caroline mode, to enact a celebration of a love in the midst of questioning the point and dignity of life altogether, and to let the contrary motives stand as balancing opposites, gracefully posing a basic human question.

It isn't only that seventeenth-century poets are always conscious of ultimate issues in affirmation of love. Dante and the neo-Platonic writers were no less aware of those. What haunts these poems are the forces that negate or undermine love, from change and death to man's first disobedience and the concupiscence of Adam and Eve. They present love as a human commitment, which is therefore subject to all human chance in a universe that doesn't favour us. The perception may be expressly related to the alarms of the times, as in Jordan's 'A Cavalier's Lullaby for his Mistress', the Audenism of the sixteen forties:

> Sweet! sleep; lie still, my dear!
> Dangers be strangers
> For ever, unto thy eye or ear;

But the invocation only localizes the imperative attempt to find stability in a universe of unrest. There's a temper of urgency, precisely realized by Hall's vision of things flying and fleeting into which his poem strikes to hold a momentary stasis:

> *Romira*, stay,
> And run not thus like a young Roe away,
>   ('The Call')

Here too the immediate issue is the finding of peace, an assurance for love in the midst of wars and the suspicions wars arouse:

> No enemie
> Pursues thee (foolish girle) tis onely I,
> I'le keep off harms,
> If thou'l be pleas'd to garrison mine arms;
> What dost thou fear
> I'le turn a Traitour?

But the final concern of the poem is the irreconcilableness of love with our condition altogether. Sitting down on the plain to spin legends of 'Love Martyrs'—

> Here on this plain
> Wee'l talk *Narcissus* to a flour again;

—they do all human beings can to arrest their fate; while beyond them the sinking and setting sun points the hostility of time to lovers.

Yet these poets buy at a price the imaginative detachment that allows them to invest with a strange pastoral beauty even a sense of our inability to control or comprehend such events as love and death:

PILGRIM   Whose soile is this that such sweet Pasture yields?
              Or who art thou whose Foot stand never still?
              Or where am I?
TIME   In love.
PILGRIM   His Lordship lies above.
TIME   Yes and below, and round about
              Where in all sorts of flow'rs are growing
           Which as the early Spring puts out,
              Time fals as fast a mowing.
    (Townshend, 'A Dialogue betwixt Time and a Pilgrime')

All Townshend can make of that at last is a trite choral sentiment, that they are happy whose threads Fate twists together 'and yet draws her the longer'. It's a typical let-down; for most of these poems fail one in the end. Some Caroline love poets, caught between delight and unease, show no wish to do more with their conflicting apprehensions than hold them in graceful poise, tingeing exhilaration with wistfulness like Herrick or striking a low-keyed witty poignancy for its own sake:

        Go lovely Rose,
    Tell her that wastes her time and me,
              (Waller)

Repeatedly the issues are trivialized by the resolution they find in the poem itself or the plain evidence that the poet doesn't know what to make of his own perception. Stanley can manage no more with his revitalized violet than a conceited praise of the lady's breasts whose only force is its feeble eroticism:

      Since thou from them dost borrow scent,
      And they to thee lend ornament

the snipsnap couplet-antithesis quite belying the rich suggestiveness of his previous sense of the flower. Hall's peremptory summons to Romira leaves them nothing to do when they have made their truce with time but to confirm a platitude:

        Nay, thou maist prove
    That mans most Noble Passion is to Love.

Conceits remain conceits. Carew suggests no sense in which a lady's eyes really do preserve the splendours of fallen stars or her voice the song of the frozen nightingale, and he offers only a vague gesture to end his poem, that the phoenix itself flies to the lady's fragrant bosom to die. For all their rich promises these poems dump one back in the world of mere conceited fancy, the game of love verse. A telling instance is Vaughan, whose early poems to Amoret are full of the metaphysical apprehensions that would fall powerfully into place within the myth of *Silex Scintillans*, but which here find only a feeble conceited force in derivative arguments:

> If Creatures then that have no sence,
> But the loose tye of influence,
> (Though fate, and time each day remove
> Those things that element their love)
> At such vast distance can agree,
> Why, *Amoret*, why should not wee.
> ('To Amoret gone from him')

It's a question, indeed, how far these poems genuinely reason anything out at all, or are truly intelligent. Few of them show any overall dialectical development; commonly, the sense is complete in the first stanza and only elaborated or varied thereafter. Stanley is a test case, a poet who repeatedly leaves one feeling that the poem has somehow slipped through one's fingers and left no trace. He disputes, he qualifies, he sharply distinguishes, but little emerges:

> Waters, plants, and stones know this:
> That they love; not what Love is.
> ('The Magnet')

Nothing in the poem turns on that substantial distinction and it leads nowhere. Repeatedly one catches him sliding away from a genuine resolution to seize some adventitious excitement, whose force may none the less be quite at odds with the argument itself:

> Let us twine like amorous trees,
> And like rivers melt in one.

This is no longer part of the argument but a figure; Stanley isn't proving anything about love or marriage but imagining erotic play, as though the movement of proof itself is too mechanical and dry to hold what he really wants to say. 'The Tomb' shows up the central difference between Stanley's wit and Donne's:

> When, cruel fair one, I am slain
>   By thy disdain,
> And, as a trophy of thy scorn
>   To some old tomb am borne,

Donne's force of rhythm is dissipated in a chattering lyric neatness and a mechanical chime; where Donne cuts deep in his indictment of women's pretensions and his account of erotic motives, Stanley's verse slips so easily along because it doesn't resist the mind like that, isn't engaged with life in any effective way.

The appearance of reasoning and of dialectical toughness is worked for, an effect of art; overall, it's a simulacrum of poetic logic rather than the thing itself. Stanley would have scorned comparison with Cleveland, whose poetic life is a knockabout figurative ingenuity:

> Since 'tis my Doom, Love's under-Shreive,
>   Why this Repreive?
> Why doth my She—Advowson flie
>   Incumbency?
>   ('To Julia to expedite her promise')

But both in the end leave one nowhere and say nothing, letting the play of conceited wit stand in itself as a game. Stanley studiously maintains his witty argument at the level of urbane play, cultivating a civilized anonymity, an impersonal grace of the mind. The only evidence that he felt any need to do more is that his writing continually shows a quality of mind and a force of imagination, a kind of concern with the status of human affairs, that has no scope for development or exploration in these neat witty movements. He is not playing with shreds of ideas lightly entertained but disciplining living issues into the cool poise of impersonal art. The consequence is a highly refined art, determinedly filtering out the unassimilable or chaotic forces of life itself and only thus preserving its fine grace and order; a trivial outcome by definition.

One wouldn't attribute to all mid-seventeenth-century love poets this Housman-like determination to perfect the game and to admit only so much of living experience as may be controlled and impersonalized within its terms. But their writing echoes with apprehensions which find no adequate outlet in the categories of amorous poetry. Possibly the commitment to love lyrics itself insulated poets from the serious life of the day. But for Dante, Petrarch, and Michelangelo love poetry had offered a way of dealing with their fundamental experience, and even of coming to terms with ultimate reality. After Donne, the gulf between writing of love and writing of final things seems absolute. Vaughan is the evidence that in mid-seventeenth-century England sexual love had become categorically distinct from the love that holds the universe in sway, and that a choice compelled itself between a fashionable amorousness and the imperative search for truth.

If Caroline love poetry is a backwater, as Miss C. V. Wedgwood argued,[3] it may be less because the poets were reactionaries who followed the king in wanting to do without politics altogether than because sexual love no longer offered a paradigm of the issues that then confronted men. The divorce between poetry and a career is conspicuous in those writers who had some part in the events of the sixteen forties —Lovelace, Montrose, Newcastle, Godolphin, Davenant, Waller. No doubt some of them really weren't much more than Pope's 'gentlemen who wrote with ease'.[4] Love was as ever the courtly fashion, and there are Caroline versifiers enough who stand at the tail end of a long line of jongleurs, court wits occupied with the old formulas of lyric love long after they were played out.

Yet Carew and Suckling, and Rochester later, are not like their courtly predecessors, in England or anywhere else. There's a quality which follows a distinctive understanding, a difference which may be a real index of change. The best of the Stuart love poets can afford light on what was happening to society and sexual manners in seventeenth-century England. Their grasp of their milieu and how they stand in it, as well as of their own experience, is sharp enough to make the comparison with earlier love poetry illuminating. They mark a shift in attitudes to love from 1600 to 1700, the decisive shift that defines us too.

Their poetry bears vivid witness to the temper of its society. It celebrates a lady's beauty by enacting the poet's wish to undress her as she walks before him (Suckling, 'Upon my Lady Carlile's walking in Hampton Court Garden'); finds a thousand wittily oblique ways of lingering over a mistress's pudenda, or on acts of penetration; embellishes recherché erotic situations such as that of a lady not yet

[3] 'Poets and Politics in Baroque England', *Penguin New Writing* 21 (1944), pp. 123–36.
[4] *The First Epistle of the Second Book of Horace Imitated*, line 108.

enjoyed by her husband, of one's mistress being bled by the surgeon, of plump beauty, of beauty in rags or in chains:

> But if too rough, too hard they presse,
> Oh they but Closely, closely kisse.
> (Lovelace, 'A Guiltlesse Lady imprisoned; after penanced')

Carew gives the game away when he resolves the argument for single-ness of love with the image of a wolf which starves because it can't decide between two sheep before it ('Incommunicabilitie of Love'). Yet if all these poems assume a motive of predatory appetite they are chiefly conscious of how society must inhibit its scope, and much of the poet's art goes in refining erotic provocation, or throwing a glittering veil over the raw impulse:

> and with amorous Charmes
> Mixt with thie flood of Frozen snowe
> In Crimson streames Ile force the redd Sea flowe.
> (? Carew, 'On the Green Sickness')

The focus of such displays of a decadent sensibility isn't in doubt. This image of the penetration of a virgin occurs in an account of England as a Paphos where—as Carew put it—'Whatever pleaseth lawfull is' ('To the Queene') and Henrietta Maria queens it over a Court of Love. The new style of court hyperbole defines the queen's relationship to the king in erotic terms, extolling her power to control and make stable the wild lusts of masculine nature; and the new version of order, as of chivalry, turns on the natural capacity of the right female to hold a man to herself, so centring his errant fancies and concentrating his powers:

> He, only can wilde lust provoke,
> Thou, those impurer flames canst choke;
> And where he scatters looser fires,
> Thou turn'st them into chast desires: . . .
> Which makes the rude Male satisfied
> With one faire Female by his side;
> (Carew, 'To the Queene')

The code is written large in the action of Carew's court masque *Coelum Britannicum* which elaborately mythologizes court ceremonial in terms of erotic play, rendering chivalric valour as sexual virility and beauty as the power to satisfy it:

> Pace forth thou mighty British Hercules,
> With thy choyce band, for onely thou, and these,
> May revell here, in Loves Hesperides.

So nice a mingling of Tasso and Donne, with its Jonsonian refinements of texture, suggests the limit of Carew's innovating power. The relationship of the writing to a particular society distinguishes it from earlier love poetry, as from the classical poems Carew reworked.[5] Charles's court wasn't like the great Renaissance courts; it had its own myth of state, and its own style which the queen's school of love helped to set. In particular it seems to have taken as the accepted understanding a naturalistic account of behaviour which Donne had worked out privately, as though he authorized an area of sexual experience. No doubt Donne spoke for his time and people fastened on him because he located their own understanding. At all events there could have been no place for a Spenser or a Sidney in a court which shows us an elaborate ritual of love styled Platonic[6] yet proceeding on assumptions as ironically remote from Plato's as from the Platonic notions of previous European love poetry; more to do with Horner than Diotima, indeed. Times have moved on when a quiet country parson can turn Jonson's sensuous mythologizing to cheerful erotic fantasy:

> I dream'd this mortal part of mine
> Was Metamorphoz'd to a Vine;
> Which crawling one and every way
> Enthrall'd my dainty *Lucia*.
>   (Herrick, 'The Vine')

or when the distinguished translator of a prime text of neo-Platonic love is himself a thoroughgoing relativist who locates a woman's beauty in her power to arouse male desire.[7]

---

[5] See K. A. McEwen, *Classical Influences upon the Tribe of Ben* (Cedar Rapids, 1939).

[6] See K. M. Lynch, *The Social Mode of Restoration Comedy*, New York, 1926, especially chapters iii to v; and F. O. Henderson, 'Traditions of *Précieux* and *Libertin* in Suckling's Poetry', *English Literary History*, IV (1937), pp. 274-98.

[7] Thomas Stanley translated Pico della Mirandola's Commentary on the Canzone of Celestial and Divine Love of G. Benivieni, as *A Platonick Discourse upon Love* (1651).

The new understanding of love gets its coherence from its social focus, complicating erotic impulse with considerations of prestige and style. The poems of this court circle tacitly suppose a few basic motives which are restrained in their scope only by each other, but chiefly by the fact that they can't be realized outside civil society and are therefore to be held in play with the requirements of civil convention and the satisfactions which that too offers. None of these motives operates simply, for social standing is itself at odds with the assumption of common desires and appetites, and so are the conventions that govern women's conduct; moreover the rivalry between women and men is a struggle for advantage in which both desire like ends and each has a power the other wants. A woman's fame and her attractive power too may draw from men's desire, and their willingness to celebrate her so as to express or satisfy it. The terms on which Carew undertakes to praise a lady are that she give herself to him for their mutual pleasure; he'll spend his treasure if she'll unlock hers—'so we each other blesse' ('To a Lady that desired I would love her'). Waller's 'The Story of Phoebus and Daphne, Applied' is a mythic embroidering of this bargaining game, falling so flaccidly because it finds an easy way out:

> He catched at love, and filled his arm with bays.

The struggle reduces to a simple issue between desirous chase, and chastity; and the fame that accrues, explicitly to the poet, implicitly to the lady, is just the unlooked-for by-product of hispoetic pursuit which he contemplates with equal self-satisfaction.

Carew's poetry in particular idealizes a civil order founded in the mutual accommodation of natural drives. It's an order infinitely more precarious, neo-Hobbesian indeed, than the old Tudor understanding, since it assumes a nice equipoise of basic impulses with no extrinsic regulation. Donne's insights impel the moves of a coterie game.

In the sixteen thirties this is the court game of love. One is always aware in Carew and Suckling and Lovelace of the enclosed court circle and its sense of strain, outwardly expressed in sophistication: 'If it pleases, it's lawful', pulls against 'If it's lawful then it will please'. A highly guarded manœuvring, far removed from Queen Elizabeth's draconian regimen, follows out the sense of allowed natural impulses which require at once outlet and regulation. Celebrity now centres in the power to excite, or in the advantage one can gain over desire without denying it or finally refusing it. Practical exigencies of a kind reduce poetic art to an ideal projection of the manners of an over-refined circle, whose first concern is to bring powerful motives into negligent control. On the men's side the style itself is the outward means to that, the assumption of an elegant rakishness, or of cool detachment rather than servitude. Style won't resolve the clash of interests even so. Carew's artistic superiority is that he sets up a self-consistent poetic poise whereas his associates fall back on extraneous supports, on sentimental loyalties or the rituals of party or coterie.

Carew's best lyrics invite comparison with Petrarchan love poems, but they suppose a wholly different relationship from those and imply altered attitudes:

> Then shalt thou weepe, entreat, complaine
> To Love, as I did once to thee;
> ('Song: To my inconstant Mistris')

'To my inconstant Mistris' promises a revenge not because the lady has scorned a suitor out of her invincible chastity, but because she has been unfaithful to an established lover. The poem assumes that she was once obdurate, yielded, swore oaths of fidelity, and then betrayed him; so that it's he who now rejects her for the promise of a firmer bliss with another mistress, 'Which my strong faith shall purchase me'. This is no clash of moral absolutes but a comedy of society intrigue where hopeful sentiment offsets a whim of sexual appetite. Yet Carew's vision is nothing like so radical as Donne's. He is sceptical and relative only so far as will quicken the easy grace of song, for his poems are not really part of a world of infidelities and momentary appetites masquerading under the styles of morality. They seek to come to terms with their circumstances, and their measured coolness is the condition of his finding an accommodation, bringing the clashing motives into urbane equipoise. 'Ingratefull beauty threatned' redresses old odds by weighing the real disposition of forces between a lover and his mistress, balancing her pride against his capacity to give her fame and the occasion of pride, the public against the private satisfactions of sexual power:

> That killing power is none of thine,
> I gave it to thy voyce, and eyes:
> Thy sweets, thy graces, all are mine;

To argue that the effect of her beauty isn't inherent but a consequence of her fame, which he has given her, is to do something more than to play for advantage or to discard a European tradition of love poetry:

> Thou art my starre, shin'st in my skies;

The possessive marks the gulf between Carew and those idealizing affirmations that the lady is truly a star—'Un'alta stella di nova bellezza,/che del sol ci to' l'ombra la sua luce' (Dino Frescobaldi, c. 1300). It argues that a woman's power accrues to her not only from our desire for her but from the celebrity it gives her when it is promulgated, and that her chief praise and real beauty isn't her invincible chastity but the fame her lovers accord her.

Carew's moral grasp amounts to a wary discrimination, which takes down presumptions with deadly nuances of tone:

> Thou hadst, in the forgotten crowd
> Of common beauties, liv'd unknowne,

His rhetoric enacts a cool sanity, opposing to the orthodox ardours a suave detachment that cuts love down to the measure of a civilized social activity. The quality of his poems, as their intelligence, lies in a nice fidelity to the complex truth of that vision. If they move dialectically it's not with Donne's dynamic life. They hold a poise and offer at most the urbane tension of disharmony resolved, an imbalance redressed. 'To my inconstant Mistris' shows a precisely calculated symmetry which has moral force in the way it works out opposite fates from contrary causes, but presents a different order of mental activity from the unpredictable movement of, say, 'Womans constancy'. It unfolds the consequences implicit in the given order of things with no surprise, no probing energy, no pregnancy of reference; the economy of the poem is a lucid balanced articulation which models the law of a moral universe where justice is exactly done. Carew's lyrics advance by reversing some vested prescription and then sharply drawing out the consequences, so as to redress the balance his way, moving always to the *mot juste*, the exact clinching stroke. His real mental distinction is his power to hold a complicated chain of argument together and give it dramatic tension by his lyric syntax; but the order is syntactical not syllogistic in that it offers the static articulation of a finished pattern rather than a live movement of the mind.

Carew's wit has to do with his complete mastery of a lyric rhetoric, the easy yet precisely articulated modulation of the sense across the elaborate stanza pattern. Its character is implicit in its means, which are an infinitely delicate poising and placing of forces, a sensitive control of tone and nuance, the subtle varying of the tension between syntax and formal scheme to point, edge, inflect. There's no doubt that Carew really did put in the meticulous labour Suckling twitted him with (in 'A Sessions of the Poets') and that it went to suggest intelligence in tight control; so that each stanza models the resolved structure of a complex thought held whole and taut in the mind. His much praised intelligence doesn't amount to any trenchancy of thought; one locates it in the cool suppleness of the poise, the sensitive grasp of all the implications, the colloquial ease that yet preserves the movement of song.

Suckling was a hedonist who engaged for no such artistic pains as Carew took—because he sought only to strike a pose—but who saw as clearly as Rochester what fashionable life now offered. His poetry offers our earliest example of a life centred in a style, which in his case draws out of a lively but in the end desperately sceptical view of sexual activity as a focus of life altogether. His recurrent figures for love— a flame which rarely burns just at the right height but 'would die, /Held down or up too high' ('Song: No, no, fair heretic'), or a clock that strikes 'Strange blisses/And what you best like' only at an unpredictable critical moment ('That none beguiled be')—show him preoccupied with the uncertainties of tumescence and orgasm. He writes out of an experience that repeatedly confirms the precariousness of attachments founded in involuntary appetite or taste, quickly satiated, or in adventitious fancy:

> I am confirm'd a woman can
> Love this, or that, or any other man:
> ('Verses')

In our circumstances consummated experience always disappoints for the reality can never come up to the imagined expectation; women can keep their hold on us only by delaying fruition—

> Fruition adds no new wealth, but destroys,
> And while it pleaseth much the palate, cloys;
> ('Against Fruition')

—as we make ourselves free of them by bringing about a chastened detumescence:

> A quick corse, methinks, I spy
> In ev'ry woman; . . .
> They mortify, not heighten me;
> ('Farewell to Love')

As lovers we operate in an area of total uncertainty where our will is at the mercy not only of chance and occasion but of women's whims, disguised as scruples—'I hate a fool that starves her love, /Only to feed her pride' ('' Tis now, since I sate down before')—and of our own impulsions:

> For thou and I, like clocks, are wound
> Up to the height, and must move round:
> ('To His Rival')

The whole force of the writing suggests what Suckling never explicitly recognizes, that the hazardousness of love only instances the arbitrariness of our affairs altogether in the kind of universe we now inhabit.

Love in Suckling's poetry as sometimes in Donne's is a sport or chase, a predatory hawking in a spirit of desperation. But he is no compulsive Don Juan. His poems define a social activity, and their style and voice follow out his sceptical diagnosis of love by way of regulating the relationships of men and women in polite society: for one thing, proposing the kind of bargains they can make with themselves and with each other—'I offer'd forty crowns /To lie with her a night or so . . .' ('Proffer'd Love Rejected'). So he found a way of accommodating in lyric verse the easy throwaway manner of coffee house or salon, just at the moment when Milton was meditating the apotheosis of artificial style:

> I prithee spare me, gentle boy,
> Press me no more for that slight toy,
> That foolish trifle of an heart;
> ('Song')

The pose of negligent indifference or bland self-mockery is a means of preserving self-respect, one's cool independence of a humiliating enslavement which can pervert social style:

> Then hang me, ladies, at your door,
> If e'er I dote upon you more.
> ('Verses: I am confirm'd a woman can')

Love may at least be kept in its place among the affairs of a man of the world or the town:

> When I am hungry, I do eat,
> And cut no fingers 'stead of meat; . . .
> I visit, talk, do business, play,
> And for a need laugh out a day:
>   ('The Careless Lover')

The careless elegance is studied; for style and taste are the one way of distinguishing in love between gentleman and clown—'th'unhallow'd sort of men' ('Against Fruition')—where there's no difference at all in the motives themselves and men's condition is common. Ben Jonson passed on to the Caroline poets his sense of a traditional conviviality, but they render it as a gentlemanly ritual, consciously maintained to mark a status. Their association of love with tippling—Suckling's vivid evocations of tavern scenes, Lovelace's ardent pledges—is truly the enactment of a social stance or style where style is just about all they can hold on to.

A witty style perforce gave an opening to intelligence, and the wit of the poets of Charles's court, often a means of heightening erotic excitements, became an open struggle to make sense of things. Lovelace was a barefaced poetical voluptuary, but his best lyrics show him trying to strike the right accommodation between the divergent elements of a creed, with the apt swagger to carry off the gesture. His wit is a matter of playing off against each other a few fixed claimants to his allegiance and clinching the issue with the fit sentiment:

> I could not love thee (Deare) so much,
> Lov'd I not Honour more.
>   ('Song: To Lucasta, Going to the Warres')

His sole way out of the self-posed dilemma between one love and another, his mistress and martial valour, is to flourish the profession that satisfies both sides, the talisman which all must approve.

Lovelace's shorter poems commonly offer the appearance of a genuine dialectic. 'To Althea, From Prison'—'When Love with unconfined wings'—plays off a physical imprisonment against the bondage of love, getting its witty bite from the conceited reversal of the physical fact which makes imprisonment in a just cause the only freedom worth having. Love, as itself a liberating imprisonment, here gets typically taken up into a larger style of caste allegiance—wine and loyal pledges, the king, freedom. These are the articles of Lovelace's chivalric code and they can only be declaimed with spirit; thereafter he simply reiterates the gesture, inweaving it with the witty proof as though there really is something for intelligence to work on. But all the poem can offer at last is the warm evocation of the situation itself and the fine assurance of the generous impulse.

The brittleness of a faith founded in the end on prescriptive enthusiasms shows up in the one poem which tries to face up to reality, 'To Lucasta. From Prison'. This time Lovelace soon slips aside from the ostensible witty play of one bondage against another to engage in a real testing of the sense in which freedom of soul is now possible. He uses the momentary liberty imprisonment gives him to try his loving allegiance around the several causes that offered for it in the sixteen forties, rejecting each in turn as unworthy or no longer accessible in the circumstances—peace, war, religion, Parliament, liberty, property, political reform, the public faith. Finally he falls back on the one object outstanding:

> What then remaines but th'only spring
> Of all our loves and joyes? The KING.

But his celebration of the king's power and right is itself plainly felt to be a forlorn gesture in a situation where 'now an universall mist/Of Error is spread or'e each breast'; and the poem finishes with a bewildered plea to the king—or it may be God—for light to see 'How to serve you, and you trust me'. Here is the cavalier style at the end of its resource, attaching everything to a personal loyalty in a way which gives some substance to Miss Wedgwood's claim that the political irrelevance of these poets shows us why the king's cause was bound to fail.[8] With the king gone too the mist would soon engulf Lovelace and his ilk.

Lovelace miserably lived out the holocaust and his poems are as much evidence art can offer of the way the court culture crumbled or was already crumbling at the time of the Civil War. Carew died just before war broke; and Suckling fled the country after failing to rescue Strafford in 1641, to kill himself (as report was) in France a year later. Vaughan's turn from Amoret to lost innocence and countries beyond the stars, his imperative sense that it's every man for himself in the oncoming cataclysm, gives us a measure of the psychic shock Royalists

[8] 'Poets and Politics in Baroque England', pp. 127-8.

sustained by the events of 1648–9 and what love poetry counted for then.

When the Cavalier voice is heard again there's a difference:

> I have been in love, and in debt, and in drink,
>   This many and many a year;

Love; sottishness; debt: this is Brome, pungently hitting off a character ('The Mad Lover') and in that vein readily represented as the sleazy voice of fagged out Royalism.[9] Rochester confirms the altered style:

> While each brave *Greek* embrac'd his Punk,
> Lull'd her asleep, and then grew drunk.
>   ('Grecian Kindness: A Song')

The deeds around Troy and the city's doom reduce themselves in the end to the common human solaces, coolly pinned down in the diction.

Brome in one way as Rochester in another reveals the crisis of love poetry as the seventeenth century wore on. In Italy love dwindles to a clever-pretty Arcadian formula; at home people are still desperately trying to say something real, and they do in fact say something desperate. Love poetry itself becomes a search for something to hold on to, some vestige of the order that underpropped the civil culture of the humanist Renaissance courts. Christopher Hill points out that whereas the Tudor court had been the focus of national life and culture the Stuarts precipitated a flight to the country, of realistic as well as disgusted courtiers.[10] The poetry itself witnesses a new concern with the country and with rural activities. If Ben Jonson's celebrations of great country houses suggest a seventeenth-century version of civil culture,[11] then Fanshawe's ode of 1630 on the king's proclamation *Commanding the Gentry to reside upon their estates in the Country* celebrates what seems to have been a conscious attempt to root English society in the landed gentry and in the big country estates:

---

[9] As by C. V. Wedgwood in *Poetry and Politics under the Stuarts* (1960), pp. 11–13.

[10] *Intellectual Origins of the English Revolution* (Oxford, 1965), pp. 11–13.

[11] See L. C. Knights, 'On the Social Background of Metaphysical Poetry', *Scrutiny* XIII (1945), pp. 37–52.

> you will find
> In that sweet life more solid joys,
> More true contentment to the mind,
> Than all town toys.

Contentments, one observes, which draw from Eden-like innocence
as the discontents of the court from guilt:

> 'Tis innocence in the sweet blood
> Of cherries, apricocks, and plums
> To be imbued.

That at least was something to hold on to; and that too went under
Cromwell. The issue between town society and country retirement
was a seventeenth-century crux which became a moral crisis. The
post-war love poets suggest, however exaggeratedly, that there was a
social crisis here too in the dwindling down to sexual relationships
alone of the old humanist arts and satisfactions of civil life; or rather
to sexual relationships and style, of which love poetry is the index.
They seek in love something that will give life a grace, when the order
which poetic love grew from is disintegrating. So that love poetry itself
is no longer a symbolic game, metaphysical or moral as may be, but
the record of extremity, a ritual of search and emptiness held briefly
together by the Restoration coterie-life centred on St. James, Covent
Garden, and 'the Fields of Lincolns Inn' (? Rochester, 'Song').

The love poetry that follows the Restoration shows no novel grasp
of love but the style has changed with the circumstances. Etherege and
Buckhurst aren't so much urbane as knowing, and ribald; the delicate
poise is gone and there's nothing that holds things together save the
chase itself, or the act itself:

> Cuffley! whose beauty warms the age,
> And fills our youth with love and rage,
> Who like fierce wolves pursue the game,
> While secretly the lecherous dame
> With some choice gallant takes her flight
> And in a corner fucks all night.
> (Etherege, 'Mr. Etherege's Answer')

These lyrics and verse-letters signal the shift of focus from court to
town, from the manners of an enclosed circle to sexual adventure in
the Holborn streets. Their mark is a Boswellian character of lively

engagement in the sport with a temper of sharp self-appraisal, a zestful candour about sexual motives:

> Against the Charmes our *Ballocks* have,
>   How weak all humane skill is?
> Since they can make a *Man* a *Slave*,
>   To such a *Bitch* as *Phillis*.
>   (Rochester, 'Song')

The *coup de grâce* couldn't be neater. Love, already impugned by the conceit that beauty is the lover's gift, reduces at last to the basic urge that draws us to a woman in spite of ourselves and of her. And far from offering us independence the revision supposes something desperate, an abject slavery to our own erotic state.

In respect of our common nature these poems pointedly play off our social discriminations against virile prowess, and negate the orthodox accounts of love:

> Thus she who Princes had deny'd,
>   With all their Pomp and Train;
> Was, in the lucky Minute try'd,
>   And yielded to a Swain.
> (Rochester, 'A Song: As *Cloris* full of harmless thoughts')

The notion of single fidelity gets a sharp deflating thrust:

> 'Tis not that I'm weary grown
> Of being yours, and yours alone:
> But with what Face can I incline,
> To damn you to be only mine?
>   (Rochester, 'Upon his Leaving his Mistress')

A nice erotic observation stands courtly servitude on its head:

> That much she fears, (but more she loves,)
>   Her Vassal should undo her.
>   (Rochester, 'To Corinna: A Song')

Pastoral idyll comes down to the sexual feats of Strephon, Phillis and Coridon under a tattered blanket in Lincoln's Inn Fields; or to the undoing of Cloris in a pig-sty:

> Now pierced is her Virgin Zone
> She feels the Foe within it;

> She hears a broken amorous Groan,
> The panting Lover's fainting moan,
> Just in the happy Minute.
> (Rochester, 'A Song: To Chloris')

A casual scepticism, following out Donne to the brutal extreme, brings down the whole house of cards that Platonic metaphysicians had erected upon the supposition of an absolute beauty:

> This shows Love's chiefest magic lies
> In women's cunts, not in their eyes:
> (Etherege, 'Mr. Etherege's Answer')

Quality apart these verses speak of a world and a mode of behaviour. They give substance to the ethic of a coterie and are themselves coterie acts, like tippling, to keep up the spirit and fellowship of the game. No doubt they present idealized projections of living pursuits, gaming, drinking and drabbing turned into graceful witty song by prescriptive use; but they are nakedly the outcome of the hunt for orgasm and wine, keeping erotic excitements in prospect and turning on erotic laws.

It can't be a local matter when this becomes the accepted style of young English aristocrats, and hence the poetic mode. The point isn't of course the perennial pastimes of moneyed youth but the moral temper of art, whose shifts from the twelfth century on one might gauge by the sense that successive poetic circles gave to 'nobility' itself. The idealism of a Cavalcanti or a Sidney has gone, and the sport of the Town becomes the exemplary use, almost a faith. For love poets at any rate the relationships of sex, and possibly of this world to the next, had been tacitly settled that way. There will be no more serious talk of beauty as a ray of the Divine Essence or of women as unattainable miracle-working stars; of a hierarchy of the faculties from the sensible to the intelligible, and a transcendence from sense to Idea, Idea to Form.

For the fact is that whether or not neo-Platonism went out of the window with pseudo-Dionysius, the assumption of a world of sense and a world of spirit is obsolete. The metaphysical basis of medieval and Renaissance love poetry has quietly dissolved, and left . . . Rochester, Etherege, Buckhurst and their peers. Salvation now is the right social pose, a style of living and of gentlemanly conduct not a moral refinement or a metaphysical transcendence. If young bloods and rakes take over love poetry this isn't a mere modish annexation.

c

It's an index of what love means and what it no longer means, and perhaps of what life no longer means. We must ask ourselves when it is that we next encounter a considerable body of love poetry in English.

By the century's end 'love' is no longer the figure of a relationship between our nature and a higher order. It is whatever we can personally make of the human attraction between men and women; in particular it is mutual erotic passion and the search for sexual satisfaction. The mode these poets enact at least gives the hunt for satisfaction the dignity of an approved way of life. Their verses make sense of love that way, as in its own way did the poetry of the *dolce stil novo* or of Michelangelo.

Rochester presses this sense as far as it will go towards giving life a point. What another writer might have left as a stereotyped witty play, in him repeatedly suggests a real concern to wring a faith from our errant devotions:

> Lest once more wand'ring from that Heav'n,
>   I fall on some base heart unblest;
> Faithless to thee, False, unforgiv'n
>   And lose my Everlasting rest.
>   ('A Song: Absent from thee I languish still')

He has a discomforting way of putting life in pawn with a ribald gibe:

> Love a Woman! you're an Ass,
>   'Tis a most insipid Passion; . . .
>
> Let the Porter, and the Groom,
>   Things design'd for dirty Slaves;
> Drudge in fair *Aurelia's* Womb,
>   To get Supplies for Age and Graves.
>   ('A Song')

But it's characteristic of him, too, to express his revulsion against the activity because it thus unbecomingly levels gentleman with drudge when his fitter employment might be witty converse and drink.

If Rochester's poetry is the extreme endeavour to bring love down to a flourish upon the momentary sexual pleasure, it looks further because of the concern he shares with greater seventeenth-century poets to find metaphysical sense in his experience and to make his discontents a sceptical judgement upon our condition now. His heightened awareness of the promises of life, or a few aspects of it, only measures the failure of our experience ever to live up to them:

> How blest was the Created State
> Of Man and Woman, e're they fell,
> Compar'd to our unhappy Fate,
> We need not fear another Hell!

'The Fall: A Song' follows Donne's 'Farewell to Love' in ironically rendering our falling short of the innocent state wholly in terms of erotic pleasure and the shortcomings of sexual performance now:

> Naked, beneath cool Shades, they lay,
> Enjoyment waited on Desire:
> Each Member did their Wills obey,
> Nor could a Wish set Pleasure higher.

But it makes this sense a character of our present existence as 'poor Slaves to Hope and Fear', where we can never have a secure hold on our joys:

> They lessen still as they draw near,
> And none but dull Delights endure.

'The Fall' is a quintessential seventeenth-century poem—Donne via Suckling—in the way it places inquietude so precisely in a universal myth. But when Rochester turns it all to a bland throwaway ending, unlike Stanley and the rest he finds something real to say:

> Then, *Cloris*, while I Duty pay,
> The Nobler Tribute of my Heart,
> Be not You so severe to say,
> You love me for a frailer Part.

What looks like an ironic exhortation is in fact a pathetic one. It asks her to keep up the pretence of a sentimental loyalty though the reality is frailer, because that's the only way by which they can preserve any illusion of satisfaction and of permanence.

   Rochester's decisive stroke is to make sexual experience the telling instance of human instability. He shares with his circle a commitment to the momentary bliss, but his 'Love and Life' amounts to something as different from Etherege's 'To a Lady, Asking Him How Long He Would Love Her' as from Suckling's old 'No such constant Lover':

> All my past Life is mine no more,
>   The flying hours are gone:

With the past lost and the future not yet his then 'The present Mo-ment's all my Lot', which he dedicates 'as fast as it is got' to his mistress. And this casual reassurance is the only constancy we can hold:

> Then talk not of Inconstancy,
>   False Hearts, and broken Vows:
> If I, by Miracle, can be
> This live-long Minute true to thee,
>   'Tis all that Heav'n allows.

There's a poignant irony in the way a flippant article of a rake's creed deepens to make a judgement on life altogether and to disturb our sense of identity and of permanence. The poem takes scepticism further, because it implies behind this relativity of human assurances a universal condition of which our lack of grasp on ourselves and on our own experience is only the most immediate evidence. Like other poems of the day 'Love and Life' places love in respect of the little time we have and of the point of human life at large. As earlier European lyric poetry it takes love for a type of men's activities, pointing the insecurity of our human circumstances thus. What is distinctive, and by contrast shock-ing, is the profession of amorous intrigue which brings love down to the momentary truth of a passing liaison and presses that sceptical insight through to life as a whole. There seems more at stake than a tradition of love poetry when erotic bliss is taken for the summation of our existence, and the fragility of sexual pleasure for a map of life. At the risk of melodramatizing a slight poem one might think that this is not only poetic love but a mind at the end of its tether.

Rochester curiously places love in a historical process of decline—it's love now not love at large—while removing the Christian implications of the myth. For all the count he takes of disobedience, sin, or grace, the Fall meant no more than the loss of a Golden Age. He plays on his secular rendering too, for the fall of his poem is also the untimely fall of one's member, the inherent inadequacy of men's powers to match their appetite and will. The implication of sex in the Fall itself allows this blasphemous reduction of the point of the event to its progressive effect on our sexual prowess. But the paradox of Rochester's poetry is that it reduces life to secular experience, what we can make of things here and now, while enforcing a sense of some original rightness which we fall ever further short of. It looks to a degeneration from a first perfect state to account for the way life fails us centrally, the gap between the way things might be and the way they are. Rochester falls too pat as a case of an apprehension looking for a faith, an aspirant to the abyss or to dramatic conversion. But his dilemma points the failing of seventeenth-century love poets, which now locates itself in the inadequacy of love, so understood, to sustain what they want to make of it and to offer in itself a coherent experience of life or a certitude to live by. The recurrent failure of their richest poems truly marks their inability to get beyond the recognition that in some manner love is bound up with the way life both surprises and disappoints us, with its splendours and promises which fail and fade, or always fall short.

Seventeenth-century love poets differ from their predecessors above all in that human love had ceased to present an issue between sense and spirit, and hence didn't confront a lover with the inherent depravity of sense or the unreality of this sensible world. The idea of a degeneration from the created human state puts it upon us neither to renounce nor to transcend our human capacities but to recover and to realize them fully. A yearning for lost innocence, felt or affected, pervades seventeenth-century lyric poetry with its vibrations of wistfulness or guilt. Comparing personable young girls with short-lived flowers is one way of playing off innocence against blasting lust; another is to pose an innocent affection which has now matured into desire:

> Ah! Chloris! that I now could sit
> As unconcerned as when
> Your infant beauty could beget
> No pleasure, nor no pain.
> (Sedley, 'To Chloris')

Versions of the traffic between a young girl and an older admirer run from the delicate to the perverse, from Bold's warnings of the power innocent beauty has over men ('Chloris, forbear a while') to Rochester's 'A Song of a Young Lady to her Ancient Lover'. Their elegaic poignancy mingles celebration and regret, as if the desire to praise in itself sadly confirms our ambiguous fallen state, that we can't now love innocently.

The equivocal standing of passion in the affairs of Adam and Eve doesn't compel us to mark off love from sexual desire. Seventeenth-century poets don't distinguish between a lower love and a higher, but put forward an indivisible sexual impulse which pulls two ways, to innocence and life but also to corruptness and death. Love offers no choice of courses, and no conflict; indeed to choose would be naïve for we can't alter our condition and the disregarded impulse is there none the less. In this, love is itself a type of the contradictions the world now confronts us with, the opposite impulses we find in ourselves—that 'double heart' Marvell spoke of [12]—and must preclude total commitments to our human ends. Short of abandoning society altogether our only reasonable response must be a working accommodation with ourselves and others, so as to gain what we can without relinquishing too much:

> MIRABELL: Well, have I liberty to offer conditions—that when you are dwindled into a wife, I may not be beyond measure enlarged into a husband?
> (Congreve, *The Way of the World*, IV. v)

The altered status of love in the seventeenth century reflects an inclination to assess actions historically, that is relative to each other in time, rather than as absolute metaphysical events. Love, as a critical instance of our present state, invites not moral decision but placing. So that love poetry loses its dynamic character and becomes a lyric realization of the way things are with us, defining the ambiguity of an impulse which thus accompanies its promises with the recognition of inevitable falling short. It's a haunted art, because it balances the one prospect against the other and holds both in play by way of heightening our apprehension of how far love is bound by time.

The moral decisions that bore upon love poetry were now more sweeping, and imperative. A heightened apprehension of where our world and we ourselves stand in time committed seventeenth-century writers to sense where earlier moralists had spurned it. They attended to natural processes so as to try our circumstances against the created life around us, acknowledging that all fallen existence is subject to the same laws. Reading nature aright one may glimpse the original state in the present decay. In the seventeenth century the effort to see things as they really are was a search for the condition of our lost Eden.

The crucial issue for these people was how we can accept the way things stand with us and yet go on living in society at all. The one

[12] See C. Hill, 'Society and Andrew Marvell', *Modern Quarterly* 4 (1946), pp. 6–31.

choice which really mattered was that between living in the corrupted world and living apart from it, striking the best terms one could with one's fellows or making the only total commitment now possible. The dynamic impulse in seventeenth-century poetry was the lonely effort to bring home our fallen condition so as to remake oneself nearer the first state. After Donne, sexual love offered no way to that.

Note

Verse Epistles

The first to be printed in English were those by Thomas Lodge in *A Fig for Momus* (1595). Donne's verse letters, like most of his poetry, were not published until they appeared in the *Poems* of 1633, two years after his death. Samuel Daniel's epistles were included in his *A Panegyricke Congratulatorie to the King's Maiestie* in 1603. Several of Jonson's epistles were collected in *The Forrest* (*Workes*, 1616), and in *The Under-wood* (*Workes*, 1640); but many of his ungathered occasional poems are also epistolary in form. Michael Drayton's *Elegies upon Sundry Occasions* (1627) contains his epistles.

Modern Editions. The principal quotations are taken from the following texts: *Horace: Satires, Epistles, and Ars Poetica*, with an English translation by H. R. Fairclough (Loeb Classical Library, London and New York, 1926). *Seneca: Ad Lucilium Epistulae Morales*, with an English translation by Richard M. Gummere (3 vols., Loeb Classical Library, London and New York, 1917–25). *Essays by Michel Lord of Montaigne*, translated by John Florio (1603) (3 vols., Everyman's Library, London and New York, 1910). *John Donne: The Satires, Epigrams and Verse Letters*, edited with an introduction and commentary by W. Milgate (Oxford, 1967) (page references cited as 'Milgate'). *Poems of Ben Jonson* edited with an introduction by George Burke Johnston (The Muses' Library, London, 1954). *Poems of Michael Drayton* edited with an introduction by John Buxton (2 vols., The Muses' Library, London, 1953). *Samuel Daniel: Poems and A Defence of Ryme* edited by Arthur Colby Sprague (Cambridge, Mass., 1930, Chicago, 1950).

Scholarship and Criticism. There is no published study of the verse epistle in this period, although Wesley Trimpi, in *Ben Jonson's Poems* (Stanford, 1962), deals at some length with the epistolary tradition from ancient times in relation to Jonson's revival of the classical plain style. F. P. Wilson's *Elizabethan and Jacobean* (Oxford, 1945) succinctly illustrates and analyses the general context of literary change during the period.

III

The Verse Epistle

D. J. PALMER

★

THE introduction of the verse epistle in English poetry during the fifteen nineties is closely related to those complex changes in style and sensibility which, however they are defined, distinguish between what F. P. Wilson called the 'Elizabethan' and the 'Jacobean'. The epistolary form answered well to a new desire for a more informal use of language and a more empirical sense of reality, for 'deeds and language such as men do use'.[1] Unlike the pretty fictions of courtly pastoral and sonnet, the verse epistle openly declares its basis in actual experience, and reveals the poet in his own person; the letter-writer is far removed from Sir Philip Sidney's conception of the poet who 'nothing affirmeth'. Moreover, since the letter is not a pure art form, but occupies an ambiguous place on the periphery of literature, it eschews rhetorical artifice in prose or verse:

> It was a quaint difference the Ancients did put 'twixt a *Letter* and an *Oration*; that the one should be attir'd like a Woman, the other like a Man: the latter of the two is allow'd large side Robes, as long Periods, Parentheses, Similies, Examples, and other parts of Rhetorical flourishes: But a *Letter* or *Epistle* should be short-coated, and closely couch'd; a Hungerlin becomes a *Letter* more handsomly than a Gown. Indeed we should write as we speak; and that's a true familiar Letter which expresseth one's Mind, as if he were discoursing with the Party to whom he writes, in succinct and short Terms.
>
> (James Howell, *Epistolae Ho-Elianae*, 1645 edn., Book I, Section I)

In terms of the traditional rhetorical divisions between the high, middle and low styles, the epistle calls for the low, or familiar style. Its appearance as a literary form at the end of the sixteenth century,

---

[1] The Ovidian heroic epistle is a fictional form, and as such has no bearing on the subject of the present chapter.

73

however, coincides with that anti-rhetorical bias towards 'matter not words', which is reflected, for instance, in Montaigne's scorn for those who admired Cicero's letters only for their style:

> They are not frivolous, idle, and triviall Epistles, and only compact and held together with exquisite choise words, hudled-up and ranged to a just smoothe cadence, but stufft and full of notable sayings, and wise sentences; by which a man doth not only become more eloquent, but more wise, and that teach us, not to say well, but to doe well. Fie on that eloquence, which leaves us with a desire of it, and not of things.   (*Essays*, XXXIX, i. 266)

The English verse letter is a revival of the form used by Horace. His own description of his epistles as '*sermones*', or 'conversations', was appropriate to their familiar style, and their main themes—the praise of retiredness and the discussion of literature—became the principal subjects of the sixteenth- and seventeenth-century epistle. Yet Horace was not the only begetter; the poets followed a general prescription of epistolary form inherited from the classical tradition, in which Seneca's moral epistles were of almost equal importance.

Characteristic of the way in which classical influences were assimilated during the English Renaissance, the verse letter was grafted to an already existing literary convention. Complimentary poems addressed to noble patrons and fellow-poets were customarily associated with the publication of important works; the first part of *The Faerie Queene*, for instance, was ushered into the world in 1590 accompanied by a whole panoply of such sonnets. Yet there is a distinction between formal tributes of this kind and the true verse letter. Fundamental to the nature of the epistle is its reflection of the author himself; as the first-century rhetorician Demetrius wrote, 'It may be said that everybody reveals his own soul in his letters. In every other form of composition it is possible to discern the writer's character, but in none so clearly as in the epistolary.' Furthermore, little if any of the Elizabethan verse written to patrons and fellow-authors has real literary value, while the epistles of Donne, Jonson, and others are not only better poetry, but also occupy a position central to their art as a whole.

Within three or four years of the first appearance of Spenser's epic, Donne was writing his earliest epistles, also in sonnet form, and thus pouring new wine into an old bottle. The poem 'To Mr. R. W.' (Milgate, p. 66) illustrates the characteristically subjective point of view of the epistle, as Donne uses the conceit of the four elements to praise his friend's 'Song' in terms of the effects it has wrought upon himself:

> Kindly'I envy thy Songs perfection
>   Built of all th'elements as our bodyes are:
>   That litle of earth that' is in it, is a faire
> Delicious garden where all Sweetes are sowne.
> In it is cherishing fyer which dryes in mee
>   Griefe which did drowne me: and halfe quench'd by it
>   Are Satirique fyres which urg'd me to have writt
> In skorne of all: for now I admyre thee.
>   And as Ayre doth fullfill the hollownes
>   Of rotten walls; so it myne emptines,
> Wher tost and mov'd it did begett this sound
> Which as a lame Eccho of thyne doth rebound.
>   Oh, I was dead: but since thy song new life did give,
>   I recreated, even by thy creature, live.

The style, plain in diction, with a syntax cutting freely across the metrical pattern within each quatrain, expresses a sequence of thought: 'and . . . which . . . for . . . And as . . . so . . . when . . . which'. It is as a letter should be, an index of the writer's mind.

The poetic epistles of Lodge, Donne, Daniel and Drayton were not attached to any public event, unlike Elizabethan complimentary verse, but were collected and printed as free-standing poems in their own right. Several of Jonson's epistles, on the other hand, are not so extrinsically different from the dedicatory and commendatory verse of the earlier period; some appeared in *The Forrest* and *The Under-wood*, but others were printed in the traditional way with the works of the authors to whom they were addressed. It is Jonson who transforms the convention by making it a vehicle for familiar address and serious critical appraisal, instead of merely well-turned compliment, and behind Jonson's commendatory poems lies the Horatian epistle. Subsequently, as a result of Jonson's influence, the distinction between the epistle proper and other kinds of complimentary verse becomes virtually impossible to define.

Like formal satire, the verse epistle was closely associated during the fifteen nineties with the literary circles of the Inns of Court. Thomas Lodge described himself as a member of Lincoln's Inn on the title page of *A Fig for Momus* in 1595, and this collection of eclogues, satires and verse letters represents three forms sharing a common association with the low style. Addressing 'the Gentlemen Readers whatsoever', Lodge claimed that 'For my Epistles, they are in that kind, wherein no Englishman of our time hath publiquely written.' In the sense that Donne's earliest epistles to fellow-members of Lincoln's Inn, such as Christopher Brooke and Thomas and Rowland Woodward, were not 'publiquely written', Lodge may have the precedence he claims. But *A Fig for Momus* is a false start, for Lodge hardly realizes the potential of the form as it was to be developed in subsequent years. Most of his epistles are informal treatises, offering counsel on such homely topics as dreams, spending and saving and, in the epistle 'To his Mistress A. L.' (probably his sister), the problem of overweight. This piece of practical advice begins by tumbling from the sublime into the ridiculous, which is sufficient to illustrate Lodge's management of the low style:

> In that same month wherein the spring begins
> And on that day when *Phoebe* left the twinnes
> (Which was on Saturday, the twelft of *March*)
> Your servant brought a letter seal'd with starch,
> Which by my soule (sweet mistres) when I op'te
> And read your motion far from that I hop'te,
> Beleeve me (had not troubles tir'd me quite)
> Might be enough to make me laugh outright:
> You pray me to advise, and tell you what
> Will take away your pursines and fat,
> You pray me without any let or pause,
> To write of both the remedie and cause,
> And in a short discourse to let you know
> The *Antidote* of that mislikes you so.
>
> (G2 verso)

Lodge associates the low style with humble subject-matter, and therefore the bathos, it must be presumed, is intentional. Only his fifth epistle, 'To Master Michael Drayton', anticipates the shape of things to come in dignity of theme and in its address to a fellow-poet. Here Lodge celebrates the art of poetry itself, but his language in doing so becomes more figurative and elevated, and achieves an almost Augustan balance in the phrasing of the couplets:

> Looke as the sunne-beame in a burning glasse
> Doth kindle fire, where ever it doth passe,
> But freely spred upon th'ingendring earth,
> Egs on the spring, and kils the cause for dearth:

So poetrie restraind in errors bounds,
With poisoned words, & sinful sweetnes wounds,
But clothing vertue, and adorning it,
Wit shines in vertue, vertue shines in wit:
True science suted in well couched rimes,
Is nourished for fame in after times.
Thou then sweet friend, grieve not though folly thrive,
Fame got by it, dies ere it is alive:
Be thou a prentize to a blessed Muse
Which grace with thy good words will still infuse.

(H3 recto)

'Wit shines in vertue, vertue shines in wit' epitomizes the function of
the verse epistle as Donne, Jonson and their contemporaries exercised
it, but when Lodge writes of poetry 'adorning' virtue, he shows that
he still thinks as an Elizabethan, without that urge to analyse and
'anatomize' experience which is the characteristic purpose of the low
style in the hands of Donne and Jonson.

Lodge's experiments with the epistle were not highly successful,
because he failed to grasp that the low style has a discipline of its own,
with qualities appropriate to the treatment of any subject, great or
small. These qualities were described in the treatise on the epistle composed in or about 1599 by John Hoskyns, himself an Inns of Court man
and friend of Donne. Hoskyns's *Directions for Speech and Style* opens with
a section entitled 'For Penninge of Letters', which he adapted from the
Institutio Epistolica of Justus Lipsius. It enumerates four qualities of
epistolary style, beginning with brevity, 'for letters must not be
treatises, or discourcings, except it be amonge learned men and eaven
amongst them, there is a kinde of thrift or saving of words . . .
brevity is attayned by the matter in avoyding . . . superfluous and
wanton Circuits of figures, and digressions.' 'The next good propertie
of Epistolarie style,' he continues, 'is perspicuitie and is often tymes
indangered by the former quallity (*Brevity*) oftentimes by affection of
some witt ill angled for, or ostentation of some hidden termes of art;
few wordes they darken the speech, and soe doe too many.' Hoskyns's
third requisite is plainness, 'which is . . . to use (as Ladies use in their
Attyre) a kind of diligent negligence.' Finally comes 'Respect', or the
decorum which adjusts style to the relationship between the writer
and the recipient.[2]

---

[2] L. B. Osborn, *The Life, Letters, and Writings of John Hoskyns, 1566–1638*

Hoskyns was not specifically writing of the verse epistle, but the considerations are essentially the same for verse and prose. Indeed the fact that Jonson transcribed the entire passage on the epistle into his *Discoveries*, as a treatise on style in general, illustrates the significance of the new form in the context of the changing ideals of style at the end of the sixteenth century. Brevity, perspicuity, and plainness are the hallmarks of these ideals; and if, as Professor Trimpi argues, Donne was inclined to offend against the second canon 'by affection of some witt', as far as his verse letters are concerned he has on his side Seneca himself, who allowed that wit was a fit companion of moral philosophy (Epistle LXXV). For wit in Donne's case is a way of perceiving reality, not a means of adorning it: it is a property of his mind rather than of his language.

These stylistic ideals are governed by the principle that language is subordinate to subject-matter. Where the writer has something of importance to say, he should deliver it with the directness and im-mediacy that its importance demands; if he has nothing to say of significance, he should remain silent. The familiar epistle, with its basis in personal intimacy, particularly requires this immediacy of expression, and the sententious gravity which became associated with the form reflects a concern for what Howell calls 'strength of matter'. Thus, as far as their chronology can be determined, Donne's verse letters develop from his early compliments to friends at the Inns of Court towards a concern with virtue and the moral life, and in so doing, they become more classical in spirit. For instance, the letter to Sir Henry Wotton (Milgate, pp. 71–3) treats a familiar classical theme in com-paring the differences between life in the country, the court, and the town. Donne rejects each in turn, and concludes with the stoical advice to find content within the mind itself:

> Be then thine owne home, and in thy selfe dwell;
> Inne any where, continuance maketh hell.
> And seeing the snaile, which every where doth rome,
> Carrying his owne house still, still is at home,
> Follow (for he is easie pac'd) this snaile,
> Bee thine owne Palace, or the world's thy Gaole.
>
> (lines 47–52)

(New Haven, 1937), pp. 118–19. The abbreviated spelling of the original has not been retained in the above quotations.

The lofty idea is wittily presented in the homely image of the snail, and Donne's ability to strike an intimate, playful note even while speaking in earnest, a kind of wit so appropriate to the epistle, is seen in the application of his analogy, 'Follow (for he is easie pac'd) this snaile.' As a piece of moralizing, such a commonplace thought hardly calls for the identification of a particular source, but the strong vein of stoicism in Horace's epistles suggests why Donne turned in this direction to give his letters moral depth. Thus Horace debates with the bailiff of his farm on the respective merits of town and country life:

> I call him happy who lives in the country; you him who dwells in the city. One who likes another's lot, of course dislikes his own. Each is foolish and unfairly blames the undeserving place; what is at fault is the mind, which never escapes from itself.
>
> (Book I, Epistle XIV, lines 10–13)

In another epistle, Horace offers similar counsel to Bullatius:

> Whatever hour God has given for your weal, take it with grateful hand, nor put off joys from year to year; so that, in whatever place you have been, you may say that you have lived happily. For if 'tis reason and wisdom that take away cares, and not a site commanding a wide expanse of sea, they change their clime, not their mind, who rush across the sea.' Tis busy idleness that is our bane; with yachts and cars we seek to make life happy. What you are seeking is here; it is at Ulubrae, if there fail you not a mind well balanced.
>
> (Book I, Epistle XI, lines 22–30)

That Donne thought the stoic emphasis upon living to oneself particularly appropriate to the epistle is clear from the frequency with which he returns to this theme. The letter to Rowland Woodward, 'If, as mine is, thy life a slumber be' (Milgate, pp. 64–5), expresses his sense of frustration at the delays preventing his departure for glory and riches in the Azores expedition of 1597–8, but it ends with a rejection of worldly fortune in favour of the treasure that lies within the self. Characteristic of Donne is the Christian application he gives the theme:

> But if (as all th'All must) hopes smoake away,
> Is not Almightie Vertue'an India?
>
> If men be worlds, there is in every one
> Some thing to'answere in some proportion

> All the worlds riches: And in good men, this,
> Vertue, our formes forme and our soules soule, is.
> (lines 27–32)

Similarly, in another epistle to Rowland Woodward, 'Like one who'in her third widdowhood doth professe' (Milgate, pp. 69–70), Donne regrets the vanity of his poetic ambition, and adds a special Christian significance to the Horatian discussion of motives to virtue ('oderunt peccare boni virtutis amore': 'The good hate vice because they love virtue', Book I, Epistle XVI, line 52):

> There is no Vertue, but Religion:
> Wise, valiant, sober, just, are names, which none
> Want, which want not Vice-covering discretion.
>
> Seeke wee then our selves in our selves; for as
> Men force the Sunne with much more force to passe,
> By gathering his beames with a christall glasse;
>
> So wee, if wee into our selves will turne,
> Blowing our sparkes of vertue, may outburne
> The straw, which doth about our hearts sojourne.
> (lines 16–24)

Compared with Donne's attitude of Christian humility, Jonson's treatment of the same stoical theme often assumes a kind of majestic pride in his own integrity:

> Live to that point I will, for which I am man,
> And dwell as in my Center, as I can,
> Still looking to, and ever loving heaven;
> With reverence using all the gifts thence given.
> ('An Epistle answering to one that asked to
> be Sealed of the Tribe of Ben,' The Under-
> wood, XLVII, lines 59–62)

These lines recall the end of Horace's epistle to Lollius:

> May I have my present store, or even less; may I live to myself for what remains of life, if the gods will that aught remain. May I have a goodly supply of books and of food to last the year; nor may I waver to and fro with the hopes of each uncertain hour. But 'tis enough to pray Jove, who gives and takes away, that he may grant me life, and grant me means: a mind well balanced I will myself provide.   (Book I Epistle XVIII, lines 107–12)

Throughout Jonson's epistles, in fact, the Horatian ideal of equanimity is at the basis of their dignity and ethical weightiness. We do not often associate Samuel Daniel with Jonson or Donne, nor is he usually thought of as a poet interested in the new forms that brought about the re-orientation of Elizabethan literature. But the stoic sententiousness of his six verse letters is the feature that justifies his description of them as being 'after the manner of Horace'. They were printed in 1603, together with the titular poem to the new monarch, *A Panegyricke Congratulatorie to the King's Maiestie*, which unfortunately was not panegyrical enough to attract the royal favour. Daniel addresses three epistles to statesmen and courtiers, namely Sir Thomas Egerton, the Lord Keeper of the Great Seal (and Donne's employer), Lord Henry Howard of the Privy Council, and the Earl of Southampton, who had fallen from grace for his part in the Essex rebellion of 1601. To the first two he writes of private integrity in public affairs, while the epistle to the unfortunate Southampton celebrates that inner fortitude which adversity alone can give to a man: stoicism is a creed for all seasons. The other three epistles are addressed to ladies, including the unhappy Countess of Cumberland, and her daughter Lady Anne Clifford, whose tutor Daniel had formerly been. These are his finest letters, especially his discreet and decorous con- solation of the Countess, whose private griefs he knew as a member of her household; yet he avoids an impertinent familiarity in admiring her courage and self-possession. 'You in the region of your selfe remaine,' he writes,

> Knowing the heart of man is set to be
> The centre of his world, about the which
> These revolutions of disturbances
> Still roule, where all th'aspects of miserie
> Predominate, whose strong effects are such
> As he must beare, being powreless to redresse,
> And that unless above himself he can
> Erect himselfe, how poore a thing is man?
>
> (lines 92–9)

Like Webster's Duchess of Malfi, the Countess sustains 'a behaviour so noble/As gives a majesty to adversity'. This virtue is reflected in the quality of the style itself, as the sobriety and plainness of the diction, drawn from the commonest materials of the language, adds its own strength to the argument; while the syntax, moving freely through conjunctives across the formal regularity of the six-line stanzas, is shaped not by rhyme, metre, or verbal patterning, but by the stress of the thought. Daniel's plain style here achieves nobility and beauty, and his own description of his aim in the long poem, *The Civil Wars*, might appropriately be applied to the epistolary ideal: 'to versify the truth, not poetize.'

The stoical emphasis upon self-knowledge reappears in the epistle to Lady Anne Clifford, as Daniel advises his pupil on those virtues she must cultivate in the life for which she is destined by birth and breeding. 'How carefull must you be/To be your selfe,' he says, warning her against the betrayal from within:

> And none, we see, were ever overthrowne
> By others flattery more than by their owne.
> For though we live amongst the tongues of praise
> And troopes of soothing people, that collaud
> All that we do, yet 'tis within our harts
> Th'ambushment lies, that evermore betraies
> Our iudgements, when our selves be come t'applaud
> Our owne abilitie, and our owne parts.
>
> (lines 76–83)

Daniel also addressed an epistle 'To The Lady Lucie Countesse of Bedford', the recipient of several of Donne's greatest verse letters, and Jonson's 'Lucy the bright', a lady celebrated for her learning as well as for her patronage and friendship to poets. She therefore has a special association with the verse epistle, and Daniel's tribute to her studies is no empty praise, but a stoical reflection on the 'true glory' which derives from the self rather than from others, 'since all the good we have rests in the mind';

> All glory, honor, fame, applause, renowne,
> Are not belonging to our royalties,
> But t'others wills, wherein th'are onely growne.
> And that unlesse we finde us all within,
> We never can without us be our owne:
> Nor call it right our life, that we live in:
> But a possession held for others use,
> That seeme to have most int'rest therein.
>
> (lines 59–66)

The thought suggests what differences lie between the epistle, with its ethical seriousness directed towards the life of the inner self, and the poetry of courtly compliment, the formal commemoration of public virtues with which earlier Elizabethan poets had honoured greatness.

★ ★ ★

The theme of these epistles, 'seeke wee then our selves in our selves', is appropriate to a form which was conceived to be a true image of the writer's mind, for the stoic virtues of self-knowledge and integrity are entailed by the epistle's evaluation of personal experience. In the sense that empiricism has to do with knowledge tested and authenticated in experience, it is closely related to stoicism in the epistle by a common emphasis upon the authority of the self.

When Donne writes to Sir Henry Wotton, 'Sir, more then kisses, letters mingle Soules;/For, thus friends absent speake' (Milgate, p. 71, lines 1–2), or when he tells Rowland Woodward (Milgate, p. 65),

> That I rejoyce, that unto where thou art,
> Though I stay here, I can thus send my heart,
> As kindly'as any enamored Patient
> His Picture to his absent Love hath sent,
>
> (lines 11–14)

he echoes a well-known letter of Seneca:

> I thank you for writing to me so often; for you are revealing your real self to me in the only way you can. I never receive a letter from you without being in your company forthwith. If the pictures of our absent friends are pleasing to us, though they only refresh the memory and lighten our longing by a solace that is unreal and unsubstantial, how much more pleasant is a letter, which brings us real traces, real evidences, of an absent friend!
>
> (Epistle XL, Loeb edn. i. 263–5)

The remainder of Seneca's letter is devoted to a discussion of the proper style for expressing moral truth: 'quod quae veritati operam dat oratio, inconposita esse debet et simplex' ('speech that deals with the truth should be unadorned and plain'). Donne and his contemporaries may have been led to associate Seneca's preference as a moralist for the plain style with his conception of the letter as a revelation of its author, by a passage from another letter in which Seneca commends the conversational idiom of the epistle:

> I prefer that my letters should be just what my conversation would be if you and I were sitting in one another's company or taking

> walks together—spontaneous and easy; for my letters have nothing
> strained or artificial about them. . . . Let this be the kernel of my
> idea: let us say what we feel, and feel what we say; let speech
> harmonize with life.   (Epistle LXXV, Loeb edn. ii. 137)

Thus the epistle, in which the writer intimately reveals himself, is an
ideal vehicle for moral truth, since it deals directly with actual experience. As an influence on the scope of the English verse epistle, the
stoicism of Seneca blends naturally with its Horatian counterpart.

In the essay, that other Senecan form revived in the same period,
Montaigne's sceptical empiricism is an extreme case of the reduction
of all experience to a reflection of the mind itself:

> For, howsoever, these are but my humors and opinions, and I
> deliver them but to show what my conceit is, and not what ought
> to be beleeved. Wherein I ayme at nothing but to display my selfe,
> who peradventure (if a new prentiship change me) shall be another
> to morrow.   (*Essays*, XXV, i. 152)

The epistle does not allow soliloquy, since it presents the self in
communication with a known reader, but Montaigne's use of the
familiar style is certainly parallel to that of the Jacobean verse epistle:

> It is a naturall, simple, and unaffected speech that I love, so written
> as it is spoken, and such upon the paper, as it is in the mouth, a pithie,
> sinnowie, full, strong, compendious and materiall speech, not so
> delicate and affected, as vehement and piercing . . . Rather difficult
> than tedious, void of affection, free, loose and bold, that every
> member of it seeme to make a bodie.   (*Essays*, XXV, i. 182–3)

Such a style follows the contours of the writer's mind intimately and
flexibly; it is shaped by the very processes of his thinking and feeling,
not according to a rhetorical pattern or design. So the reader is brought
into immediate contact with the writer's personal being. It was to
achieve this aim that Hoskyns had advised the letter-writer, 'to examyne
the clearest passages of your understanding, and through them to
convey your sweetest and most significant *English* wordes, that yow
can devise, that yow may the easier teach them the readyest way to
another mans conceipt.'

'Letters must not be treatises,' writes Hoskyns, for their truth is
relative to the immediate personal situations of the writer and his
recipient; the reality they refer to is local and particular. This is well
illustrated in the two verse epistles which Donne composed while on

the Azores expedition in 1597. 'The Storme' and 'The Calme' (Milgate, pp. 55–9) are companion pieces often misread as purely narrative or descriptive poems. They are, however, so neatly complementary in theme, their subjects being two contrasted extremes of experience, that when taken together they suggest something more than literal records of events. Each is concerned with an experience illuminating the fragility of man's estate and his dependence upon God. 'The Storme' concludes with the apocalyptic imagery of the end of the world:

> Darknesse, lights elder brother, his birth-right
> Claims o'r this world, and to heav'n hath chas'd light.
> All things are one, and that one none can be,
> Since all formes, uniforme deformity
> Doth cover, so that wee, except God say
> Another *Fiat*, shall have no more day.
>
> (lines 67–72)

Similarly, the final lines of 'The Calme' find in the uselessness of the becalmed man-o'-war an image of the futility of human enterprise:

> What are wee then? How little more alas
> Is man now, then before he was? he was
> Nothing; for us, wee are for nothing fit;
> Chance, or our selves still disproportion it.
> Wee have no will, no power, no sense; I lye,
> I should not then thus feele this miserie.
>
> (lines 51–6)

In fact, as B. F. Nellist has shown, 'they are poems about the place of fortune, of the unaccountable and uncontrollable in the affairs of men. But as usual his poems are not simply a commentary upon the idea. They are concerned with the passions aroused by participation in the situation.'[3] Donne does not merely describe the scenes visually; through the witty imagery of terror, horror, and grotesque comedy, he re-enacts his experience of them, so that their moral significance is intimated as sensation rather than as thought.

> Some coffin'd in their cabbins lye,'equally
> Griev'd that they are not dead, and yet must dye;
> And as sin-burd'ned soules from graves will creepe,
> At the last day, some forth their cabbins peepe:

[3] B. F. Nellist, 'Donne's "Storm" and "Calm" and the Descriptive Tradition', *Modern Language Review*, LIX (1964), pp. 511–15.

> And tremblingly'aske what newes, and doe heare so,
> Like jealous husbands, what they would not know.
> ('The Storme', lines 45–50)

Temperamentally Donne has much in common with Montaigne, whom he certainly read with profit. They share that sense of the mind as its own place, that complex self-awareness which is a meeting-point of stoicism and scepticism, while their ironic sense of the vagaries and incertitude of man's condition is reflected in the character of their religious‛faith. The technique of 'The Storme' and 'The Calme' shows that Donne, like Montaigne, used the familiar style to verify moral truth empirically, by representing his theme as a mental event. It is a technique, appropriate to the epistle as a literary form, which justifies T. S. Eliot's famous observation that 'a thought to Donne was an experience.'

Donne's later epistles, particularly those addressed to ladies such as the Countesses of Huntingdon and Bedford, have not won much favour among subsequent readers, whatever their original reception. Even during the modern revival, when Donne was enjoying a critical esteem denied to Milton, his epistolary poems attracted little attention save a general disapproval of his apparent attempts to flatter his way into the good graces of a patroness. The more considered judgement of Douglas Bush is sufficiently damning to the epistles, 'in which intellectual ingenuity is so seldom fused with feeling, not to mention the letters to the Countess of Bedford, in which ingenuity and feeling are so seldom restrained by taste.'[4] At least it may be said that Donne in some measure anticipated this unsympathetic criticism, when he wrote to that same Countess, 'At New-yeares Tide' (Milgate, pp. 98–100),

> So, my verse built of your just praise, might want
>   Reason and likelihood, the firmest Base,
> And made of miracle, now faith is scant,
>   Will vanish soone, and so possesse no place,
>   And you, and it, too much grace might disgrace.
> (lines 21–5)

As Donne prophetically implies, these poems have been more often undervalued than understood.

[4] D. Bush, *English Literature in the Earlier Seventeenth Century* (Oxford, 1945), p. 131.

An interesting light is thrown on the character of these later epistles by one of his prose letters, possibly addressed to Sir Henry Goodyer in 1604,[5] where Donne offers his own conception of the epistolary form:

No other kinde of conveyance is better for knowledge, or love: What treasures of Morall knowledge are in *Senecaes* Letters to onely one *Lucilius?* and what of Naturall in *Plinies?* . . . But it is the other capacity which must make mine acceptable, that they are also the best conveyers of love. But, though all knowledge be in those Authors already, yet, as some poisons, and some medicines, hurt not, nor profit, except the creature in which they reside, contribute their lively activitie, and vigor; so, much of the knowledge buried in Books perisheth, and becomes ineffectuall, if it be not applied, and refreshed by a companion, or friend. Much of their goodnesse, hath the same period, which some Physicians of *Italy* have observed to be in the biting of their *Tarantala*, that it affects no longer, than the flie lives. For with how much desire we read the papers of any living now, (especially friends) which we would scarce allow a boxe in our cabinet, or shelf in our Library, if they were dead? And we do justly in it, for the writings and words of men present, we may examine, controll, and expostulate, and receive satisfaction from the authors; but the other we must beleeve, or discredit; they present no mean.

Here also, perhaps, Donne foresees the judgement of posterity, for if the active truth of his epistles lies buried with their author, leaving us to 'beleeve, or discredit', then there is no doubt which has been generally preferred. Donne describes the essentially personal nature of the letter, and we should remember that, unlike his contemporaries Lodge, Daniel, Drayton and Jonson, he did not intend his epistles for publication.

In the sense that Donne gives to the word, the series of verse epistles he addressed to great ladies between about 1605 and 1614 are love letters. The 'knowledge' with which they are concerned, as in his earlier letters, is the knowledge of virtue. Their 'lively activitie, and vigor', without which such knowledge 'perisheth, and becomes in-effectuall', is the wit that serves as the 'conveyer of love'. Donne's wit, simultaneously playful and serious, is the mode of address that sets the intimate but decorous tone of these epistles.

[5] The date and identity of the recipient are tentatively suggested by the editors in *John Donne: Selected Prose* (Oxford, 1967), chosen by Evelyn Simpson and edited by Helen Gardner and Timothy Healy, p. 121.

As we have seen, Donne uses the familiar style to write, not so much as he speaks, but rather as he thinks and feels. His language mirrors his mind in action, and wit is a faculty of the mind. It signifies keener perception, not merely verbal technique, which delights in truths beyond the scope of 'reason and likelihood'. It apprehends purely personal truths and finely attunes one mind to another, like the nuances and inflexions of a familiar voice. Donne's witty analogies in these epistles often refer to the process of wit itself, as the means to a more absolute, more personal kind of knowledge:

> MADAME,
> Reason is our Soules left hand, Faith her right,
>   By these wee reach divinity, that's you;
> Their loves, who have the blessing of your sight,
>   Grew from their reason, mine from far faith grew.
>
> But as, although a squint lefthandednesse
>   Be'ungracious, yet we cannot want that hand,
> So would I, not to'encrease, but to expresse
>   My faith, as I believe, so understand.
>
> Therefore I study you first in your Saints,
>   Those friends, whom your election glorifies,
> Then in your deeds, accesses, and restraints,
>   And what you reade, and what your selfe devize.
>
> But soone, the reasons why you'are lov'd by all,
>   Grow infinite, and so passe reasons reach,
> Then back againe to'implicite faith I fall,
>   And rest on what the Catholique voice doth teach.
>
>   ('To the Countesse of Bedford',
>   Milgate, p. 90, lines 1–16)

'Made of miracle, now faith is scant', these epistles may 'tast of Poëtique rage or flattery', as Donne is aware; we are reminded of Ben Jonson's criticism of the *Anniversaries*, which he found 'profane and full of blasphemies':

> That he told Mr. Done, if it had been written of ye Virgin Marie it had been something to which he answered that he described the Idea of a Woman and not as she was.
>   (*Conversations with William Drummond of Hawthornden*)

Donne's use of the language of religious faith is not the inflated rhetoric of a sycophant, but itself an image of that inspired leap of insight by which wit moves. The bar of common sense has no jurisdiction over him; instead, the appeal is to the nature of the letter itself, for 'more then kisses, letters mingle soules.' In reaching the 'soule' of the lady to whom he writes, Donne also reveals his own.

The passages in these epistles which might have been more suitably addressed to Our Lady, in the eyes of readers who take Jonson's part, are those in which Donne attributes to his Lady the quality of absoluteness, of perfect wholeness of being. Thus he writes to the Countess of Huntingdon (Milgate, p. 84):

> But (madame) I now thinke on you; and here
> Where we are at our hights, you but appeare,
> We are but clouds you rise from, our noone-ray
> But a foule shadow, not your breake of day.
> You are at first hand all that's faire and right,
> And others good reflects but backe your light.
> You are a perfectnesse, so curious hit,
> That youngest flatteries doe scandall it.
> For, what is more doth what you are restraine,
> And though beyond, is downe the hill againe.
> We have no next way to you, we cross to'it:
> You are the straight line, thing prais'd, attribute;
> Each good in you's a light; so many'a shade
> You make, and in them are your motions made.
> These are your pictures to the life. From farre
> We see you move, and here your *Zani's* are:
> So that no fountaine good there is, doth grow
> In you, but our dimme actions faintly shew.
>
> (lines 77–94)

The Countess of Bedford is no less a paradigm of all that is good and lovely:

> If good and lovely were not one, of both
>   You were the transcript, and originall,
> The Elements, the Parent and the Growth,
>   And every peece of you, is both their All:
>   So'intire are all your deeds and you, that you
>   Must do the same thing still: you cannot two.
>
> (Milgate, p. 93, lines 55–60)

If this is not merely the *reductio ad absurdum* of courtly compliment, what serious meaning does it have? And what connection is there between this and the sententious gravity of his earlier epistolary theme, 'seeke wee then our selves in our selves'? In fact the thought which underlies these later epistles is exactly that which concludes his earlier letter to Rowland Woodward (Milgate, p. 65), quoted above:

> If men be worlds, there is in every one
> Some thing to'answere in some proportion
> All the worlds riches: And in good men, this,
> Vertue, our formes forme and our soules soule, is.

'Vertue' signifies the very quality by which a thing exists as well as moral excellence: the two meanings are both present in Donne's use of the word. In reaching the identity of the lady, her 'formes forme' and 'soules soule', Donne also draws upon the traditional system of analogies ('if men be worlds'), which recognizes that the lady contains 'all' within herself by virtue of her humanity: he describes 'the Idea of a Woman' which exists in each of the ladies he addresses.

Donne does not accept the familiar notion of man as a microcosm, or little copy of the world, arguing that he is in truth the greater world. Such is the burden of his letter of 1611 'To Sir Edward Herbert, at Julyers' (Milgate, p. 81):

> Since then our businesse is, to rectifie
> Nature, to what she was, wee'are led awry
> By them, who man to us in little show;
> Greater then due, no forme we can bestow
> On him; for Man into himselfe can draw
> All; All that his faith can swallow,'or reason chaw.
> All that is fill'd, and all that which doth fill,
> All the round world, to man is but a pill.
>   (lines 33–40)

As the editor of the epistles points out,[6] Donne took the idea seriously enough to repeat it in a sermon:

> The properties, the qualities of every Creature, are in man; the Essence, the Existence of every Creature is for man; so man is every Creature. And therefore the Philosopher draws man into too narrow a table, when he says he is *Microcosmos*, an Abridgement of the world

6 Milgate, pp. 241–2.

in little: *Nazianzen* gives him but his due, when he calls him
Mundum Magnum, a world to which all the rest of the world is but
subordinate.

Thus the neo-Platonic analogies in the epistles, which make the lady
an Idea of goodness and beauty, whose creative power gives form and
meaning to all, refer not to some absurd impossibility, but to a definition of the self as entire and absolute. As identity is single and uniform,
so it is not a part of something greater than itself, but that quality in its
entirety. (In this connection, Laurence Stapleton has shown the use
Donne makes of the Platonic doctrine of virtue as indivisible.[7]) Donne
addresses himself to the very concept of identity, 'to speake things
which by faith alone I see':

> That is, of you, who are a firmament
> Of virtues, where no one is growne, or spent,
> They'are your materials, not your ornament.
>
> Others whom wee call vertuous, are not so
> In their whole substance, but, their vertues grow
> But in their humours, and at seasons show . . .
>
> We'are thus but parcel guilt; to Gold we'are growne
> When Vertue is our Soules complexion;
> Who knowes his Vertues name or place, hath none.
>
> Vertue'is but aguish, when 'tis severall,
> By'occasion wak'd, and circumstantiall.
> True vertue'is *Soule*, Alwaies in all deeds *All*.
>
> ('A Letter to the Lady Carey, and
> Mrs. Essex Riche', Milgate, pp.
> 105–7, lines 13–18, 31–6)

The similarity of thought between this and the theme of Donne's
earlier epistles,

> There is no Vertue but Religion:
> Wise, valiant, sober, just, are names, which none
> Want, which want not Vice-covering discretion,
> ('To Mr Rowland Woodward', Milgate, p. 70)

[7] L. Stapleton, 'The Theme of Virtue in Donne's Verse Epistles', *Studies in
Philology*, LV (1958), pp. 187–200.

illustrates their remarkable continuity. The greater subtlety with which the thought is translated into experience in the later epistles is reflected in their movement towards the very centre or 'soul' of personal being:

> She [virtue] guilded us: But you are gold, and Shee;
>   Us she inform'd, but transubstantiates you;
> Soft dispositions which ductile bee,
>   Elixarlike, she makes, not cleane, but new.
>
> Though you a wifes and mothers name retaine,
>   'Tis not as woman, for all are not soe,
> But vertue having made you vertue,'is faine
>   T'adhere in these names, her and you to show,
>
> Else, being alike pure, wee should neither see;
>   As, water being into ayre rarify'd,
> Neither appeare, till in one cloud they bee,
>   So, for our sakes you do low names abide.
>   ('To the Countesse of Huntingdon',
>   Milgate, pp. 85–8, lines 25–36)

Like the 'Songs and Sonets', the epistles express that heightened awareness of individuality which is for Donne the essential experience of love. While his lyrics celebrate love as the mutual incorporation of two in one, that inter-animation which creates an entire and absolute world, in his verse letters to ladies the relationship is obviously on a different plane, but it is nevertheless one in which the lover finds his own identity through knowing, and being filled with the knowledge of, the lady's essential self. Instead of making one little room an everywhere, his epistles translate one person into an everything. And if letters reveal the self, then Donne's highly developed sense of self is felt in the singularity of his wit, which is as authentically personal as a signature.

★   ★   ★

'Language most shewes a man; speak, that I may see thee.' The epistle was admirably suited to Jonson's linguistic ideals, and to that moral concern for truth of which his style is the mirror. While Donne's wit, addressed to ladies, suggests that 'the truest poetry is the most feigning', Jonson, writing more often to men, expresses himself in a style plainspoken, vigorously direct, and sparing of metaphor and epithet. Both poets use the epistle as a vehicle for moral truth apprehended by personal experience, but for Jonson truth is characterized by its simplicity.

Jonson is at his best when dealing on equal terms. Thus, commending his friend John Selden's *Titles of Honour* in 1614, he begins his letter with a declaration in favour of the plain, curt style:

> I know to whom I write. Here, I am sure,
> Though I am short, I cannot be obscure:
> Lesse shall I for the Art or dressing care;
> Truth and the Graces best, when naked are.
> > (*The Under-wood*, XIV, lines 1–4)

Moreover, he knows Selden will approve the latter observation as an axiom, for they share the same stylistic interests. When Jonson praises Selden's language, he might be describing the characteristic qualities of his own verse:

> To marke the excellent seas'ning of your Stile!
> And manly elocution, not one while
> With horrour rough, then rioting with wit!
> But to the Subject, still the Colours fit
> In sharpnesse of all Search, wisdome of Choise,
> Newnesse of Sense, Antiquitie of voyce!
> > (lines 55–60)

Such properties of the plain style, forceful but without affectation in its 'manly elocution', matching the expression exactly 'to the Subject', informal but without slackness or superfluity, incisive and penetrating in judgement, and eschewing eccentricity to achieve that authoritative 'Antiquitie of voyce', summarize the classical temper of Jonson's epistles. He means just what he speaks, no more or less; there are no suggestive undertones or added complexities resonating beyond the surface meaning of the words. The style is therefore a pledge of the man's own sincerity and candour:

> I have too oft preferr'd
> Men, past their termes, and prais'd some names too much,
> But 'twas with purpose to have made them such.
> Since being deceiv'd, I turne a sharper eye
> Upon my selfe, and aske to whom? and why?

And what I write? and vexe it many dayes
Before men get a verse: much lesse a Praise;
So that my Reader is assur'd, I now
Meane what I speake: and still will keepe that Vow.
(lines 20-8)

As the voice of probity and truthfulness, Jonson's epistolary style is noble and dignified, though without grandiloquence or rhetorical heightening. If he is characteristically conscious of his moral dignity, it is because he turns 'a sharper eye/Upon my selfe'; there is no suspicion of complacency. The stoic equanimity of Horace, that particular 'Antiquitie of voyce' which is Jonson's ideal in the epistle, is grounded upon the inner strength of vigilant self-knowledge and self-respect. In lines already quoted, Horatian by origin, but wholly Jonsonian in context, application, and emphatic force, he declares to 'one that asked to be Sealed of the Tribe of Ben':

Live to that point I will, for which I am man,
And dwell as in my Center, as I can,
Still looking too, and ever loving heaven;
With reverence using all the gifts thence given.
(*The Under-wood*, XLVII, lines 59-62)

Passages of direct self-description, rare in Donne's epistles, are frequent in Jonson's.

The sovereign virtue of living to oneself is for Jonson the very basis of friendship, since he who would be true to others must first be true to himself. Thus in 'An Epistle to a Friend' (*The Under-wood*, XXXVII) he defends himself with urbane dignity against the charge that he is 'too severe/Rigid and harsh':

It is an Act of tyrannie, not love
In practiz'd friendship wholly to reprove,
As flatt'ry with friends humours still to move.

From each of which I labour to be free,
Yet if with eithers vice I teynted be,
Forgive it, as my frailtie, and not me.

For no man lives so out of passions sway,
But shall sometimes be tempted to obey
Her furie, yet no friendship to betray.
(lines 25-33)

'''Tis vertue alone, or nothing that knits friends,' he writes to Arthur Squib, advising him to test the inner integrity of whoever professes friendship:

> Turne him, and see his Threds: looke, if he be
> Friend to himselfe, that would be friend to thee.
> For that is first requir'd, A man be his owne.
> But he that's too-much that, is friend of none.
> (*The Under-wood*, XLV, lines 21-4)

Jonson's counsel, 'First weigh a friend, then touch, and trie him too', is typical of his concern to verify, to see and present things as they really are. The epistle's engagement with the reality of personal experience strongly appealed to the empiricist in him. His moral insights are not developed by philosophical argument, but reflect the world of concrete particulars from which they derive.

The satirical element in several of Jonson's epistles also expresses this ethical realism, where the aim is not ridicule, as in his great stage comedies, but vehement denunciation of the corruption and degeneracy of the times. The epistle to Colby, 'to perswade him to the Warres' (*The Under-wood*, XV), is the most notable and sustained example, since all but the final exhortation to Colby is in the following trenchant vein:

> Our delicacies are growne capitall,
> And even our sports are dangers! what we call
> Friendship is now mask'd Hatred! Justice fled,
> And shamefastnesse together! All lawes dead
> That kept man living! Pleasures only sought!
> Honour and honestie, as poore things thought
> As they are made! Pride, and stiffe Clownage mixt
> To make up Greatnesse! and mans whole good fix'd
> In bravery, or gluttony, or coyne,
> All which he makes the servants of the Groine,
> Thither it flowes; how much did Stallion spend
> To have his Court-bred-fillie there commend
> His Lace and Starch? And fall upon her back
> In admiration, stretched upon the rack
> Of lust, to his rich Suit and Title, Lord?
> (lines 37-51)

In the passionate intensity of such lines is felt the same moral energy, the same uncompromising candour, which Jonson reveals throughout his epistles. The satirist's characteristic urge to speak out, his sense of outrage and disgust at the debasement of 'honour and honestie', are identified with the personal qualities of the letter-writer. Jonson grafts satire to the epistle without straining the proper limits of the form. Horace offered a precedent by describing both his satires and his epistles as '*sermones*'; moreover, in Jonson's case, the plain style combines a desire for truth to experience with the naked severity of the satirist's exposure of the world.

Jonson's epistles are part of the substantial body of his familiar verse, which includes other classical forms like his epigrams, odes and elegies, and also numerous complimentary and commemorative poems not collected in *The Forrest* or *The Under-wood*. The difficulty of formally distinguishing between his epistles and other verse addressed to fellow-authors is illustrated by the letter to Selden (*The Under-Wood*, XIV). It is Horatian in the sense that Horace's epistle to Augustus (Book II, Epistle I), for instance, is concerned with poetry and with the poet's definition of the ideals by which he works; but, originally prefixed to Selden's book, it is also akin to such other complimentary poems as 'To the Worthy Author M. John Fletcher' (published in Fletcher's *The Faithfull Shepherdess*, 1609–10?), 'To his much and worthily esteemed Friend the Author' (namely John Stephens, in *Cinthia's Revenge*, 1613), 'The Vision of Ben. Jonson, on the Muses of his Friend M. Drayton' (for the volume which Drayton published in 1627), not to mention the celebrated verses for the First Folio, 'To the Memory of my Beloved, the Author, Mr. William Shakespeare'. Perhaps Jonson did not trouble himself with the distinction, although he could well have regarded the lines to Selden as a genuine epistle, since to a much greater extent than his other complimentary verses these directly reveal his own poetic concerns. Certainly the kind of poems he produced for these conventional occasions are longer, more familiar in address, and show greater critical judgement, than their Elizabethan predecessors, and it seems likely that Jonson had in mind the canons of epistolary form in making these changes.

★   ★   ★

In the miscellaneous verse epistles of the Caroline period, Jonson's influence is not far to seek. Yet, apart from the quasi-epistolary complimentary poems, the true verse letter is not a popular form among the later poets, and beyond their Jonsonian echoes and their common debt, to a greater or lesser degree, to Horace, their epistles have little in common with each other. They lack a sense of distinctive form, as though they were merely a fading reflection of poetic aims no longer felt to be relevant or appropriate.

The last poet to publish his epistles as a series, and as an intimately revealing series, was Michael Drayton, in his *Elegies upon Sundry Occasions* (1627). Born a year before Shakespeare, Drayton preserved many of the attitudes and ideals of a late Elizabethan, and his epistles reveal a man out of sympathy with the trends of a new age. As laments for the passing of a greater age, Drayton's Horatian epistles of friendship truly belong with their accompanying elegies (the unHoratian epistle, 'Of his Ladies not Comming to London', is really an elegiacal complaint).[8] 'To Master George Sandys', the translator of Ovid and Treasurer of the Virginia Colony, and 'To Master William Browne', the pastoral poet, are both satirical complaints over the decay of English poetry and society. The latter poem, sub-titled 'of the evill time', concludes on that stoical note which had been so often associated with the epistle:

> Then noble friend the next way to controule
> These worldly crosses, is to arme thy soule
> With constant patience.
>
> (lines 123–5)

The best of Drayton's epistles, 'To My Most Dearely-loved Friend Henery Reynolds Esquire: of Poets and Poesie', opens with a charming image of the Horatian ideal of literary friendship, without Jonson's stoic severity:

> My dearely loved friend how oft have we,
> In winter evenings (meaning to be free),
> To some well chosen place us'd to retire;
> And there with moderate meate, and wine, and fire,
> Have past the howres contentedly with chat,
> Now talk'd of this, and then discours'd of that,
> Spoke our owne verses 'twixt our selves, if not
> Other mens lines, which we by chance had got.
>
> (lines 1–8)

[8] F. W. Weitzmann, in 'Notes on the Elizabethan Elegie', *Publications of the Modern Language Association of America*, L (1935), pp. 435–43, refers to a similar conflation of the elegiac and epistolary modes in a poem from Davison's *Poetical Rhapsody* (1602), 'An Elegie or Letter in Verse'. Doubtless this is an Ovidian conception of the epistle.

After an autobiographical digression, which good-humouredly relates his naïve boyhood ambition to be a poet, Drayton moves to his real theme, a summary of the English poetic achievement, with particular emphasis upon the great Elizabethans. Nostalgia for the spirit of that age is blended with critical penetration in a series of perceptive but informal literary judgements, and, perhaps recalling Horace's proud refusal to court fashionable popularity (Book I, Epistle XIX), Drayton ends his epistle to Reynolds by expressing his scorn as an old professional for the younger generation of amateurs now holding sway:

> For such whose poems, be they nere so rare,
> In private chambers, that incloistered are,
> And by transcription daintyly must goe;
> As though the world unworthy were to know,
> Their rich composures, let those men that keepe
> These wonderous reliques in their judgement deepe,
> And cry them up so, let such peeces bee
> Spoke of by those that shall come after me,
> I passe not for them.
>
> (lines 187–95)

Although Drayton marks it as a symptom of decay, the decline of the epistolary form during the second half of the period had really little to do with the amateur tradition, which was just as strong in Drayton's youth. More to the point was the disappearance of the familiar style as a vehicle for analysing and evaluating personal experience. As Donne's wit becomes too often among later poets a decorative mannerism rather than a way of perceiving reality, so Jonson's vigorous plainness is subjected to refinement, his urbanity confused with gentlemanly ease. Donne had virtually no influence upon the later epistle. There is possibly something owing to him in his friend Lord Herbert of Cherbury's poems, 'To the C[ountess[of D[orset]?' and 'Platonic Love', and in the feeble neo-Platonism of Habington's 'To the Right Honourable Countess of C.' Crashaw's 'Letter to the Countess of Denbigh: Against Irresolution and Delay in Matters of Religion' is a superb poem, grounded, like most of Donne's epistles, upon the devotional truths of Christianity, but that is about all they have in common. Although Jonson was not short of imitators and followers, none used the epistle for that intimate and candid self-appraisal which is the main feature of his own verse letters. The Horatian praise of country life, which Jonson celebrated in the epistle to Sir Robert Wroth (*The Forrest*, III), inspired two delightful poems by Robert Herrick, 'A Country Life: to his Brother' and 'The Country Life: to Endimion Porter', as well as Carew's 'To my Friend G. N. from Wrest' and Henry Vaughan's 'To his retired friend, an Invitation to Brecknock': the Caroline poets were less confirmed city-dwellers than Jonson and Donne. On the other hand, Francis Beaumont's 'Letter to Ben Jonson, written before he and Mr Fletcher came to London' actually inverts the Horatian preference by contrasting the dullness of existence in the country with the wit and conviviality of the city, and Suckling's epicurean, not to say hedonistic, 'Epistle' adopts a similar attitude in summoning a university friend from his books to the pleasures of London. Yet even where the stoic virtue of living to oneself remains the central theme of the epistle, as in Herrick's Horatian image of the country as the home of the contented mind, or in Lovelace's sententious 'Advice to my Best Brother', the poet is not writing about himself. When Donne wrote 'Seeke wee then our selves in our selves', his style mirrors his meaning, translating the thought into experience, as the reader participates in his processes of thinking and feeling. But the extravagance of Donne's wit, and the nakedness of Jonson's candour, by which they both reveal themselves, yield to new stylistic ideals, as the smoother and more polished versification of the middle decades of the century prepares the way for the tone of the Augustan epistle, whose neat and measured antitheses reflect the poise and equilibrium of a new sensibility:

> How blest is he, who leads a country life,
> Unvex'd with anxious cares, and void of strife!
> Who, studying peace and shunning civil rage,
> Enjoy'd his youth, and now enjoys his age:
> All who deserve his love, he makes his own;
> And, to be lov'd himself, needs only to be known.
> (John Dryden, 'To my Honor'd Kinsman,
> John Driden', lines 1–6)

In describing his kinsman, Dryden formulates a type, the representative of a social ideal. Thus, while to speak of 'a dissociation of sensibility' creates more problems than it solves, the 'politeness' of Dryden's verse moves in an opposite direction from the individualizing qualities of the low style used by Donne and Jonson.

Note

Modern Editions

The principal quotations are taken from the following texts: *The Poems of Robert Southwell, S.J.*, edited by James H. McDonald and Nancy Pollard Brown (Oxford, 1967). This admirable new edition, with an important introduction and notes, at last makes plain Southwell's importance as the first significant poet in the Elizabethan and seventeenth-century line of devotional poets. *The Sonnets of William Alabaster*, edited by G. M. Story and Helen Gardner (Oxford, 1959). This important edition, with a very illuminating introduction and commentary, dates the sonnets *c.* 1597–8, and presents them in a modernized text. The numbering of the sonnets in this edition has been followed in the present chapter, but quotations from Alabaster have been taken from the text presented in *The Anchor Anthology of Seventeenth-Century Verse*, Vol. 1, edited by Louis L. Martz (Garden City, N.Y., 1969). The other texts used are *John Donne: The Divine Poems,* edited by Helen Gardner (Oxford, 1952). *The Works of George Herbert*, edited by F. E. Hutchinson (Oxford, 1941). *The Works of Henry Vaughan*, edited by L. C. Martin (Second edition, Oxford, 1957).

Critical Studies. Professor Martz's book, *The Poetry of Meditation* (Second edition, New Haven, 1962) is a major contribution to the study of the religious poetry of the period, demonstrating the importance of traditional devotional methods and themes to poetic structure and meaning. For studies of the individual poets see the following: Arnold Stein, *George Herbert's Lyrics* (Baltimore, Md., 1968); Joseph H. Summers, *George Herbert, His Religion and Art* (1954); Rosemond Tuve, *A Reading of George Herbert* (1952); Ross Garner, *Henry Vaughan: Experience and the Tradition* (Chicago, 1959); F. E. Hutchinson, *Henry Vaughan: A Life and Interpretation* (Oxford, 1947); E. C. Pettet, *Of Paradise and Light: A Study of Vaughan's Silex Scintillans* (Cambridge, 1960); Austin Warren, *Richard Crashaw; A Study in Baroque Sensibility* (Baton Rouge, La., 1939).

IV

The Action of the Self:
Devotional Poetry in the Seventeenth Century

LOUIS L. MARTZ

★

THE basic principle of devotional poetry in the seventeenth century is prefigured in a poem by Robert Southwell entitled 'Looke home', written sometime around 1590:

> Retyred thoughts enjoy their owne delights,
> As beawtie doth in selfe beholding eye:
> Mans mind a myrrour is of heavenly sights,
> A breefe wherein all marvailes summed lye.
> Of fayrest formes, and sweetest shapes the store,
> Most gracefull all, yet thought may grace them more.
>
> The mind a creature is, yet can create,
> To natures paterns adding higher skill:
> Of finest workes wit better could the state,
> If force of wit had equall power of will.
> Devise of man in working hath no end,
> What thought can thinke another thought can mend.

It is no accident that these lines from an Elizabethan poet should prefigure the famous stanza in Marvell's 'Garden' which speaks of how 'the Mind . . . Withdraws into its happiness':

> The Mind, that Ocean where each kind
> Does streight its own resemblance find;
> Yet it creates, transcending these,
> Far other Worlds, and other Seas;

while at the same time four other lines from Southwell's 'Looke home'

seem to foreshadow certain lines in the middle of Marvell's 'On a
Drop of Dew':

> Mans soule of endles beauties image is,
> Drawne by the worke of endlesse skill and might:
> This skilfull might gave many sparkes of blisse,
> And to discerne this blisse a native light.

> So the Soul, that Drop, that Ray
> Of the clear Fountain of Eternal Day,
> Could it within the humane flow'r be seen,
> Remembring still its former height,
> Shuns the sweat leaves and blossoms green;
> And, recollecting its own Light,
> Does, in its pure and circling thoughts, express
> The greater Heaven in an Heaven less.

In these passages by Southwell and Marvell we find enclosed the
central image of the place where the basic religious action of the period
was performed: the mind, the soul, where the images received through
the senses could be transformed by means of an inner light, the light
of human 'wit', that is, the intellect, the understanding, the power of
reason. In Southwell's poem, as in Marvell's, the emphasis falls upon
the action of thought, upon the creative power of human reason,
're-collecting' its light by remembrance, and also by collecting together
its own interior faculties.

It is the same action that another Elizabethan poet, William Alabaster,
described in one of his holy sonnets written in the very last years of the
sixteenth century, where he says:

> soe moves my love about the heavenlie spheare
> and draweth thence with an attractive fire
> the purest argument witt can desire,
> whereby devotion after may arise;
> and theis conceiptes, digest by thoughts retire,
> are turned into aprill showers of teares.
>
> (Sonnet 15)

Here is a definition of the meaning of the phrase 'devotional poetry'.
'Devotion,' says Alabaster, is a state of mind that arises after love of the

divine has searched out in heavenly things certain topics upon which the power of wit may operate. And these 'conceits', that is, these conceptions, are then digested by the retirement of thought into a state of concentrated attention in which fervent emotions are generated and thoughts are converted into tears—or into joy or into other devout manifestations.

'Devotion', then, is an active, creative state of mind, a 'poetical' condition, we might say, in which the mind works at high intensity. Thus François de Sales declares that 'devotion is no other thing than a spiritual nimbleness and vivacity, by means of which charity [i.e. the love of God] works in us, or we by her, readily and heartily.' Charity and devotion, he declares, 'differ no more, the one from the other, than the flame from the fire; in as much as charity, being a spiritual fire, when it breaks out into flame, is called devotion: so that devotion adds nothing to the fire of charity, save the flame which makes charity ready, active and diligent, not only in observing the commandments of God, but in practising the heavenly counsels and inspirations.'[1]

The phrase 'devotional poetry' should not, then, be taken to indicate verse of rather limited range, 'merely pious' pieces without much poetic energy. Devotion is for these poets a state of mind created by the 'powers of the soul' in an intense, dramatic action, focused upon one central issue. Thus, for example, Alabaster concentrates upon the image of the Cross:

> Now I have found thee, I will ever more
> embrace this standerd where thou sitest above:
> feed greedy eyes, and from hence never rove,
> sucke hungrye Soule of this eternall store.
> Issue my hearte from thy two leaved dore
> and lett my lipps from kissinge not remove.
> O that I were transformed into Love
> and as a plante might springe upp in his flowre,
> like wandring ivy, or sweete hony suckle,
> how would I with my twine aboute it buckle!
> and kiss his feete with my ambitiouse bowes
> and clime alonge uppon his sacred brest
> and make a garland for his wounded browes!
> Lord, soe I am if here my thoughtes might rest.   (34)

[1] St. François de Sales, *Introduction to the Devout Life*, edited and translated by Allan Ross (Westminster, Md., 1948), pp. 38–9.

Here again we have the emphasis upon the power of thoughts, with a highly emotional and dramatic concentration of the senses upon the image of the crucified Christ.

In another of his sonnets Alabaster gives an explicit account of how these thoughts operate upon images:

> The sunne begins uppon my heart to shine:
> now lett a cloude of thoughts in order traine
> as dewy spangles wonte, and entertaine
> in many drops his Passione Divine,
> that on them, as a rainbow, may recline
> the white of innocence, the black of paine,
> the blew of stripes, the yellow of disdaine,
> and purple which his blood doth weell designe.   (70)

That is, purple which well signifies or represents Christ's blood. This poem is entitled in one manuscript 'A Morninge Meditation', and, of course, the sun that begins to shine upon the speaker's heart is at first the physical sun. But we become gradually aware that it is ultimately the Son of God whom the speaker is contemplating and that this Son is warming his heart. This is no random thinking, but rather 'thoughts in order': a process of 'passionate paradoxical reasoning which knits the first line to the last'—to use Grierson's old description of the metaphysical style.[2] The poem concludes with a passage that represents the search for unity in multiplicity, which is the true nature of a metaphysical action, in the strict sense of that word 'metaphysical.'[3]

> And lett those thousand thoughts powre on mine eyes
> a thousand tears, as glasses to beehould him,
> and thousand tears, thousand sweete words devise
> uppon my lipps, as pictures to unfold him.
> Soe shall reflect three rainbowes from one sunne:
> thoughts, tears, and words, all end in Actione.

'In Actione'—that is, devout, unified, concentrated action: a nimble, vigorous state of mind perhaps better represented in the alternative ending that one manuscript gives for this sonnet: 'yet actinge all in one'.

[2] See *Metaphysical Lyrics and Poems of the Seventeenth Century*, edited by Herbert J. C. Grierson (Oxford, 1921), p. xxxiv.

[3] See the indispensable essay by James Smith, 'On Metaphysical Poetry', which originally appeared in *Scrutiny* in 1933, and is now fortunately available in *A Selection from Scrutiny*, compiled by F. R. Leavis (2 vols., Cambridge, 1968), II, 157-71.

Finally, to take one more example from this interesting precursor of the seventeenth-century line of religious poets, Alabaster sums up in a brilliant little drama the action that he has here been describing:

> When without tears I looke on Christ, I see
> only a story of some passion
> which any common eye may wonder on,
> butt if I look through tears Christ smiles on mee,
> yea there I see my selfe: and from that tree
> he bendeth downe to my devotione . . .   (71)

Here again the word 'devotion' occurs as the outcome of a vigorous internal drama: through the power of the speaker's mental action he sees Christ smile on him and bend down to assist the activity of the human soul.

By combining the techniques of devotion with the techniques of the Elizabethan sonnet, Alabaster has here produced poetry of a strongly 'metaphysical' cast. His sonnets thus suggest that we should be extremely cautious in estimating the influence of Donne upon the course of devotional poetry in the seventeenth century. And indeed, the more we ponder the peculiar quality of Donne's religious consciousness, the more we realize that his Hymns and Holy Sonnets do not lend themselves to imitation.

Let me explain and illustrate what I mean by the inimitable peculiarity of Donne's religious consciousness. Two Holy Sonnets will perhaps serve to make my point. First, Holy Sonnet 9, which develops a remarkably intricate series of dramatic postures.[4] The poem is at first spoken furtively to the self as if God were not present and would not hear the blasphemous thoughts that the speaker is uttering, as he tries to evade his human responsibilities:

> If poysonous mineralls, and if that tree,
> Whose fruit threw death on else immortall us,
> If lecherous goats, if serpents envious
> Cannot be damn'd; Alas; why should I bee?

It is the *tree's* fault that death came upon us; and we can see a further bit of hypocrisy and wilful misunderstanding in the word 'serpents', because we know very well that one 'serpent' has been damned to eternity. And that cry, 'Alas; why should I bee?' is implicitly answered

[4] Number 5 in the first sequence of the Holy Sonnets as presented in Miss Gardner's edition.

in the very next line, as though an answer had occurred to the self-deluding speaker between the lines, for he goes on to ask:

> Why should intent or reason, borne in mee,
> Make sinnes, else equall, in mee, more heinous?

He knows perfectly well the traditional answer: it is the power of reason that makes man damnable when 'mineralls' or trees cannot be damned. But 'borne in mee' turns the blame towards the Creator; and he has a further complaint which he goes on to express in his querulous way:

> And mercy being easie, and glorious
> To God, in his sterne wrath, why threatens hee?

It is as though the mention of the name of God reminds the speaker that he is, however he may pretend, speaking in the presence of his God. Suddenly his whole resistance breaks down in anguish and fear:

> But who am I, that dare dispute with thee?
> O God, Oh! of thine onely worthy blood,
> And my teares, make a heavenly Lethean flood,
> And drowne in it my sinnes blacke memorie.
> That thou remember them, some claime as debt,
> I thinke it mercy, if thou wilt forget.

In that last line the speaker seems to be saying that perhaps the best he can hope for is that he will be utterly forgotten and wiped out of God's mind, although he would prefer to have only his sins forgotten. The poem stands on the edge of despair, but never quite falls into the pit. What is most striking here is the continuously shifting nature of the argument, the way in which the speaker's mind seems to be racing ahead of itself, answering questions implicitly even while they are being asked. It is this constantly shifting nature of the speaker's stance within a given poem that makes Donne's poems basically inimitable. His search for the One moves along the edge of a quicksand, with a feeling that the steps of reason are always on the verge of disaster; yet reason never does collapse; in fact, it emerges triumphant in the sestet of this sonnet, with an exact command of the theology of redemption, in spite of all the evasions and curious questions raised en route.

We can see a similar shifting of the mind in a sonnet that is not often analysed, though frequently mentioned, Holy Sonnet 17, written after

the death of Donne's wife. Here again, one is struck by the fact that the
opening posture, in this case, one of serenity, is utterly deceptive:

> Since she whome I lovd, hath payd her last debt
> To Nature, and to hers, and my good is dead,
> And her soule early into heaven ravished,
> Wholy in heavenly things my mind is sett.
> Here the admyring her my mind did whett
> To seeke thee God; so streames do shew the head . . .

Thus far the speaker's state of mind seems secure and even placid,
strangely serene for Donne. But it is all illusory, for the next two lines
tell us that this speaker is, as always, dissatisfied:

> But though I have found thee, and thou my thirst hast fed,
> A holy thirsty dropsy melts mee yett.

He longs for the satisfaction of his love for God, and so another and
a more perplexing question follows with a repetition of the word 'but':

> But why should I begg more love, when as thou
> Dost wooe my soule for hers; offring all thine:

This is Grierson's reading, based on the Westmoreland manuscript,
and it is indeed a perplexing one. As it stands it seems to say that God
is wooing the speaker's soul in order to rejoin it with the soul of his
beloved lady; God's love brings to perfection the true love of two
human beings. Yet Miss Gardner's emendation is attractive,[5] which
makes the question read thus:

> But why should I begg more love, when as thou
> Dost wooe my soule, for hers offring all thine:

As Miss Gardner explains, the speaker is then asking why he needs to
beg for more love when God is offering God's love in place of his lady's
love. From one standpoint this meaning leads better into the next
two lines:

> And dost not only feare least I allow
> My love to saints and Angels, things divine, . . .

Donne may be alluding to his lady here under the traditional Petrarchan category of saints and angels. On the other hand, there seems to be
a clear allusion to the theological problems raised by Catholic devotion
to saints and angels, a practice of course forbidden, or severely restricted,

[5] See Miss Gardner's discussion, *Divine Poems*, p. 79.

by the Protestants. In either case (and we may take both interpretations simultaneously) the last four lines of the poem flow together to produce a curious sense of latent threat to the opening security:

> And dost not only feare least I allow
> My love to saints and Angels, things divine,
> But in thy tender jealosy dost doubt
> Least the World, fleshe, yea Devill putt thee out.

Donne seems to be saying here that God may very well have some reason to fear that the speaker will love saints and angels, things divine, but it is an excess of tender jealousy for God to fear that, at this stage of his life, the world, the flesh, or the devil could ever put God out of the speaker's heart. And yet the very mention of the world, the flesh, and the devil at the end indicates the speaker's awareness that this is a danger, this is a just fear. As in many of Donne's poems, the ending is a most precarious resolution and leaves the reader with no sense that the ever-recurrent instability of this speaker's mind has really been overcome.

The contrast between Donne's instability and Herbert's deeply achieved security makes the poetry of these two men vastly different. I think we do not do Herbert's poetry a favour when we seek to emphasize its restlessness. What we have in his poetry as presented in the whole *Temple* is the *memory* of states of restlessness now securely overcome and retrospectively viewed as dangers overpassed. As Herbert's *Temple* now exists it is an edifice in which the praise of God is securely rendered, from a vantage point of victory. It is probably only an accident of the modern temper that we should regard a state of continuous instability as more interesting than a state of achieved security. Certainly the seventeenth century did not regard Donne as a greater religious poet than Herbert. Vaughan, as we know, revered Herbert as a 'Saint' and imitated his poetry almost as though it were holy writ.

Herbert's poetry at its best is represented in that well-known poem 'Vertue', which will show clearly the enormous difference between the basic state of mind and consequently the basic poetical techniques of Donne and Herbert:

> Sweet day, so cool, so calm, so bright,
> The bridall of the earth and skie:
> The dew shall weep thy fall to night;
>   For thou must die.

Sweet rose, whose hue angrie and brave
Bids the rash gazer wipe his eye:
Thy root is ever in its grave,
            And thou must die.

Sweet spring, full of sweet dayes and roses,
A box where sweets compacted lie;
My musick shows ye have your closes,
            And all must die.

Onely a sweet and vertuous soul,
Like season'd timber, never gives;
But though the whole world turn to coal,
            Then chiefly lives.

The poem creates that sense of deliberate architectural building, block by block, which marks the Herbertian technique, and which he shares with Ben Jonson and the Sons of Ben. As in the design of a classical building, one seems to see at once how it is put together, why it produces this effect of total serenity and full command. The parallelism in the opening phrases of the first three stanzas is explicit, all being neatly bound together in the middle of the poem, in the ninth line. Then all the repetitions of 'sweet' are bound together once again in the opening line of the final stanza. On the other side of the stanzas, the rhymes are carefully built. The second and fourth lines of the first three stanzas contain the same rhyme, meeting on the word 'die', three times repeated; thus a melancholy oscillation is produced between 'Sweet' and 'die' at beginning and end of these three stanzas. Then, in the last stanza, the shift in the position of 'sweet', and the change in rhyme, mark a change towards a positive, optimistic mood.

Meanwhile, underneath all this carefully built symmetry there is a rich and fluent sub-structure of association developing out of the repetitions of that word 'sweet', used with many implications. Consider all that the word 'sweet' may imply as recorded in the OED, in addition to indicating a pleasant flavour. As applied to smell it means: having a pleasant odour, fragrant. As applied to hearing it means: having a pleasant sound, being musical, harmonious. As applied to sight it means: lovely, charming. Or, to give the richest of the OED definitions, the word means: 'free from offensive or disagreeable taste or smell; not corrupt, putrid, sour, or stale; free from taint or noxious matter; in a sound or wholesome condition.' Furthermore, as in

'sweetheart', it may of course mean: beloved, precious, dear—as in
Lovelace's poem: 'Tell me not (Sweet) I am unkind.' All these meanings are compacted in the five repetitions of the word 'sweet', along
with the central and summary use of the noun 'sweets', meaning
perfumes or fragrant flowers, not chocolates. Then at the very close
the poem takes a double turn, for although the 'sweet and vertuous
soul' is like 'season'd timber' in its strength, it is unlike timber in a final
regard, because even seasoned timber will turn to ashes, after a long
time: but the 'sweet and vertuous soul' will live. As in the design of a
classical building, what seems at first so clear and obvious grows from
a very subtle convergence of lines and perspectives. Such art as this is
founded upon security, can arise only from security. It lies at the
farthest remove from the vehement, rushing, questioning and often
querulous action of Donne.

   We should note, too, that Herbert's technique of repetition pervades
the entire *Temple*. A similar repetition of the word 'sweet', for instance,
binds 'Vertue' and 'The Odour' together, though they are separated by
some eighty pages in the standard edition; and of course the word
'sweet' occurs dozens of times in the intervening poems and elsewhere.
There are many other words which stretch their tentacular affiliations
throughout the full range of Herbert's book, sometimes dominating
single poems, at other times linking many poems: words such as 'grief',
'blood', 'heart', 'love', 'dust', 'musick', along with kindred terms, and
many other repeated words which every reader will wish to emphasize
for himself. Thus, after 'The Sacrifice' has presented the words of Christ
from the Cross: 'Was ever grief like mine', the next poem, 'The
Thanksgiving', picks up the word 'grief' and savours its various
meanings: suffering, sorrow, injury, pain, 'the grief of a wound':

> Oh King of grief! (a title strange, yet true,
>   To thee of all kings onely due)
> Oh King of wounds! how shall I grieve for thee,
>   Who in all grief preventest me?
> Shall I weep bloud? why, thou hast wept such store
>   That all thy body was one doore.

Then, in 'The Agonie' three key words, 'love', 'sweet', and 'bloud',
are brought together in the final lines:

> Love is that liquour sweet and most divine,
> Which my God feels as bloud; but I, as wine.

Upon the fabric established by these repetitions, Herbert weaves an astonishing variety of designs, including some of the boldest familiarity with God found anywhere in literature. I think, for example, of 'The Bag', which opens with a firm rejection of 'despair', by alluding to the occasion when Jesus calmed the waves of the sea (*Matthew* 8. 24–7):

> Away despair! my gracious Lord doth heare.
>   Though windes and waves assault my keel,
>   He doth preserve it: he doth steer,
>   Ev'n when the boat seems most to reel.
>   Storms are the triumph of his art:
> Well may he close his eyes, but not his heart.

Within this context of security Herbert then proceeds to tell 'a strange storie' about the Incarnation and the Crucifixion, all done in the most intimate fashion:

> But as he was returning, there came one
>   That ran upon him with a spear.
>   He, who came hither all alone,
>   Bringing nor man, nor arms, nor fear,
>   Receiv'd the blow upon his side,
> And straight he turn'd, and to his brethren cry'd,
>
> If ye have any thing to send or write,
>   I have no bag, but here is room:
>   Unto my Fathers hands and sight,
>   Beleeve me, it shall safely come.
>   That I shall minde, what you impart,
> Look, you may put it very neare my heart.
>
> Or if hereafter any of my friends
>   Will use me in this kinde, the doore
>   Shall still be open; what he sends
>   I will present, and somewhat more,
>   Not to his hurt. Sighs will convey
> Any thing to me. Harke, Despair away.

The letter-bag, we see, turns out to be Christ's own side, with allusion to the *Gospel of John*, 10. 9: 'I am the door: by me if any man enter in, he shall be saved, and shall go in and out, and find pasture.' At the same time, when we look at the shaping of these stanzas, turning them on the side, it appears as though each stanza represents the shape of a bag. This effect is quite in line with the sort of visual wit that Herbert works in other poems. But my point is the way in which this witty intimacy lives within the state of security and could not otherwise exist.

The same is true of 'Conscience', where the speaker intimately addresses his conscience as though it were a troublesome, foolish babbler, or a child causing difficulty by its chattering:

> Peace pratler, do not lowre:
> Not a fair look, but thou dost call it foul:
> Not a sweet dish, but thou dost call it sowre:
> Musick to thee doth howl.
> By listning to thy chatting fears
> I have both lost mine eyes and eares.

He proceeds in the next stanza to state the ideal which he seeks and within which his poems work:

> Pratler, no more, I say:
> My thoughts must work, but like a noiselesse sphere;
> Harmonious peace must rock them all the day:
> No room for pratlers there.
> If thou persistest, I will tell thee,
> That I have physick to expell thee.

Then, picking up the word 'physick', he develops it into a theological metaphor, that the medical prescription will be the blood of Christ tasted at his table:

> And the receit shall be
> My Saviours bloud: when ever at his board
> I do but taste it, straight it cleanseth me,
> And leaves thee not a word;
> No, not a tooth or nail to scratch,
> And at my actions carp, or catch.

> Yet if thou talkest still,
> Besides my physick, know there's some for thee:
> Some wood and nails to make a staffe or bill
> For those that trouble me:
> The bloudie crosse of my deare Lord
> Is both my physick and my sword.

Notice how the troublesome conscience is treated as a dramatic character quite distinct from the speaker's whole self. The blood of Christ is not only the speaker's own cure, but it also provides a tough

THE ACTION OF THE SELF

weapon against conscience itself. The curiously bantering tone of the poem could only be successful within the familiar confidence that Herbert has achieved in speaking in the presence of his God.

Henry Vaughan, in his creative, deliberate imitation of George Herbert's poetry, has frequently attempted to achieve the intimacy in which Herbert so securely lives. But Vaughan's consciousness lives in a different universe, an unstable and insecure state of mind, in which the speaker attempts to maintain the memory of certain moments of illumination: especially that moment represented in the engraved title-page and prefatory poem to *Silex Scintillans* (1650), when the power of God struck him and his rocky heart flashed with the fire of love. Vaughan's mystic consciousness lives in the effort to recover that event, the beginning of his spiritual life. Thus, instability and a groping movement seem to be essential to the action of Vaughan's poetry, even when he is most closely imitating Herbert. One poem, filled with echoes of Herbert, will illustrate the difference: 'The Resolve'. The title is, of course, reminiscent of Herbert's way of entitling many of his poems, such as 'The Reprisall', from which Vaughan takes his opening line, echoing word by word the first line of Herbert's poem:

> I have consider'd it; and find . . .

But each poet is considering quite a different thing. Herbert is considering how he may repay the love of God, as described in the preceding poem, 'The Thanksgiving', where he honours Christ as the King of Grief in the passage quoted previously; how he might deal with Christ's 'mighty passion'. He goes on to explain that he will solve this problem 'by confession' in which he 'will overcome/The man, who once against thee fought.' Significantly, Vaughan is not considering the Passion; his poetry, unlike Herbert's, is not centred on the Cross. What Vaughan's centre is, the poem gradually and gropingly reveals:

> I have consider'd it; and find
>   A longer stay
> Is but excus'd neglect. To mind
>   One path, and stray
> Into another, or to none,
>   Cannot be love;
> When shal that traveller come home,
>   That will not move?

> If thou wouldst thither, linger not,
>   Catch at the place. . . .

The last phrase, 'Catch at the place', is an echo of the phrase in Herbert's poem 'Affliction (I)', where Herbert says his 'sudden soul caught at the place' (line 17), that is to say, the place in the ministry of the Church into which God has 'enticed' him. In Herbert's poem we know exactly where the 'place' is, for he has spoken of the joys in the service of God which he has hoped to find. But in Vaughan's poem, characteristically, we do not know what place the speaker is seeking, we do not know what path he 'minds', intends to follow. And Vaughan continues with his exhortations for many lines, without telling us the ultimate goal.

> Tell youth, and beauty they must rot,
>   They'r but a *Case*;
> Loose, parcell'd hearts wil freeze: The Sun
>   With scatter'd locks
> Scarce warms, but by contraction
>   Can heat rocks;
> Call in thy *Powers*; run, and reach
>   Home with the light,
> Be there, before the shadows stretch,
>   And *Span* up night;
> Follow the *Cry* no more.

Clearly, the speaker is urging a concentration of the powers of his soul upon some ultimate aim, and he is going to escape from the way of the world, 'the *Cry*' (with a reference not only to the general opinion of the world but perhaps also to the cry of a pack of hounds). Another explicit echo of Herbert's poem 'Affliction (I)', lines 19–22:

> At first thou gav'st me milk and sweetnesses;
>   I had my wish and way:
> My dayes were straw'd with flow'rs and happinesse;
>   There was no moneth but May.

is added as Vaughan continues thus:

> there is
> An ancient way
> All strewed with flowres, and happiness
> And fresh as *May*;

In Herbert's poem this sense of happiness is an illusion indicating the speaker's misunderstanding of the way of Christ; but here in Vaughan the imagery of nature and springtime indicates a true and ultimate goal, as the poem concludes:

> There turn, and turn no more; Let wits,
> Smile at fair eies,
> Or lips; But who there weeping sits,
> Hath got the *Prize*.

In the very last word, italicized by Vaughan, we understand the goal. It is that expressed by St. Paul in his *Epistle to the Philippians* (3. 14): 'I press for the mark for the prize of the high calling of God in Christ Jesus.'

What has Vaughan learned then from Herbert's poetry? He has learned how to use familiar conversation in colloquy with the self; he has learned how to use familiar allusions in the presence of God. But the structure of Vaughan's poetry lacks the kind of architectural neatness which we find in Herbert at his best. As in 'The Resolve', Vaughan's best poems move tentatively with a roving action, seeking the ancient way which Vaughan at his best frequently symbolizes in imagery from nature, from the pastoral scenes of the Bible, or from the memory of the innocence of those 'early days' of his own childhood.

A more elaborate indication of these aspects of Vaughan's poetry may be found in the longer poem 'Ascension-day', in which all the finest aspects of Vaughan's art are brought together. Here is a poem in which he uses many of the traditional modes of religious meditation.[6] The opening 'aspirations' are followed by the use of all the senses to apprehend vividly ('as though one were present') the action in the scene:

> I greet thy Sepulchre, salute thy Grave,
> That blest inclosure, where the Angels gave
> The first glad tidings of thy early light,
> And resurrection from the earth and night.
> I see that morning in thy Converts tears,[7]
> Fresh as the dew, which but this dawning wears!
> I smell her spices, and her ointment yields,
> As rich a scent as the now Primros'd-fields:
> The Day-star smiles, and light with thee deceast,
> Now shines in all the Chambers of the East.
> What stirs, what posting intercourse and mirth
> Of Saints and Angels glorifie the earth?

[6] For details see my study, *The Poetry of Meditation* (2nd edition, New Haven, 1962), especially chapters 1 and 2.

[7] Vaughan adds a note identifying the 'Convert' as St. Mary Magdalen.

> What sighs, what whispers, busie stops and stays:
> Private and holy talk fill all the ways?
> They pass as at the last great day, and run
> In their white robes to seek the risen Sun;
> I see them, hear them, mark their haste, and move
> Amongst them, with them, wing'd with faith and love.

In this 'composition of place', directed towards this scene of light, Vaughan is able to bring to bear the ancient technique of using the senses in a spiritual exercise, a technique which he has been unable to use effectively in other poems where he has attempted to meditate upon Eucharistic scenes. He cannot, for example, grasp the Passion of Christ visually, although he tries to do so in his very weak poem entitled 'The Passion', a poem cast in the past tense, unable to achieve the presence of God. But here the sense of presence is achieved as the speaker proceeds to associate the scene of the Ascension with the early days of *Genesis* and the beauties of nature as Vaughan himself could visualize them. Three areas of action then are brought together here: the fields of Bethany on the Ascension day, the scene in Eden in the days before the Fall, and the vestiges of that original beauty which still can be seen in nature at present:

> I walk the fields of *Bethani* which shine
> All now as fresh as *Eden*, and as fine.
> Such was the bright world, on the first seventh day,
> Before man brought forth sin, and sin decay;
> When like a Virgin clad in *Flowers* and *green*
> The pure earth sat, and the fair woods had seen
> No frost, but flourish'd in that youthful vest,
> With which their great Creator had them drest:
> When Heav'n above them shin'd like molten glass,
> While all the Planets did unclouded pass;
> And Springs, like dissolv'd Pearls their Streams did pour
> Ne'r marr'd with floods, nor anger'd with a showre.

In this setting, bright with natural beauty and with memories of the Bible, Vaughan is able to fulfil the quest that he began in the first part of *Silex Scintillans* in his poem 'The Search', where he roved through the traditional places of Christ's residence, and was unable to find his Lord. But now

> With these fair thoughts I move in this fair place,
> And the last steps of my milde Master trace;

I see him leading out his chosen Train,
All sad with tears, which like warm Summer-rain
In silent drops steal from their holy eyes,
Fix'd lately on the Cross, now on the skies.
And now (eternal Jesus!) thou dost heave
Thy blessed hands to bless, these thou dost leave;
The cloud doth now receive thee, and their sight
Having lost thee, behold two men in white!
Two and no more: *what two attest, is true,*
Was thine own answer to the stubborn Jew.
Come then thou faithful witness! come dear Lord
Upon the Clouds again to judge this world!

Thus the poem concludes with two precise biblical allusions; first to
the scene of the Ascension itself (*Acts* I. 9–11), and secondly to the verse
of the *Gospel of John* (8. 17), where Jesus answers the Pharisees by
saying, 'It is also written in your Law, that the testimony of two men
is true.' In a way characteristic of Vaughan's best work, this poem then
ends abruptly with a brief prayer.

This poem is very little indebted to George Herbert and not at all to
John Donne. Its roving action is an original achievement by Vaughan,
working within a mode of versification characteristic of the Sons of
Ben Jonson, where the development of couplet-rhetoric was moving
towards its Augustan culmination.

Meanwhile, in exile on the continent, Richard Crashaw was bringing
to conclusion his efforts to achieve ecstatic expression in the continental
mode of the baroque. One poem must serve here as an example of the
way in which Crashaw was departing from the central modes of
English poetry, adapting the phraseology of Herbert, the couplet-
rhetoric of Ben Jonson, the techniques of the Elizabethan love-song,
and bringing all these modes into an idiom that was essentially foreign
to the English tradition. Crashaw's poetry remains an anomaly in
English literature, an example of a continental importation which
never struck a firm hold upon the English scene, and in the end had
to seek its proper nourishment in exile. I choose his poem on the
Assumption of the Virgin Mary, a poem that may have been written
before Crashaw left England in the early sixteen forties, since it was
published in part in the first edition of *Steps to the Temple* (1646). Here,
however, a passage of sixteen lines (19–34) is lacking, which appeared
in the edition of 1648 where we find the longest version of the poem;

the posthumous edition of 1652 omits ten other lines (47–56), whether on Crashaw's authorization or not, we shall never know. I take the version of 1648 to be the best as well as the longest, and it is on this that I base my comments.[8]

The poem opens in the manner of a formal meditation with a composition of the scene of the Virgin Mary's Assumption:

> Hark! she is call'd, the parting houre is come.
> Take thy farewell, poore world! Heav'n must goe home.
> A peece of Heav'nly Earth, purer and brighter
> Than the chast stars, whose choice lamps come to light her,
> While through the Christall orbes, clearer than they,
> She climbs; and makes a farre more milky way.

Now the speaker, being present at the scene, hears the song of Christ, as in the *Song of Solomon* (2. 10–13), calling his beloved, while the poem modulates gracefully from pentameter couplets into a song of neatly balanced tetrameter couplets:

> She's call'd. Harke how the deare immortall *Dove*
> Sighes to his silver mate. *Rise up my Love,*
> *Rise up my faire, my spotlesse one,*
> *The winters past, the Rain is gone:*
> *The spring is come, the Flowers appeare,*
> *No sweets but thou are wanting here.*

Then, picking up the biblical 'come away', Crashaw transmutes the measure into the verse form of an Elizabethan song, echoing the invitation found in many Elizabethan song-books, as in Campion's lyric:

> Come away, arm'd with loves delights,
> Thy sprightfull graces bring with thee;

or in Dowland's lyric:

> Come away, come sweet Love,
> The golden morning breakes:
> All the earth, all the ayre
> Of love and pleasure speaks;

[8] I quote from the 1648 edition of *Steps to the Temple*; see the text of this poem in *The Anchor Anthology of Seventeenth-Century Verse*, vol. 1. The Oxford edition of Crashaw's *Poems*, edited by L. C. Martin (2nd edition, Oxford, 1957), prints only the versions of 1646 and 1652.

or in Ben Jonson's song:

> Come away, come away,
> We grow jealous of your stay.[9]

In this popular mode Crashaw then presents his sacred parody in a madrigal of Christ:

> Come away my love,
> Come away my dove,
> Cast off delay:
> The Court of Heav'n is come,
> To waite upon thee home;
> Come, come away.

Then, in the long passage missing in 1646, the speaker subtly effects a shifting of voices suggested by the fact that the above madrigal is not italicized as the voice of Christ alone, but is rather presented as a song in which the human speaker may also be singing. But now the voice clearly shifts to that of the human speaker, developing the imagery of the *Song of Solomon* into his own fallen landscape, as he longs for the presence of the Virgin who can help to heal all mortal sorrow:

> The Flowers appeare,
> Or quickly would, were thou once here.
> The spring is come; Or if it stay,
> 'Tis to keepe time with thy delay.
> The raine is gone, Except as much as wee,
> Detain in needfull *Teares*, to weep the want of thee.
> The winters past,
> Or if he make lesse haste,
> His answer is, Why, she doth so;
> If summer come not, how can winter go?
> Come away, come away,
> The shrill winds chide, the waters weep thy stay,

[9] See *The Works of Thomas Campion*, edited by Walter R. Davis (Garden City, N.Y., 1967), p. 108; see also Campion's song, 'Come away, bring thy golden theft', in *The Lords Maske*, p. 252. For Dowland's lyric see *England's Helicon*, edited by Hyder Edward Rollins (2 vols., Cambridge, Mass., 1935), I, p. 158. Jonson's song appears in his *Masque of Blacknesse*; see the edition of *Ben Jonson*, by C. H. Herford, and Percy and Evelyn Simpson (11 vols., Oxford, 1925–52), VII, 178; it was published in Alfonso Ferrabosco's *Ayres*, 1609. See *English Madrigal Verse, 1588–1632*, edited by E. H. Fellowes and revised by Frederick W. Sternfeld and David Greer (3rd edn., Oxford, 1967), pp. 388, 460, 512.

> The fountaines murmure; and each loftiest Tree,
> Bowes lowest his leavy top, to looke for thee.

But now the madrigal of Christ is heard again:

> Come away my love,
> Come away my dove, &c.

Thus the speaker finds that Mary must indeed now leave this earth, and he accepts the loss, finding his consolation in her praise:

> She's call'd again; And will she goe?
> When Heav'n bids come, who can say No?
> Heav'n calls her, and she must away,
> Heav'n will not, and she cannot stay.
> Goe then, goe (*glorious*) on the golden wings
> Of the bright youth of Heav'n that sings
> Under so sweet a burden, *Goe*,
> Since thy dread *Son* will have it so.
> And while thou goest, our Song and wee,
> Will as wee may reach after thee.
>   *Haile, holy Queen*, of humble Hearts!
>   We in thy praise wil have our parts . . .
>
> Though our poore joyes are parted so,
> Yet shall our lips never let goe
> Thy gracious name, but to the last
> Our loving song shall hold it fast.

In this determination the speaker now creates his own earthly madrigal, in an intricate pattern of trimeter, tetrameter, and dimeter, concluding with a firm tetrameter couplet:

> Thy precious Name shall bee
> Thy self to us, and wee
> With holy care will keep it by us.
>   Wee to the last
>   Will hold it fast;
> And no Assumption shall deny us.
>   All the sweetest showers
>   Of our fairest flowers,
> Will wee strow upon it;
>   Though our sweets cannot make
>   It sweeter, they can take
> Themselves new sweetnesse from it.

> *Maria*, Men and Angels sing,
> *Maria*, Mother of our King.

Thus the celebration has achieved its climax. After a short pause, the poem then quietly modulates into its final movement, where, with full serenity, the speaker expresses his faith that Heaven and Earth are still united in the praise and presence of Mary, despite her bodily removal to Heaven. First, the poet speaks in stately, elegant pentameters, and lastly, in direct and simple four-foot lines, with an effect of intellectual poise and control:

> *Live, Rosie Princesse, live*, and may the bright
> Crowne of a most incomparable light
> Embrace thy radiant browes: O may the best
> Of everlasting joyes bath thy white brest.
> Live our chaste love, the holy mirth
> Of heav'n, the Humble pride of Earth.
> Live, crowne of women, Queen of men;
> Live Mistrisse of our Song; And when
> Our weake desires have done their best,
> *Sweet Angels come, and sing the Rest.*

The poem represents Crashaw's art of baroque celebration at its best, with its subtly shifting voices, varied repetitions, multiple perspectives, and modulating verse forms, all its variety held together under the artful control of the human speaker, whose simple language opens and concludes his hymn.

Crashaw died at Loreto in 1649, and Vaughan's inspiration ebbed away in the second part of *Silex Scintillans* in 1655; the great era of English devotional poetry thus ended with the coming of the Puritan Commonwealth. Devotional poetry flourished in England during a period of some fifty years, while the established church provided a way of resolving the religious issues of the time. It was a brief era in which all the currents of religious life, both continental and English, could meet and make a little stay. But the inner tensions of the time could not for long be tempered to the spirit of devotion. John Milton found that he could not complete his poem on the Passion, but had to wait until his strenuous, indomitable genius could find the larger forms in which his voice could master the warring issues of his day.

Note

Works
A little before his death, Herbert sent his poems to his friend Nicolas Ferrar, with instructions that they should either be burned or printed. Ferrar decided to print, and a transcript was made for the purpose. This survives in the Bodleian Library (Tanner 307). The poems were printed as *The Temple*, 1633. Sixty-nine of the poems in the 1633 edition, together with six not found there or in the Bodleian manuscript, exist in manuscript form in Dr. Williams's Library (Jones B 62). Herbert's prose treatise, *The Country Parson*, was first published in 1652 under the title of 'A Priest to the Temple' in *Herbert's Remains*.

The Temple was very popular in the seventeenth century, and thirteen editions appeared up to 1709. Both *The Temple* and an expanded volume of *Remains* were printed in an attractive nineteenth-century edition by William Pickering, who included Coleridge's notes on the poems.

Modern Editions. The standard annotated edition of Herbert's *Works* from which quotations in the following essay are taken is that by F. E. Hutchinson (1941, revised 1945); G. H. Palmer's commentary in his 1905 edition (revised 1907) is also useful. The Nonesuch Press published in 1927 an edition based on the Bodleian manuscript. A facsimile of *The Temple* has been produced by the Scolar Press (1968).

Scholarship and Criticism. Izaak Walton's *Life* (1670) has often been reprinted, and there is a modern biography by Margaret Chute in *Two Gentle Men* (1959).

By far the best critical study is Joseph H. Summers: *George Herbert, his Religion and Art* (1954). Margaret Bottrall's *George Herbert* (1954) has insight and enthusiasm. There are very full stylistic analyses in Arnold Stein's *George Herbert's Lyrics* (1968). The liturgical and iconographic tradition behind the poems is discussed by Rosemond Tuve in *A Reading of George Herbert* (1952); and Louis Martz's *The Poetry of Meditation* (1954) relates them to the devotional practice of the time.

Among many articles and short discussions, the following are worth special notice: Chapter III of A. Alvarez's *The School of Donne* (1961); the chapters on Herbert in Robert Ellrodt's *L'Inspiration personelle et l'esprit du temps chez les poètes metaphysiques anglais* (1960); Fredson Bowers: 'Herbert's sequential imagery: "The Temper" ', in *Modern Philology* 59 (1962); Chapter VI of Rosemary Freeman's *English Emblem Books* (1948); A. M. Hayes: 'Counterpoint in Herbert', *Studies in Philology* 35 (1938); L. C. Knights: 'George Herbert', in *Explorations* (1945); Alicia Ostriker: 'Song and Speech in the Metrics of George Herbert', *Publications of the Modern Language Association* 80 (1965); Mary E. Rickey: 'Herbert's Technical Development', *Journal of English and Germanic Philology* 62 (1963); E. B. Greenwood: 'George Herbert's Sonnet "Prayer" ', *Essays in Criticism*, 15 (1965).

V

Something Understood:

The Nature of Herbert's Wit

M. M. MAHOOD

★

A TIME when many poets are more than half way to becoming graphic
artists is a time ripe for reconsidering the views of Dryden and Addison
about the picture poems of the seventeenth century. It may well be that
their condemnation of what was to them a false form of wit was
aesthetically sound; it did at least spring from an instinctive recognition
of the limits of the sister arts as Lessing was to define them. Whatever
its typographic character, a poem is not a shape, but an event; that is
to say, it yields its meaning only as the reader progresses from its
beginning through its middle to its end. Recent explications and
justifications of Herbert's 'hieroglyphs' make this very point, for they
demonstrate above all the forward movement of thought in such
poems: the rhythmic rise and fall of 'Easter-wings', corresponding first
to the fall and redemption of man and next to the depression and
elevation of the poet's own spirits; the welding of 'Sinnes round' into
a firm and vicious circle such as makes the Concretist trick of printing
'revolve' in a circle seem very mild wit. Other recent criticism, by
showing how many of the lyrics in *The Temple* are constructed on the
plan of a formal meditation, has served to emphasize further this
feature of ordered progress towards a distinct end in Herbert's verse.
The aspirant to a devout life was urged to meditate upon his meditations; to ask himself, that is, if his thoughts had been so ordered that
they moved forward to the point where they could issue in prayer. As
in a poem, the end crowned all.

As meditations, Herbert's poems are colloquies with himself and
with God. They are also conversations with the reader. The poet who
so clearly described the art of good talk in 'The Church-porch', knew

123

perfectly how to control his reader's response throughout a poem, satisfying his expectations and stimulating his curiosity by 'the lullings and the relishes of it', to a conclusion that would leave him with the deep satisfaction of (to quote the end of the sonnet 'Prayer') 'something understood'. Among the Augustans, no one mastered better than Pope this art of manipulating the reader's interest by the right mixture of anticipation and surprise; and whatever lesser poets of the time had to say about *The Temple*, Pope was 'a great reader' of Herbert.

Pope also knew that the mixture of anticipation and surprise had to be adjusted according to the type of poem he was writing. The shocks of satire would be out of place in a pastoral; but the slack stock response had to be forestalled in the latter, with as much skill as was required in the former to allay the anxiety of listening to a talker who was too clever by half. In its small compass *The Temple* also covers a great range of poetic types and moods· it has been suggested that Herbert sought to include an example of each kind of short poem current in his time. In many of these, the reader's pleasure is one of familiarity: the recognition of an Horatian theme in 'Constancy', or of a famous passage from Ovid in 'Vertue'; enjoyment of a canticle's orderly survey of the wondrous works of God in 'Man' or 'Providence'; the 'now it's time for the sermon' expectancy that greets such homilies as 'The Churchporch' or 'Lent'. In all these types of poem Herbert has to use, in his own phrase, 'millions of surprises' to prevent the pleasure of recognition becoming a tired familiarity.

There are also quite different poems in which it appears that it is Herbert who is in a sense surprised. In these, though Herbert is in fact still talking to the reader, the reader has the sensation that he is listening to the poet at meditation or at prayer, eavesdropping on the 'many spiritual Conflicts' of Herbert's inner life in his last years at Bemerton. Just as the more didactic poems are often in danger of being over-explicit, over-organized, so these poems exploratory of adventures of the soul often risk disintegration. As a collection, *The Temple* perhaps loses some of its poetic distinction towards its middle, and recovers it only near the end. The reason may well be that these late poems, which include some of the very finest, but also some of the least shaped and ordered, are placed in the Bodleian manuscript between two series of the carefully revised pre-Bemerton poems. Illness and a short life robbed Herbert of time he must have craved for their revision, and 'The Forerunners' shows that he was troubled by the thought of failing powers. In itself this poem, by its skilful use of the 'sweet phrases, lovely metaphors' which threaten to abandon him, reasserts Herbert's mastery of his art; but its theme signals his distress that so many other poems fail to achieve the perfect ordering of this, or of 'The Collar', 'Aaron' or 'The Flower'.

*   *   *

A concern with dramatic form, with ordered movement towards a timely conclusion, guides Herbert in his choice and use of all the technical resources of his poetry: diction, imagery, sentence-structure, stanza forms, rhyme and rhythm. In his choice of words in particular Herbert is acutely sensitive to the dangerous Scylla and Charybdis of the over-facile and the too remote. When the reader's response may slip too easily into a groove, words need to be chosen for their denotative force. 'Faith' is, for Herbert, a long poem; its eleven stanzas play such witty variations on the power of faith to make all things possible that Herbert's inventiveness makes it difficult for him to terminate the poem in any manner that will achieve a real ending. It is done at last by a conclusion in which nothing is concluded:

> What though my bodie runne to dust?
> Faith cleaves unto it, counting evr'y grain
> With an exact and most particular trust,
> Reserving all for flesh again.

The telling exactness of the verbs *runne* and *cleaves* clinches the argument with the force of a physical gesture such as was sometimes used to end an oration or a sermon; one thinks of Donne picking up the hour-glass on the edge of the pulpit and saying, 'If there be a minute of sand left (There is not).' So here the disintegrating, soft-sift-in-a-glass effect of *runne* is powerfully matched and overcome by the cohesive force of *cleaves*.

Verbs again serve to vitalize what might otherwise have the deadness of the over-familiar in the second 'Jordan'. The notion that 'There is in love a sweetnesse readie penn'd' had been a commonplace ever since Sidney's 'look in thy heart and write', but it is here given new life by a string of tactile, sensuous verbs that not only describe the struggle to be ingenious but also exemplify the kind of verse that results—in, for example, Giles Fletcher's poetry—when thoughts begin 'to burnish, sprout, and swell', and the poet 'bustles' to 'weave' himself into the sense. Here the reader's too easy expectations, which have to be out-witted, come from the form of the poem, a sonnet; in 'Faith' they came rather from the poem's repetitive structure. Like 'Faith', 'The Quip' is built out of a connected series of conceits, and here too verbal sharpness gives precision just where it is needed. Our interest in the world's trained bands as they pass under review might flag as Glory follows so inevitably on the heels of Beauty and of Money—if Glory did not startle us by 'puffing by In silks that whistled'. As an entrance, this cannot be bettered, and a fresh device is needed to hold our interest in the succeeding figure of Wit-and-Conversation. The surprise is that Wit turns out to be on the poet's side; Herbert's only worldly office was that of Public Orator. But Wit's long-winded oration is no answer to the world's scorn. Only God can give that. 'Say I am thine,' Herbert demands; and the ambiguity of 'I' and 'thine' is typical of these late and powerfully Christocentric poems in which Herbert's will becomes indistinguishable from the will of God.

From such ambiguity it is a short step to playing with several mean-ings in a single word. Herbert insisted 'I like our language'—perhaps in defiance of his brothers, who considered him a better poet in Latin and Greek. What he especially liked about it on this occasion ('The Sonne') was its wealth of homophones. He makes lavish use of these for a variety of purposes and effects. Some are introduced, in the manner of the telling *mots justes* already noticed, to startle into attention the reader who might otherwise be lulled by the familiarity of the more didactic lyrics in *The Temple*. 'The Church-porch' is directed at a young wit and abounds in word-play:

> If reason move not Gallants, quit the room,
> (All in a shipwrack shift their severall way)

—where *gallants*, as well as meaning 'fine gentlemen', has nautical overtones;

> Slight those who say amidst their sickly healths
> Thou liv'st by rule;

and

> Onely a herauld, who that way doth passe,
> Findes his crackt name at length in the church-glasse

—where *crackt* means 'bankrupt' as well as 'damaged'; lastly,

Dare to look in thy chest, for 'tis thine own:
And tumble up and down what thou find'st there.

This last example gives a clue to a concealed pun in another homiletic poem, 'Ungratefulnesse'. This takes a dramatic turn when man is shown to possess, besides the two 'cabinets of treasure' bestowed upon him in the Trinity and Incarnation, a 'poore cabinet of bone' enclosing a heart he is not willing to render to God. The image is brought about through an unspoken play upon the meanings of *chest* such as occurs also in 'The Method': 'Go search this thing, Tumble thy breast, and turn thy book'. In the same way 'Love', the last and culminating poem in *The Temple* turns upon an unspoken pun on the word *host*. This gives the poem a Eucharistic reference, though its place in the sequence of lyrics shows it to be primarily about the soul's entry to heaven. The two interpretations, disputed by modern critics, would have coexisted comfortably for the seventeenth-century reader as the allegoric and anagogic meanings of the poem.

Although Herbert can thus pun openly or obliquely to stimulate the reader into thinking in more than one direction, his favourite use of word-play is to hold together a wealth of images and allusions in those more self-exploratory poems in which he tumbles up and down the thoughts of his own heart. Sometimes he does this by a wittily figurative title which acts as a signpost to the areas that are to be explored; it has been noticed that such titles—'Vanitie', 'The Sonne', 'The Crosse' —are a feature of the Bemerton poems. But they also occur in the earlier collection of the Williams manuscript. The title 'The Temper', in the first poem that bears it, not only signifies the elasticity given to steel by the process of hardening it with alternate heat and cold, but has also medical, musical and other meanings which help to hold together a poem that threatens to explode under the stress of Herbert's racked emotions. This word-play also makes it, as Fredson Bowers has shown, a nodal poem in the collection, bringing together the themes of the lyrics which surround it in this part of *The Temple*.

Word-play can also have a unifying effect when it occurs at the end of a poem and draws together its otherwise disparate images and their significances. 'Repentance' opens in the manner of many Psalms with a series of images that fly apart in all directions under the stress of painful feelings, and the penultimate stanza of the poem suggests a disintegration in shame of the whole personality, like that of the body's

decomposition that leaves nothing but dry and disjointed bones. But a
cry of anguish cannot be a poem. Something has to be predicated,
some statement made about the emotion expressed; and within the
Christian framework of Herbert's thought and experience this means
seeing the individual's grief as part of God's purpose. And in the last
stanza the images are transformed from those of physical destruction
into images of harmony by the help of double meanings in *set*, *broken*,
fractures and *bones* (a name for an Elizabethan form of percussion):

> But thou wilt sinne and grief destroy;
> That so the broken bones may joy,
> And tune together in a well-set song,
> Full of his praises,
> Who dead men raises;
> Fractures well cur'd make us more strong.

Discord is here brought to an harmonious close, similar to that sought
at the end of 'Employment' (I):

> I am no link of thy great chain,
> But all my companie is a weed.
> Lord place me in thy consort; give one strain
> To my poore reed.

In the earlier version of this poem represented by the Williams manuscript, this stanza ended: 'Lord that I may the Sunns perfection gaine
Give mee his speed.' This did not satisfy Herbert; it introduced at too
late a stage a new image unrelated to the rest of the poem. What he
knew to be needed was some metaphor in keeping with the flower
images with which the poem began, which would effect a turn in the
thought from the idea of fruitless blossoming to that of a purposeful
existence. Herbert accomplished this in the end by his use of *reed*: the
most fragile of plants, but yet the one which can be made into a musical
instrument and in particular the instrument which traditionally stands
for the poet's art.

   The sonnet 'Prayer' has often been praised for its powerfully sequential imagery. Our first passing impression as we read is of a heap of
conceits; but it is impossible to reach the end of the poem without the
images forming themselves, though below the conscious level, into a

double sequence. Prayer is earth raised to heaven, but it is also—since heaven gives man the grace to pray and hears his prayers—heaven brought to earth. The two thoughts are twisted, as closely as the sugarstick pillars of the time's architecture, through image after ambiguous image. 'Sinners towre' is not only a refuge from the world, a heaven-on-earth, but also a Babel-like structure threatening heaven; manna came down from heaven in the first place before it could be 'exalted' by man in the form of prayer—and so on. This duality of idea becomes especially forceful at the line 'Heaven in ordinarie, man well drest'. Not only is prayer heaven in workaday clothes and man in his Sunday best, but also it is heaven condescending to the public table of an inn as well as man served up—'well drest'—at the Church's banquet (the poem's opening image). Placed thus in the eleventh line of the sonnet the words *ordinary* and *dressed* impart overtones of sensuous pleasure to 'The milkie way, the bird of Paradise'; the celestial bird was footless and could not perch, but nevertheless exotic birds were often the centrepiece of a seventeenth-century banquet. This blend through word-play and imagery of material and immaterial pleasure is carried a stage further in 'Church-bels beyond the starres heard, the souls bloud', where we are in doubt whether the bells are earth's heard by heaven or heaven's heard from earth, and the last phrase is especially mysterious; and it is finally clarified in the ultimate refinements of sensuous and of intellectual pleasure, the one representing the apprehension of distant joys in earth's craving for heaven and the other heaven's enlightenment of earth: 'The land of spices; something understood.'

★   ★   ★

Poems such as 'Prayer', in which Herbert's usual terseness is intensified by the sonnet form, abound in one-word images. For this reason, no clear demarcation is possible between Herbert's diction, including his word-play, and his imagery. A single word, not in itself exactly a pun, can be so placed towards the end of a poem as to gather together a number of images from its earlier stanzas. 'The Pearl' offers a striking example. In this poem Herbert surveys, through three unusually elaborate stanzas of nine ten-syllable lines each, the worlds of Learning, Honour and Pleasure, countering the claims of each with the simple refrain: 'Yet I love thee.' Clearly the refrain anticipates some very

E

powerful counterclaim in the last stanza. As if uneasily aware of this, Herbert calls into play in the closing stanza two images that are potentially highly effective: the one of a falcon returning to her owner and the other, implied in the poem's title, of the merchant who sold all he had in order to buy the pearl of great price. But although it is possible to work out some logical connection between these—the falcon is ready to surrender her prey—the two images mix uncomfortably because the first suggests irrationally spontaneous or conditioned actions, the second an action resulting from reasoned calculation. This disparity can be felt in the changing movement of the verse:

> I know all these, and have them in my hand:
> Therefore not sealed, but with open eyes
> I flie to thee, and fully understand
> Both the main sale, and the commodities;
> And at what rate and price I have thy love;
> With all the circumstances that may move.

The tone becomes hesitant, uncertain. Neither his own desires nor his reasoning can explain the strength of Herbert's allegiance, which must have a source beyond his own powers. The rhythmically firm concluding lines acknowledge this:

> Yet through these labyrinths, not my groveling wit,
> But thy silk twist let down from heav'n to me,
> Did both conduct and teach me, how by it
>   To climbe to thee.

The image of a labyrinth was familiar to readers of contemporary emblem books. Herbert could have met it in Hermann Hugo's *Pia Desideria*, of which there were many editions from 1624 onwards. One plate there shows the pilgrim Anima picking her way through a maze while keeping a firm hold on the love-twist (to use Henry Vaughan's word) which has been let down for her by Divine Love from his high tower. The poet too, at this point in the poem, has picked an intricate way through the preceding stanzas, and the word *labyrinths* relates to each of these: to the opening image of the pipes of a winepress which moves quickly on, through a quibble on *press*, to the world of learning and the labyrinthine brain; to the corridors of power through which the ambitious man has to tread with labyrinthine ingenuity; and to the double theme of music and passion in the third stanza, the one represented by the convolutions of the time's music (and perhaps the labyrinth of the inner ear), the other recalling the lair of the Minotaur. The word thus subsumes all that has gone before in the poem. At the same time the related image of the silk twist, the clue through the labyrinth, replaces the confused assertions that began this last stanza by a metrically poised expression of the poet's dependence on grace.

Only occasionally does Herbert have to rely on such a powerfully charged word as *labyrinths* to fuse together a poem's images. At other times they are held together throughout by a firm allegorical framework such as that constructed for 'Love' or for 'The Pulley'. The choice of such a framework is not however in itself a guarantee of poetic success, as can be seen from a comparison of the sonnet 'Redemption' with that on 'Christmas'. The latter starts with an adaptation of a Petrarchan conceit such as was usual in a 'holy sonnet': the poet, wearied with the hunt in which his body is his horse and his affections, or passions, the hounds, arrives at an inn and finds there his 'dearest Lord', ready 'To be all passengers most sweet relief'. But here the allegory breaks down; there is no literal way in which the child in the crib can relieve travellers, and the sestet introduces new confusion between the horse as the body and man as 'brutish' but more in need of Christ's presence than the ox and ass. The poem virtually dissolves after its fine start, whereas 'Redemption' is sustained throughout by the firmly legalistic idea of the atonement current in Herbert's day, as well as by a play of meaning between the legal and the theological senses of the title. These enable Herbert to develop the poem, with great dramatic force, from the grumble of a dissatisfied tenant to the awe and gratitude of redeemed man.

The sonnet form lends itself well to the poetic structure of definition through a series of images, as countless Elizabethan examples show. Yet only a gifted poet can establish a close harmony between his images; Shakespeare, say, in 'That time of year . . .' or 'Let me not to the marriage of true minds . . .', Herbert in 'Prayer' or 'The Answer'. And even Herbert, despite his conscious artistry, has left a number of sonnets such as 'The Holy Scriptures' (I) in which the images, though individually striking, do not cohere, or move together to any kind of climax. Probably Herbert's dissatisfaction with this sonnet led him to attempt another more successful one on the same theme, in which he skilfully elaborates the metaphor of biblical texts as stars into the notion that the practised reader can combine these stars into constellations:

> This verse marks that, and both do make a motion
> Unto a third, that ten leaves off doth lie.

The image reminds us that in the designing of a poem Herbert, besides ordering his ideas through nodal imagery or through the use of allegory, could draw on long-established connections between different biblical episodes, especially between those of the Old and of the New Testament. These associations were already well established in the mind of the seventeenth-century reader, thanks to their persistence in art and to the stock grouping of 'exampla' in innumerable sermons. Herbert's first readers can have had no difficulty, in reading 'Aaron', in grasping the affinity between Aaron the high priest, Christ the great high priest, and Herbert the parish priest; or in recognizing, when they read 'The Bunch of Grapes' that the bunch of Eshcol was a type of Christ, the true vine of the new covenant as Noah's vine had been a pledge of the old.

In such poems, Herbert's delicate balance of his readers' expectation and surprise can be recaptured only by the modern reader who is sensitive to the seventeenth-century association of words and images. It is easy to be mystified by what was not at all mystifying in 1633; conversely, it is not always easy to grasp that Herbert is out to startle in a particular poem. Much of his imagery reflects the solid domestic comforts of the Caroline gentry, their world of feather beds, ingenious clockwork and elaborate joinery. For us these constitute Herbert's 'homeliness'; they have the remote charm of a seventeenth-century Dutch interior. It takes an imaginative effort to realize that for Herbert's first readers these things represented their own up-to-the-minute conspicuous expenditure. Allusions to enclosures or to land-drainage in the more didactic poems must have been aimed at jolting the reader out of any stock response to pious verse. So too would the abrupt colloquialism of 'Wilt eat thy cake and have it?' or of 'Thou pullst the rug, and wilt not rise'. Above all these hortatory poems sustain the reader's interest to the end, and make their point with inescapable force, by their deft placing of the most familiar and yet most striking image at the climax: the picture in the penultimate stanza of 'Lent'—verging on the sentimental when taken from its context but absolutely right in it—of God turning to take the traveller in a hard way by the hand; the 'famous stone' of the alchemists, 'That turneth all to gold' at the end of 'The Elixir'; and perhaps best of all, the image which concludes 'Constancy', of the bowler twisting his limbs to match the bias of his unsuccessful throw.

Of all Herbert's structural uses of imagery—and only a few have been touched upon here—none is more skilful than his use of it as a kind of dramatic irony, to prepare us subconsciously for a turn of thought that is to occur later in the poem. A major pleasure of re-reading Herbert lies in the discovery of these anticipatory images. The surprise at the end of 'The Collar' is that the voice of the taskmaster against whom the speaker has been rebelling turns out to be the voice of love. Yet paradoxically this is no surprise, because love has been present all through the poem. It is perfectly true, as the speaker claims, that 'there is fruit'; but it is to be found, not 'abroad', but on the table that the speaker strikes in his exasperation. And despite his assertion that all his harvest is a thorn, the wine and corn are there all the time, the outcome of the Passion and its thorns; we recall, and in this closely-linked collection of lyrics are probably meant to recall, the closing reference in 'The Agonie' to the 'liquor' 'Which my God feels as bloud; but I, as wine.' Most ironic of all is the defiant 'Call in thy deaths head there'; love has called it in long before.

The resolution of other poems is less dramatic than is that of 'The Collar', but the same principle is everywhere followed of skilful prep-aration of a turn in the thought. 'Mortification', for example, is a meditation on the familiar seventeenth-century theme that all life is a preparation for death. Nothing could seem to promise greater mor-bidity than the opening conceit that the clothes prepared for a child's birth are 'little winding sheets':

> How soon doth man decay!
> When clothes are taken from a chest of sweets
> To swaddle infants, whose young breath
> Scarce knows the way;
> Those clouts are little winding sheets,
> Which do consigne and send them unto death.

Yet the effect of this stanza is far from morbid. The 'chest of sweets' powerfully counters the death-in-life theme with one of life-in-death, since the sweets in question are dried herbs and rose leaves such as Herbert uses for a symbol of the soul's preservation in 'Life' and 'The Rose'. The chest, too, recalls the 'ebony box' in which man is kept safe till dawn in 'Even-song', as well as the treasure-chest of the Incarnation (also recalled by the swaddling clothes), guarantee of man's immortality in 'Ungratefulnesse'. This counterstress to the dominant idea is maintained as the succeeding stanzas progress through the ages of man's life. If the sleep of children is like death, death is also like sleep. If the music that surrounds youth is a pre-echo of 'the knell Which shall befriend him at the houre of death', the word *befriend* suggests that the passing bell, reminder that every man was a part of the continent, a piece of the main, relieved the fearfulness of death with a common awareness of mortality. The middle-aged man, settling down to build a house, seems to be preparing his own grave; but the fancy carries with it the serene and unfrightening thought of man's long home. Only the last stanza but one, in which the rheums of old age presage a final dissolution, sets up any kind of shudder; and this is immediately checked by the poem's conclusion which comes, not as a pert *sententia*, but as the inevitable climax of the poem's blend of the theme of mortality with the less overt but equally powerful theme of immortality:

> Yet Lord, instruct us so to die,
> That all these dyings may be life in death.

The underlying tenderness and confidence of 'Mortification' also informs 'Church-monuments', a meditation among the tombs which is completely free from any taint of the charnel-house. Here the counter-statement is not explicit, even at the end; but tone, diction and image all make it transparently clear to the responsive reader. The counter-statement begins in the first line—'While that my soul *repairs* to her devotion'—and is pursued in the image of the soul leaving the body among the tombs as a careful parent might leave a young child at school 'to spell his elements'; there is a further word-play here on the elements of learning and the four elements of which the body is composed. The lesson that we must all die is kindly, even humorously, imparted to the 'Deare flesh'; the pompous monuments are viewed as a vain attempt to 'sever the good fellowship of dust'. If the flesh is seen as a child at school, there must be all life before it, and a future in which the body as well as the soul will be repaired is implied in the final stanza:

> thou mayst know
> That flesh is but the glasse, which holds the dust
> That measures all our time; which also shall
> Be crumbled into dust.

Here the theme of dissolution is deliberately over-stated. The glass containing the sands of time will itself be crumbled (the word is Herbert's improvement on the original 'broken'), just as will the monuments enclosing human dust. But the parallelism of the construction with that of the preceding line leads us to take 'which' to refer not to 'glasse' but to 'time'. Time must have a stop and dissolution be at an end. This confirms the implicit serenity of the poem, and imparts to it the note of certitude that also ends 'Death':

> Therefore we can go die as sleep, and trust
> Half that we have
> Unto an honest faithfull grave;
> Making our pillows either down, or dust.

*   *   *

The recognition of an implied counter-statement in 'Church-monuments' in no way diminishes the reader's awareness of the skill with which Herbert has given the effect of dissolution. For this effect, he lies largely, as Joseph H. Summers has demonstrated, on the placing of sounds and even more on the structure of his sentences: 'The series of clauses and participial phrases, each relating to a word in some preceding clause or phrase, threaten to dissolve the sentence structure. The repetitions of "that" and "which" give the effect of unplanned prose, a prose which seems to function more by association than by logic.'[1] The seventeenth-century writer carried over from prose to poetry his rhetorical skill in handling different kinds of sentence structures. Herbert varies his syntax according to whether the poem he is writing is expository and didactic, or self-searching and intensely personal. For the second, the 'loose style' recognized by the rhetoricians of the time was most apt, since its loosely connected units of sense, corresponding to the movement of meditative thought, were able to achieve a real *peinture de la pensée*.

---

[1] *George Herbert, his Religion and Art*, p. 133.

A sharp contrast with the syntax of 'Church-monuments' is afforded by the sentence structure of 'Constancy'. Here, as in the Character or the Baconian essay, the movement of thought is radial rather than linear, in that every statement in its seven stanzas stands in an equally dependent relationship to the opening question: 'Who is the honest man?' The poem is something of a 'hieroglyph', attempting to represent in its form the thing it describes; the grave evenness of constancy is conveyed by the pairing of words through antithesis and alliteration (this last a rare trick with Herbert), and further weightiness is given by the enunciation of things in threes, in the manner of Bacon's *tricola*. The images too have a Baconian brevity. The poem is not well known, perhaps because it is considered untypical of Herbert—it is not an avowedly religious poem—and perhaps also because we feel that Wordsworth and Kipling have exhausted for us the *integer vitae* vein so richly opened by Elizabethan poets like Dyer and Campion. But it could scarcely be matched as an example of Herbert's linguistic decorum and his power to make the commonplace uncommon:

> Who is the honest man?
> He that doth still and strongly good pursue,
> To God, his neighbour, and himself most true:
>   Whom neither force nor fawning can
> Unpinne, or wrench from giving all their due.
>
>   Whose honestie is not
> So loose or easie, that a ruffling winde
> Can blow away, or glittering look it blinde:
>   Who rides his sure and even trot,
> While the world now rides by, now lags behinde.
>
>   Who, when great trials come,
> Nor seeks, nor shunnes them; but doth calmly stay,
> Till he the thing and the example weigh:
>   All being brought into a summe,
> What place or person calls for, he doth pay.
>
>   Whom none can work or wooe
> To use in any thing a trick or sleight;
> For above all things he abhorres deceit:
>   His words and works and fashion too
> All of a piece, and all are cleare and straight.

Who never melts or thaws
At close tentations: when the day is done,
His goodnesse sets not, but in dark can runne:
    The sunne to others writeth laws,
And is their vertue; Vertue is his Sunne.

    Who, when he is to treat
With sick folks, women, those whom passions sway,
Allows for that, and keeps his constant way:
    Whom others faults do not defeat;
But though men fail him, yet his part doth play.

    Whom nothing can procure,
When the wide world runnes bias from his will,
To writhe his limbes, and share, not mend the ill.
    This is the Mark-man, safe and sure,
Who still is right, and prayes to be so still.

'Constancy' derives much of its weightiness from Herbert's choice of a rhyme scheme for the poem. In each stanza considerable emphasis falls on the rhyme word in the third line, and there is a break in the sense at this point. The couplet forming the second and third lines is thus given the weighty force of a Senecan *sententia* or aphorism; and the last line of each stanza, being of the same length as the second and third and rhyming with them, underlines the couplet's meaning and adds to the firm and gnomic effect. Certain other effects of tone and manner in Herbert's poetry are achieved at least in part through rhyme. 'Time' is almost jocular. The speaker in the poem is quite unabashed by his meeting with Time the reaper, and the poem's levity comes partly from the use of feminine rhymes like *grinde it/find it, debter/ better*; and partly from rhymes using unstressed syllables or words in unstressed positions: *passe/us, be/patiently*. Another special effect is achieved by means of internal rhyme in 'Unkindnesse', where the repetition of sound in the first stanza suggests the way the speaker dances attendance on his friend and chimes in with his every wish:

Lord, make me coy and tender to offend:
In friendship, first I think, if that agree,
    Which I intend,
    Unto my friends intent and end.
I would not use a friend, as I use Thee.

The extent to which a reader's responses can be manipulated by rhyme alone is, however, very limited. The same is true of the poet's choice of line lengths. Samuel Johnson was to say scathing things about attempts to represent a long object by a long line, and Herbert perhaps saw the weakness of such kinds of imitation when he abandoned his first 'Even-song' poem (preserved in the Williams manuscript). A stanza that expanded from short lines to long had lent itself very well to the theme of 'Mattens', and Herbert was tempted to try the reverse shape for the companion poem, but was dissatisfied with the result. By and large, his only general principle in the matter of line length seems to be to use a ten-syllable line—his longest—to give the effect of a wise neutral voice in his more allegorical and impersonal poems. But he tries some experiments. As we have seen, the strikingly short line 'Yet I love thee' used as refrain in 'The Pearl' is a brave sling shot against the Goliath bulk of each stanza. An effect of exhaustion is imparted by the decreasing lines of the stanza used for 'The Temper' (I). Perhaps the most remarkable imitation achieved through lengths of line is in 'Aaron' where, as Grierson long ago pointed out, the five lines of each stanza increase and then decrease in length in a way reminiscent of the swelling and dying away of a bell's note.

It is the combination of two formal elements which are in themselves of limited effectiveness, rhyme and line length, into what has been called Herbert's 'counterpoint' that give his poetry its extraordinary range of effects. The construction of the pattern of line lengths in independence of the pattern of the rhymes is constantly used to control the reader's responses of expectation and surprise. When the rhymed lines are of the same length, the verse pattern asserts itself quickly and easily, and expectation is satisfied—indeed is in some danger of being satiated. When the rhymed lines are unequal in length, this expectation is outwitted and we are kept on the alert, not knowing quite where we are being led. This counterpointing device was first used by Sidney in his paraphrase of the *Psalms*, and Herbert also uses it for those psalm-like devotional poems in which he searches out the thoughts of his heart. If we examine (to take a manageable example) the twenty-three poems in *The Temple* which are written in five-line stanzas, we find that the symmetrically patterned, non-counterpointed poems tend to be allegories or fables related in a neutral voice, such as 'The Pulley', 'The Windows' and 'The World', whereas the poems of spiritual conflict are with one exception in asymmetrical and counterpointed verse;

the exception is 'The Glimpse', one of Herbert's least successful poems, where the incoherent imagery is in uncomfortable contrast to the tight neatness of the stanza form.

As a poetic craftsman, Herbert seems deliberately to avoid easy and obvious effects. He makes, for example, very limited use of one of the most exploited of metrical devices: the variation between metrical stress and the stress of normal speech. Actual inversions of the normal stress of the metre are so rare as to be a form of 'hieroglyph', as in 'Deniall'—

> Then was my heart broken, as was my verse.

Additional stresses are also used sparingly and for special effects, such as the disorder suggested by the two trochees which end each stanza of the same poem, until the last line restores not only the rhyme but the iambic measure as well:

> They and my minde may chime,
> And mend my ryme.

Additional stresses can suggest a speaker's agitation, as in 'Assurance':

> Wouldst thou raise devils? I see, I know,

or they can convey a sense of security, of firm ground under one's feet, as at the end of 'The Temper' (I), where there are five stresses instead of the expected three:

> Thy power and love, my love and trust
> Make one place ev'ry where.

Such effects are, however, the stock in trade of the competent poet. Much more distinctive of Herbert is a device which could be called another form of counterpointing, that of using from time to time a number of dissyllabic and trochaic words—or trissyllabic and dactylic ones—in a basically iambic line. Although this causes no distortion of normal metrical stress, or very slight distortion at most, the ear is aware that the sounds it hears group themselves differently as words and as metrical feet. The lilting, swinging tone of the first three stanzas

of 'The Pearl' comes in large part from this counterpoint in such
lines as

> In vie of favours whether partie gains;
>
> And bear the bundle, wheresoe're it goes;
>
> The lullings and the relishes of it.

The exuberance of tone in the same poem derives too from another
sound device: the tension between the pattern of the lines and the
phrasing of the thought, which arises from the use of medial pauses and
run-on lines. Again, this tension was, by Herbert's time, a much exploited poetic device. Herbert's skill consists in combining it with other
devices so that its effects vary inexhaustibly from poem to poem. In
'The Pearl', the sentence structure of each stanza is radial, emanating
from an initial brief statement: 'I know the wayes of Learning', etc.
Given the poem's theme, the run-on lines are then able to convey a
feeling of the world's rich plenitude, good measure pressed down and
running over. Yet in 'Church-monuments', where as we have already
seen the sentence structure is loose and pendative and where the rhymes
occur only at three-line intervals, enjambment results in the very
opposite effect: one of subtraction, of the world reaching the end of
its resources.

Herbert's use of enjambment is also closely linked with the control
of the reader's responses through different rhyme-schemes. Herbert
makes fairly frequent use of a stanza of five lines, but he is well aware
of one difficulty inherent in this form; unless its rhyme scheme is *abbba*
(which never occurs in *The Temple*) or *aaabb* (which occurs only once),
a completed stanza will take shape in the reader's mind—since we listen
with our inner ear as we read—after the fourth line, and the final line
will then sound tagged-on, a metrical appendix. Herbert's way of fore-
stalling such an effect is, normally, to suspend the sense at the end of the
fourth line in the opening stanzas of the poem, giving the five-line
stanza time to establish itself as an entity in the reader's mind. 'Constancy', quoted already, offers a ready example. When Herbert fails to
use enjambment of the fourth and fifth lines in the opening two or
three stanzas of such a poem, it is always with good reason. In 'To all
Angels and Saints' the reason might perhaps be considered disingenu-
ous. Herbert is plainly not happy with orthodox Anglican teaching
about prayers addressed to the Virgin Mary—'But *now*, alas, I dare not'

is a revealing phrase—and in each of the two following stanzas, the
second and third of the poem, the sense and the stanza both seem
complete by the end of the fourth line, giving an impression which
may well be deliberate that the fifth line is a breaking-out of feelings
which have been held in check:

> Not out of envie or maliciousnesse
> Do I forbear to crave your speciall aid:
>   I would addresse
> My vows to thee most gladly, Blessed Maid,
> And Mother of my God, in my distresse.
>
> Thou art the holy mine, whence came the gold,
> The great restorative for all decay
>   In young and old;
> Thou art the cabinet where the jewell lay:
> Chiefly to thee would I my soul unfold.

Medial pauses are used with a comparable skill. In 'Assurance', the
shift from the speaker's panting indignation with his own doubts to
his humble pleading that God will remember his promises, is achieved
in two stanzas; jerky questions, crowding stresses, inverted feet and
medial pauses all give way to sustained syntax, run-on lines and space-
out, barely emphasized stresses which quieten the earlier agitation and
suggest the process of 'centring down' in prayer:

> And what to this? what more
> Could poyson, if it had a tongue, expresse?
> What is thy aim? wouldst thou unlock the doore
> To cold despairs, and gnawing pensivenesse?
>   Wouldst thou raise devils? I see, I know,
>   I writ thy purpose long ago.
>
>   But I will to my Father,
> Who heard thee say it. O most gracious Lord
> If all the hope and comfort that I gather
> Were from my self, I had not half a word,
>   Not half a letter to oppose
>   What is objected by my foes.

The effect of this is perhaps a little broad, almost as if Herbert were
watching his own inner drama from some detached, elder brotherly

viewpoint; this detachment is in itself a device by which Herbert preserves a feeling of control through the most passionately introspective
lyrics. What he here does rather simply is done with great delicacy of
poetic means in 'Love Unknown'. This poem starts in a voice that is
querulous with self-pity and the conviction that there is no one to help
the speaker: 'And in my faintings, I presume your love Will more
complie than help.' The tale is one of rejection and, it appears, ill
treatment:

> The servant instantly
> Quitting the fruit, seiz'd on my heart alone,
> And threw it in a font, wherein did fall
> A stream of bloud, which issu'd from the side
> Of a great rock: I well remember all,
> And have good cause: there it was dipt and dy'd,
> And washt, and wrung: the very wringing yet
> Enforceth tears. *Your heart was foul, I fear.*
> Indeed 'tis true. I did and do commit
> Many a fault more then my lease will bear;
> Yet still askt pardon, and was not deni'd.
> But you shall heare. After my heart was well . . .

The querulous voice overrides the line divisions, effaces the quatrains
of the rhyme scheme. A dramatic break in this first voice gives the
voice of the friend—conscience, the inner light—the chance to get a
word in edgeways; his firm statement, reasserting the line division,
results in a moment of slow and honest reflection in the speech rhythm
of the first voice before it slips back into plaintive self-justifications.
The pattern thus established is repeated twice over: on the first repetition the complaint is yet shriller before it is interrupted, its shrillness
conveyed through repetition, through an agitated parenthesis, and
through the way the conjunction of vowels causes a momentary pause
before the main stress falls on 'offerers':

> My heart that brought it (do you understand?)
> The offerers heart. *Your heart was hard, I fear.*

By such resourcefulness of poetic means, Herbert here suggests all the
monotony of self-pity, without letting the poem itself become in the
least degree monotonous.

★　　　★　　　★

'Love Unknown' is a long poem for Herbert. He knew in writing it that its length caused him to run the risk of losing his remarkable rapport with his reader, and took special care against such a risk. As a general rule, except when there is good cause for prolonging a poem through many stanzas—such as was offered by the traditional six or seven ages of man's life in 'Mortification'—Herbert prefers a length of three or four stanzas. Three stanzas was a length made popular by the musical dominance of the 'air' at the beginning of the seventeenth century; in these songs with instrumental accompaniment a satisfying balance between pleasure in the words and pleasure in the music could best be maintained if the tune was heard three times over. The first of Herbert's two poems on Easter draws attention to the air's blend of voice and instrument, first by calling for speech to be made song in the first stanza—'Rise heart'—then by invoking the instrument—'Awake, my lute'—in the second, concluding in the third with a blend of the two: 'Consort, both heart and lute.' Many airs, however, ran to four stanzas; and this length of lyric was also encouraged by the one-two-three-go progression of thought that was natural to the Elizabethan sonnet with its three quatrains and concluding couplet. Of the poems already discussed, 'The Pearl' is a triumphantly successful example. Herbert nowhere shows greater mastery of his control of the reader's responses than in these poems of three or four stanzas, and this short exploration of his craftsmanship as a poet may perhaps best end with a glance at two of the most memorable of these.

'Vertue' begins in a tone of even, reflective enjoyment, quickened in the second line by a striking image which is made still more striking by the repetition of a consonant group in *bright* and *bridall*. In contrast, the third and fourth line seem to effect a turn beloved of the late Latin lyricists, the reminder that beauty is but a flower:

> Sweet day, so cool, so calm, so bright,
> The bridall of the earth and skie:
> The dew shall weep thy fall to night;
>   For thou must die.

But the third and fourth lines here are less melancholy in their effect than we might expect, and the reason for this is not just that the thought is over-familiar. A bridal is consummated at night; the sexual overtones of *dew*, *fall* and *die* all work, though at this point below the conscious level, against the direct statement of the lines. This same irony persists through the second stanza; beyond the dramatic contrast between the flower's flaunting (*brave*) colour and the dark earth there is an aware-ness that life renews itself from the soil and that the rose will blossom again *because* its root is in its grave:

> Sweet rose, whose hue angrie and brave
> Bids the rash gazer wipe his eye:
> Thy root is ever in its grave,
>   And thou must die.

The third stanza is the most difficult in this type of poem, where the thought is a literary commonplace and the form quickly anticipated as three statements and a counter-statement. Herbert skilfully turns this dangerous corner first by a piece of deft recapitulation and then by defiantly drawing attention to the poem's familiar pattern in a musical pun:

> Sweet spring, full of sweet dayes and roses,
> A box where sweets compacted lie;
> My musick shows ye have your closes,
>   And all must die.

But there is more here than graceful manœuvring; the first image here is a strong counterstress to thoughts of life's transitoriness, since a box of sweets (meaning dried herbs, or preserved fruits, or perhaps vials of scent) keeps the spring's savour into later seasons. Once again what seemed vulnerable has been preserved. Accordingly the last stanza begins—helped by a rhythmic reversal, *soul* at the end of the first line balancing *day*, *rose*, *spring* at the opening of the first lines of the other stanzas—with a clear statement of what has in fact been anticipated throughout:

> Onely a sweet and vertuous soul,
> Like season'd timber, never gives; . . .

The word *vertuous* is here as cumulative in its meaning as was the word *labyrinths* in 'The Pearl'; it harks back not only to the poem's title, but to the virtuous bride who will be the mother of children, the sap that rises into the flower in spring, the healing properties of the herbs or essences in the box of sweets. And at the very end, as if to confirm our recognition of the poem's classical ancestry, and yet to give it a Christian

turn of thought without destroying its humanist temper, there is a
deliberate development of the image of the funeral pyre in Ovid's

> Iam molire animum, qui duret, et adstrue formae
> Solus ad extremos permanet ille rogos:[2]

> But though the whole world turn to coal,
> Then chiefly lives.

'Vertue' is essentially a poem in which anticipation dominates over
discovery, in which our pleasure is to find it all so well expressed; it
represents, as it were, the classical aspect of Herbert's art, whereas the
poem called 'Love' represents the meditative aspect; it is the very last
of the 'spiritual Conflicts' in his particular pilgrim's progress. The by
now familiar story of the sense of illumination that came to the French
philosopher Simone Weil as she slowly repeated the poem to herself
conveys something of the poem's power.

> Love bade me welcome: yet my soul drew back,
>   Guiltie of dust and sinne.
> But quick-ey'd Love, observing me grow slack
>   From my first entrance in,
> Drew nearer to me, sweetly questioning,
>   If I lack'd anything.
>
> A guest, I answer'd, worthy to be here:
>   Love said, You shall be he.
> I the unkinde, ungratefull? Ah my deare,
>   I cannot look on thee.
> Love took my hand, and smiling did reply,
>   Who made the eyes but I?
>
> Truth Lord, but I have marr'd them: let my shame
>   Go where it doth deserve.
> And know you not, sayes Love, who bore the blame?
>   My deare, then I will serve.
> You must sit down, sayes Love, and taste my meat:
>   So I did sit and eat.

The almost laconic simplicity of this gives it the air of an artless tale
besides which 'Vertue' appears a high-wrought piece of Renaissance

artifice. Actually the artistry is here as elaborate as anywhere in Herbert's poetry. There is first the manipulation of the point of view, so that we are at one and the same time experiencing with the speaker, feeling both the awe that surrounded great houses in a ceremonious age and the shame of the human condition itself, 'guilty of dust', and yet standing outside the situation, watching an encounter between the sanctified Cupid and Psyche of the emblematists, Anima and Divine Love. The means to achieving this double vision, to which we have grown accustomed in poems like 'The Collar', are almost imperceptible: the separation of 'me' and 'my soul' in the first line, perhaps, and certainly the word 'slack' which, besides suggesting the speaker's reluctance to press forward, has a strong critical overtone. At the very beginning of *The Temple* ('Superliminare') the soul was invited to 'approach, and taste The churches mysticall repast'; but its response was always a slack one, as the reproaches of 'The Sacrifice' indicated, and as Divine Love was the pursuer then, so he is now, 'quick-ey'd' in his search for the soul.

The exposition is now complete and the drama proper can begin. The term is not too large for a small poem; the opening words of the second stanza are as indicative of an involved state of mind as a long speech in a play. They are modest, courtly—but not quite sincere; if God is willing to take him as he is, it is not for the speaker to wish himself somebody else. And the absolute directness of Love's reply breaks down this last defence of adopting a humble attitude. The image of sight in 'quick-ey'd' is maintained in the cry 'I cannot look on thee', and its full implication made clear in 'Who made the eyes but I?' This has all the compression of meaning we might expect from a divine pun. It conjures up the whole designed relationship between Creator and creature, in which man, made in God's image, saw with the divine vision. But man has marred what God made; once again the eye image has powerful reverberations, recalling the many legends in which blindness has stood for shame. Love is, however, redeemer as well as Creator, and his gentle reminder—'know you not . . . who bore the blame?'—is the poem's dramatic climax, bringing to the speaker a new realization of the whole relationship. He no longer thinks of leaving. He belongs here, though only as the prodigal son felt he belonged; the humility of 'I will serve' is far from the humble posture with which the second stanza opened. His will is now Love's, and in this perfect conformity the poem ends. Herbert has achieved, in this exchange of courtesies which in fact comprehends all his own inner life and the whole plan of man's existence, 'a condition of complete simplicity'; it has cost 'not less than everything' in terms of the endeavour of his art.

Note

Editions

Lines from seventeenth-century poems in this essay (except Cowley's) are quoted from the standard editions published by Oxford University Press. Lines from Cowley's works are quoted from *Poems* and *Essays, Plays and Sundry Verses*, edited by A. R. Waller (Cambridge, 1905, 1906). Most of the poems cited are included in many easily accessible collections. Quotations from seventeenth-century prose are from familiar works such as Bacon's *Essays* and *Advancement of Learning* or Milton's *Of Education* which are readily available in school texts and anthologies.

Critical Studies. The secondary literature on this subject is vast. No attempt is made here to cover the hundreds of books and articles on individual seventeenth-century writers that deal directly or indirectly with aspects of the subject. The alphabetical list at the end of the chapter presents only a selection of works published during the last decade that focus rather directly on the problem. However, a few earlier books of exceptional importance should be singled out.

Two of the most basic works for the study of this subject are Arthur O. Lovejoy's *The Revolt Against Dualism* (LaSalle, Illinois, 1930) and *The Great Chain of Being* (Cambridge, Mass., 1936). Almost equally important is Basil Willey's *The Seventeenth Century Background* (1934). Another seminal work is Hardin Craig's *The Enchanted Glass* (New York, 1936). The many outstanding articles and books by Marjorie Nicolson have deservedly exercised profound and far-reaching influence in this field. The articles have been collected in *Science and Imagination* (Ithaca, N.Y.,1956). Her most important earlier books are *Newton Demands the Muse: Newton's 'Opticks' and the Eighteenth-Century Poets* (New York, 1946), *The Breaking of the Circle: Studies in the Effect of the 'New Science' upon Seventeenth Century Poetry* (Evanston, Illinois, 1950; revised edition, New York, 1960), and *Mountain Gloom and Mountain Glory: The Development of the Aesthetics of the Infinite* (Ithaca, N.Y., 1959). Important and not widely enough known is Clarence Thorpe's *The Aesthetic Theory of Thomas Hobbes* (Ann Arbor, Mich., 1940). The work of Douglas Bush has been very influential. His *English Literature in the Earlier Seventeenth Century: 1600–1660* (Oxford, 1945; 2nd edition, 1962) contains a significant chapter and an extensive bibliography. His *Science and English Poetry: A Historical Sketch, 1590–1950* (London and New York, 1950) was reprinted in 1967. Richard F. Jones' important *Ancients and Moderns: A Study of the Background of the Battle of the Books* (St. Louis, Mo., 1936) was revised (Washington, 1961). Charles M. Coffin's *John Donne and the New Philosophy* (New York, 1937) was reprinted in 1958. Also useful on individual writers are Fulton H. Anderson, *The Philosophy of Francis Bacon* (Chicago, 1948); C. J. Ducasse, 'Francis Bacon's Philosophy of Science', *Structure, Method, and Meaning*, edited by P. Henle *et al.* (New York, 1951), pp. 115–44; Egon S. Merton, *Science and Imagination in Sir Thomas Browne* (New York, 1949); and Kester Svendsen, *Milton and Science* (Cambridge, Mass., 1956). Recent general studies of the problem are Margaret L. Wiley, *The Subtle Knot: Creative Scepticism in Seventeenth-Century England* (Cambridge, Mass., 1952) and Richard S. Westfall, *Science and Religion in Seventeenth-Century England* (New Haven, Conn., 1958). Among many good histories of science, one of the most useful is Abraham Wolf's *A History of Science, Technology, and Philosophy in the XVIth and XVIIth Centuries* (London and New York, 1935; revised by D. McKie, 1950; reprinted, New York, 1959). Two significant confrontations of the problem of science and the humanities in

The Apotheosis of Faust:
Poetry and New Philosophy in the Seventeenth
Century

ROBERT B. HINMAN

★

EXTENSIVE and diversified study of the Renaissance has not yet dispelled the widespread notions that science and art were fundamentally opposed in the seventeenth century and that the 'new philosophy' had a deleterious effect on poetry. The more nearly historical truth seems to be that artists and 'new philosophers' (i.e., both empirical scientists and what we would now call philosophers) were spiritual allies, even if they were not always aware of the alliance, and that—despite individual or occasional antagonisms—the total effect of each group upon the other was salubrious.

Historians of literature, casting science as villain, sometimes forget that Galileo was a talented poet. In discussing the adverse influence of seventeenth-century thought, they sometimes ignore the creative Faustian implications of Descartes' *Discourse on Method*, the relationship between Bacon's Atlantis and Sidney's golden world, the mythic-metaphoric structure supporting Hobbes' nominalism. Furthermore, they sometimes appear to confuse art and religious orthodoxy, for it is the threat to the latter that such contemporary obscurantists as Henry Stubbe evoke when they attack the new philosophy, and not infrequently these seventeenth-century foes of science—Meric Casaubon, for example—are foes of poetry as well.

The most widely cited evidence of the impact of the new philosophy on a poet is the melancholy passage from Donne's *First Anniversary*. But these lines do not even support an argument that the speaker's faith has been affected by science. They constitute a brief passage in a melancholy poem that questions the meaning and value of temporal

---

our time are Jacob Bronowski's *Science and Human Values* (London and New York, 1956) and Lionel Trilling's 'Science, Literature and Culture: A Comment on the Leavis-Snow Controversy', *Commentary* (June, 1962), pp. 461–77.

Further references are given in the list of works appended to the chapter.

life, as poets, including very devout ones, often do when they ponder an untimely death. The contemporary data, far from converting the speaker to materialism, contribute to his other-worldliness by rein-forcing the many older indications that the post-lapsarian cosmos is unreliable. The scepticism nourished by the new philosophy is thus creative, impelling towards faith and away from complacency or spiritual numbness, just as 'wise doubting' guides the seeker towards the 'stream's calm head' in Donne's *Satyre III*.[1]

Historians of science usually agree with literary historians that science and poetry were (and are) opposed, but rather than cast poetry as villain, they make it almost fool. They also note Donne's lament about new philosophy, but comment on his interest in alchemy and astrology. They acknowledge Milton's interest in Galileo, but focus amusedly on the Ptolemaic universe in *Paradise Lost*.[2] They tend to argue that science had little influence on poetry because poems did not at once incorporate the data pointing to a new view of 'reality'. By such logic, poetry could avoid conflict with (or indifference to) science only by trying to play science's explicit role—but in a medium so unsuitable that the effort would be doomed to failure. The poems thus produced would clearly demonstrate that the effect of science on poetry is inevitably bad, for they would be only the versified science that Aristotle describes when he differentiates between Homer and Empedocles.

No significant poet of the seventeenth century served (or damaged) the cause of science by deserting poetry in this way. But neither was any significant poet—however deeply committed to still viable older traditions—oblivious of the 'new philosophical' spirit. Content alone, even considered independently of attitude towards it or manner of treating it, reveals shared preoccupations among poets and the scientifi-

[1] Some who cite the passage are careful to distinguish between religion and poetry. Douglas Bush puts it into his customary broad and judicious perspective when he remarks that 'One could not readily name any man of the seventeenth century whose religious belief was overthrown by science. . . .' But he quotes the lines in a discussion of the impact of science on poetry and he concludes 'that for literature progress entailed far greater losses than gains, . . .' 'Science and Literature', in *Seventeenth Century Science and the Arts*, edited by H. H. Rhys (Princeton, 1961), pp. 50, 59.

[2] E.g., Stephen Toulmin in 'Seventeenth Century Science and the Arts', *op. cit.*, pp. 7–8, 19. It is only fair to add that Mr. Toulmin raises important questions about the relationship between science and poetry (though his answers are mostly conventional) and that he notes the rapidity with which poets absorbed the implications of the new astronomy.

cally inclined (both philosophers and scientists). Whether or not there is a clearly identifiable *Zeitgeist*, even the Spenserians unmistakably reflect a response to phenomena at least as similar to William Gilbert's as it is to medieval sacramentalism or allegory. As evidence we need not single out such unread curiosities as Fletcher's *Purple Island* which despite its old-fashioned mode, shares Gilbert's impulse to treat the concept of microcosm as a testable or demonstrable hypothesis. Nor do we have to fall back on Drummond's catalogue in *A Cypress Grove* of newly-observed phenomena similar to those enumerated in *The First Anniversary*. Impressive corroboration appears in places as remote from the laboratory or observatory as *Britannia's Pastorals*. Browne's golden age (II, iii) differs strikingly from that of Boethius delineated in Chaucer's 'Former Age'. Browne's technological detail, herb lore, and optical particularity do not reproduce Galilean mechanics, but something of the observing, inquiring spirit of Galileo's creative leap from lantern arc to pendulum invests Browne's lines.

It is even possible to traverse some of the imaginative distance between Boethius and Browne in the work of a single poet. In Vaughan's *Olor Iscanus* appears a paraphrase of Metrum V from Book II of the *Consolation of Philosophy* that begins 'Happy that first white age!' Though a competent rendering of what some of Boethius's lines say, the poem lacks the energy of Chaucer's version. Vaughan is reproducing a medieval *topos* without feeling its original vitality. Like the rest of the poems in *Olor Iscanus*, this one suggests the respectable poeticizing of a retired scholarly clergyman. But in *Silex Scintillans* the sparks struck from the heart are often incandescent responses to a world in which the searcher has found—not just by reading old books, but also by investigating phenomena—some new breaths of an old life. Like others of his time he has embarked on a voyage of discovery hailed as one of recovery. The 'first white age', long and frequently obscured, occasionally flashes in 'bright shoots of everlastingness', apparently because contemporary experience or influence has taught him to summon nature, to pierce 'through all her store', to track with Baconian zeal the traces of the Creator in His creation. Even if the phenomena impede and frustrate as they lure and tantalize, even if they are hieroglyphics almost impossible to read through the dark lens of human perception, they prove the only sacred script still being written, the only accessible containers 'of Paradise and light'. The old sacramentalism has been softening into superstition or hardening into dogma

or simply going dead, but a recently fostered or newly focused attention
to the meaning within names, to the things behind words, to 'a quick-
ness, which my God hath kist'—as evident in the Herbert who seeks
truth at only one remove as in the Bacon who sees 'the highest link of
nature's chain' attached to the throne of God—has inspired a poetry
every bit as dangerous to mere orthodoxy as any statement Hobbes
ever made.

Because the obscurantists and enemies of poetry were right. Doctrinal
status quo (though not reverence and spirituality), every form of being
at ease in Zion, is always threatened by imagination, by the impulse
to make anything new, for example, or one's perception of any phenomenon or by one's perspective upon the interconnections among all
things. That is the impulse that anatomizes, analyses, and then resyn-
thesizes. Both its means and its ends are disturbing to orthodoxy.
Beyond Baconian explorations of vulgar errors beckons Brownian
fideism that can accept and assimilate apparent aberrations of worship
into a saintly tolerance which transforms grotesquery into beauty, just
as divine love encompasses, contains and finally absorbs even the
darkness of death and the horror of hell. Beyond the meditations of
intensely individualistic, almost solipsistic, figures such as Descartes and
Donne expands the infinite self of Traherne transfigured into a contemporary imitation of Christ, destroying deadly sins by transmuting
each into its opposite, into fully operative charity, a worldly *agape*
whereby every soul becomes both centre and circumference of Pascal's
divine circle. The same Protestant mind that frames Cowley's *A Proposition for the Advancement of Experimental Philosophy* not only dares to
canonize a Catholic poet, but to invoke his newly made saint in trans-
ferring to the true God the worship hitherto accorded *Magna Mater*
('the monster Woman').

Cowley's desire to devote poetry, 'the heavenliest thing on earth',
to 'things divine' is the desire to turn the cosmic corner around which
the Whore of Babylon becomes the handmaiden of God. It partakes of
Bacon's eagerness to restore to their Creator a kingdom of creatures
usurped by one of the greatest among them, to defeat *goetia* by converting it into natural magic, the angelical gift to Atlantis that Cowley
calls 'the plain magic of true Reason's light'. The end of that endeavour
is a freeing of Satan—to pursue his destruction if he chooses, but also,
after he wearies of 'going to and fro in the earth, and from walking up
and down in it', to present himself with the rest of the sons of God,

bringing Job (or Faustus) with him. The end is heaven's descent to earth, or man's ascent to heaven, whether in the great thula that catalogues the achievements of a House of the Six Days Work or in a hexameral narrative of creation by an angelic poet who assumes the mask of poetic angel. To those who plainly and directly say 'My God, my King!' the commonplace has entered the realm of wonder; the literal biblical narrative remains, but it simultaneously becomes, even if it is not called, constantly renewable, individually interpretable myth. In the fertilized egg of any ordinary chicken, Harvey says, we observe the finger of God. In the creative act itself, says Milton, will be the conceiving spirit that 'from the first wast present', will be the Logos that Faust boldly renders 'die Tat'.

New philosophy imparts a Faustian dimension to the most unlikely overreachers imaginable. Although perhaps no longer seen as 'the last Elizabethan', Robert Herrick is frequently regarded as a poet virtually untouched by the ideas and events swirling about him. Yet, one of his favourite writers seems to have been Robert Burton, so mindful of that swirling as to postulate the necessity of a kind of infinite series of Democrituses to contain the cosmic laughter. Burton undertakes to improve his immediate environment (both its inner and outer weather), or, as he says, to rectify the air, only after he has indulged his longing for the seal of Solomon that will reharmonize all things, only after a descent from an imagined divine perspective, a prospect from which an all-encompassing natural philosopher might survey the universe or a voice out of a whirlwind challenge and humble the presumption of Job.

The fact that Herrick often addresses primroses and daffodils should not conceal, but indeed should reveal, that he perused Sir Thomas Browne's other book of divinity, that of the creatures, as avidly as the doctor did. In fact, Herrick's 'paganism' consists chiefly in his reading 'lovely leaves' as statements of both the human condition and divine Providence. There is virtually no difference between his manner of speaking to God and his addresses to the phenomena, whether flowers metamorphosed into girls or girls transformed into flowers. Hence, he can infuse the energy that overwhelms Job into the simple reverence of a child. So doing, for example in 'To find God', he exploits paradox and explores miracle as deftly as Donne in 'Go and catch a falling star'. Each speaker yearns—only half playfully—towards explanations for all things, solutions to all riddles, penetrations of all mysteries. But each speaks with creative scepticism. There is no way to have what one desires except to lose oneself in an *O Altitudo*, to overcome such Faustian desire by passing through it to the simplicity of acceptance called faith, to rest finally in an untested and untestable hypothesis, thereby supporting Bacon's contention that incomplete data may lead to atheism (in Donne's poem disbelief in absolute fidelity) but that more extensive investigation must finally lead to devout submission, for a paradoxical absolute remains at the end of each poem as the consequence of a programme of nearly infinite research. The eternally faithful woman, the handmaiden and helpmeet, the ordinary miracle, is always potentially right next door.

There is scarcely one of Herrick's poems, however playful, in which we cannot observe this reaching out from a commonplace, an ordinary, even a trivial, phenomenon towards ultimate, even infinite, significance. Probably many readers of 'To the little Spinners' see only a filmy and fantastic conceit in the lawn of spider web with which he would 'ease the rawness and the smart' of wounds inflicted by Love's lash. But in the rough and ready pharmacopeia of Herrick's day spider web was quite literally a specific for bleeding, a specific which empirical experience had demonstrated to be, in fact, efficacious. The remedy is ancient, and the implication that the readiness of remedy for mundane suffering assures a cosmic cure for cosmic pain appears in the interchange of secular and religious motifs in medieval lyrics. But the perception (or convincing illusion) of identity between an actual physical process realistically observed and a spiritual condition is characteristic of a time when the operation of a pulley (as in Herbert's well-known poem) or the arrest introduced by surface tension into the cycle of condensation and evaporation (as in Marvell's 'On a Drop of Dew') figures forth a state of the soul.[3]

The difference between the imaginative process in these seventeenth-century poems and that in many earlier poems seems to be that imaginative creation, an inductive leap like a leap of faith, has fused sacramentalism and empiricism. Phenomena which actually look or behave as the poet describes them point towards (or imply) love, towards a divinely regulated order that is also demonstrable natural law. They

[3] As in many other respects, Dante may be a medieval exception here. A striking example would be most of Canto II of 'Paradiso'. However, Beatrice is considerably more discursive in her use of optics than are the seventeenth-century poets in their use of phenomena as means to truth.

are tangible, often commonplace, embodiments or manifestations of what is not manifested so immediately in any other way, and therefore they can give rise to metaphors of exceptionally rich tenor which continue to maintain matter-of-fact links with their vehicles. Older sacramentalism had often depended on totally or partially false notions of phenomena, the kind of lore that fills the bestiaries. Anyone's experience could have easily exploded most of it. Hence, like the old philosophy, older sacramentalism had depended on a separation between the processes of men's minds and the objects of perception. It had depended on compartmentalization, on a fragmenting faculty psychology, and so had most of the poetry expressing it. The celebrated medieval order had been maintained only at the cost of the kind of dishonesty or blindness inherent in a concept of double truth. Theories of poetry such as Augustine's tended to degrade metaphorical language and poetic fiction to the merely decorative or concealing status implied in the distinction between kernel of doctrine and husk of fable. Naturally, many interested in preserving the orthodox purity of doctrine distrusted what appeared justifiable only as puzzle or lie set up as an obstacle whose difficulty would cause the surmounter to value more highly the traditional truth he found beyond it.

It is possible, therefore, to argue that the split between what one thought and what one felt was wider in the Middle Ages than it became in the seventeenth century, that the Renaissance was really the renewal that some modern insistence on medieval survival has minimized or obscured. Humanists, religious reformers, poets, philosophers of the Renaissance were likely to claim that they were reviving or renewing the past, and certainly the prevailing impulse was to recover a time of greater, more nearly divine simplicity and wholeness. Perhaps the most important bequest to the modern world from the best of Greek life and thought has been the sense of completeness sought in the fusion of *physis* and *gnosis*. Greek science and philosophy pursued unity. Without such a goal, without a concept of uniformitarianism and predictability, science as we know it could not have developed. The entire thrust of Aristotle's work, both as a critic of Plato's metaphysics and as a theorist of poetry, is towards the kind of integration implied in recent studies of the *Poetics*, especially in the interpretation of *katharsis* as ordering.

Although many humanists and reformers subsided into orthodoxies of their own, this integration of experience and world-view, this new myth or model-making whereby an imaginative creation or an accurate natural history come to embody truth by uniting universal and particular, seems to have been the common goal of many poets and many new philosophers, even when they did not recognize their common cause, even when they were as distrustful of premature systems or syntheses as Bacon, as unprogrammatic or anti-'school' as Donne. Thus Bacon—though revering Aristotle himself—takes issue with the *Organon* and undertakes a new one because those who elevated it into sacro-sanctitude vitiated its spirit. Even the magnificent Aquinian synthesis failed because of disproportionate rationalism. Donne—though deeply imbued with Petrarchism—takes issue with some earlier artifice and devises his own because 'Love's not so pure and abstract as they use/To say, who have no Mistress but their Muse.'

The notorious opposition between poets and new philosophers appears to be largely a modern construct projected backwards from a sense of separate cultures which even in our own day is probably stronger among technicians—whether in the arts or sciences—than it is among the genuinely creative—whether artists, physicists, or philosophers of science. The most significant condemnation of poetry made by a seventeenth-century philosopher is Locke's advice to parents in *Some Thoughts Concerning Education*. Yet Locke is not as harsh towards poetry as Cervantes claims to be towards medieval romance—and few would argue that Cervantes scorns creative imagination or its works. In fact, in his exploration of impulses to create the world, to bring it to life by interpreting sense data and received ideas imaginatively, Cervantes, one of the greatest spokesmen for poetry—its wonder and its danger—the world has seen, is probably not as distant from Locke as their differing media suggest.

At any rate, the same ordering, synthesizing, all-encompassing, imaginative surge towards 'reality', towards as much truth as man can grasp or express, seems evident in such diverse achievements as *The Temple* and *Principia Mathematica*. Though some temperaments or abilities (Newton's own, for instance) would have preferred Newton's way to Herbert's, would have found it more conducive to reverence, the reverse preference is also observable in such differingly pragmatic, 'practical' men as Nicholas Ferrar, to whom Herbert entrusted the future of his work, and Samuel Hartlib, who enjoyed and reciprocated the respect of Milton and Cowley. The distinction that labels Herbert's book 'literature of power' and Newton's 'literature of knowledge' would not have been generally accepted—or even understood—in the seventeenth century. Herbert's work is concerned with knowledge of the human heart in its gropings towards God. It is just as much concerned with demonstrating or discovering a pattern where none seems to be as Newton is. Herbert's poems express a kind of spiritual topology in which inside and outside are seen to be one, just as Newton's mathematics express an unseen connection between falling bodies and planetary motions. And the end of Newton's work, just as of Herbert's, is the power men can have by discovering real order where there had apparently been chaos. A similar purpose pervades Bacon's *Essays*, no more pragmatically 'realistic' in addressing themselves to 'men's business and bosoms' than Herbert's 'Church Porch' where verse frankly and plainly—but luminously—pursues him 'who a sermon flies'. Amidst the vicissitude of things, Bacon searches for and enshrines truth, so that his essays are as profoundly incorporated into his instauration as any other aspect of his vision of nature and learning.

In their varying degrees of personal humility, the poets, the new philosophers, the scientists seem to have breathed deeply the air of their time in history, to have felt a shared intoxication, to have looked beyond the immediate horizon and to have experienced a magian vision that assured them of Incarnation, the good news made new, or re-revealed, renewed certainty of intersection of word and flesh. The truth had been there all along in both books of divinity, but neither had been adequately read without the other.

So it came to pass that a whole troop of Magi sought the familiar, ordinary manger, not only to worship together, but individually and collectively to present their personal testaments—indeed, to worship by means of such offerings. Accurate observation of the mutable phenomena—the empiricists' role—and faithful but immutable representation—the artist's role—had to be combined if the worship was to be real, if a true sacrament of communion was to occur. A true poem, Cowley says in 'Of Wit', must include all there is, must be an ark, hence a symbol of a covenant, an image of, a preserver of, because an embodier or container of, life. But it can only reach that degree of completeness by providing a refuge from its destructive opposite, the Flood, and it can only fulfil such a function by confronting, incorporating and reconciling in a new peaceable kingdom the very elements of chaos, the mutable creatures now everywhere being examined anew. As a kind of poetic manifesto, an artistic counterpart of the new philosophical programme of entelechy, 'Of Wit' examines what wit is not. The vision or expression of orderly completeness cannot ignore the data of apparent randomness, any more than a conception of reality can be respectable if its cherisher has declined to look through Galileo's glass. The poets did not decline. A unitary field theory—whether Newton's or Einstein's, Milton's or Traherne's—will assume that God does not play dice with the cosmos, but will not ignore the rattle of bones in old urns that suggests a run of sevens. It is not too great an exaggeration to assert that the Baconian 'idols' roughly correspond to the vices and defects that Cowley describes as pretenders to the perfection of true wit, or to the demons who inhabit the hell in the human heart depicted in their several ways by both Milton and Hobbes; for the idols are those phantasms that must be at least recognized—if not entirely exorcized—before there can be any true instauration—or before Atlantis can rise from the sea.

Both poets and new philosophers, therefore, in seeking to deal newly and truly with the world, could be very disturbing to orthodoxy and obscurantism, to any lingering medievalism (and some of it lingers in nearly everyone) that preferred compartmentalization, to those who had ignored or wanted to ignore the continuous drift towards gnosticism or other forms of unresolved or unmediated dualism which persist despite ever fresh attempts at reconciliation. The visions of many of the best thinkers and best poets were unmistakably revolutionary in implication by virtue of their compelling insistence upon their primitive truthfulness, their return to fundamentals, to basic sources in myths and in data. They were revolutionary in the compelling impression they conveyed (and still convey) of having honestly confronted and harmonized the almost endless pieces of contradictory data available for observation. The unity in multiplicity often noted in much seventeenth-century writing (for it is prevalent in many works besides those poems usually called 'metaphysical') offers a paradoxical sense of rich, complex simplicity, of an apprehensible plenum. Sometimes enthusiasm for the plenum and a sense of the dignity of each element in it leads to unexpected parallels such as that between the catalogues of wonder in Traherne, especially his *Thanksgivings*, and the catalogue of realized potential in the survey at the end of *The New Atlantis*. The principle of organization in such lists, as in more tightly structured or unified visions of the time, is a deep feeling about the interrelationships of phenomena and a strong sense of reverence for them, but here a kind of rhapsodizing replaces usual structuring devices. Such rhapsodic lists may suggest the prophetic utterances of Blake or Whitman in their movement towards ecstasy from the ordinary or matter-of-fact. Such ecstatic attention to phenomena also occurs in Vaughan's work, where an eagerness to experience undimmed the refulgence gleaming fitfully in the creatures (from whom he often feels almost totally alienated) may lead him to anatomize fragments of the cracked frame of nature with a kind of impatience reflected in the breakdown of traditional forms or patterns of unity.

This reshaping or reinvesting of accepted forms, combining genres and expanding or shattering generic limitations, experimenting with received tradition, reworking conventions to accommodate personal vision is characteristic of seventeenth-century art, even where the organizing principle is less elusive than in the ecstasies just noted. Disparates are everywhere being harmonized, but often with the kind of control evident in *Leviathan*'s fusion of myth, treatise, anatomy and vision, or in Milton's combination of myth and encyclopedia of natural history in Book VII of *Paradise Lost*, or in the interpenetration of joy and contemplativeness that seeks to assimilate all experience into prophetic strain just as one poem is assimilated into another to produce 'L'Allegro/Il Penseroso'.

A more manageable example, perhaps, is the 'Argument' to *Hesperides*. Some detailed study of it may suggest, not only the extent of this remaking, but also how deceptive the apparent simplicity and simplifying of the time can be, how different this harmonizing is from the kind of unity often meant by those who describe the poets of the age as resisting rather than participating in a new world-view. The apparent playfulness of poets like Herrick and Cowley (why not of Donne?) is often treated as their avoidance of the challenge, their missing the implications of the new threat to order. Quite the reverse is true. Like Hobbes, like Milton, Herrick confronts the world's incoherence. Like them, like Burton, like Bacon, he seeks to come to terms with it.

Both the 'Argument' and the book it introduces outline a world fearfully and wonderfully made that often resembles chaos, or worse. Close observation, like that of the empiricists, provides the often minute and sometimes unpalatable data of Herrick's world. Those data, just as Bacon recognizes, will not be fully comprehended until we enter the light that illuminates the Father of Salomon's House, or until we reach Herrick's 'White Island'. In the humdrum—and frequent misery—of every day, the world scarcely seems to offer or elicit praise, of itself or its Creator—as Herbert, Traherne and especially Vaughan frequently note. But a creative leap to order, a hypothesizing intuition, can make joy where reason alone, or the data alone, would argue no joy can be. Theologically, faith may be distinguishable from poetic imagination or from the capacity to frame an hypothesis to explain contradictory data. But aesthetically and epistemologically all three can be regarded as the power to symbolize, to represent the far as near, the absent as present, the potential as actual, the unseen as seen. Only works of imagination, then, can fulfil the needs of faith, can produce the model or map for finding God. Poet and priest and magus must become one—as most poets, many priests, a number of philosophers and some scientists have always known. To worship God aright, or to utter truth (which is still an analogous act for many philosophers and scientists), the poet must utter 'holy incantation', the philosopher or scientist must create a work of art (or something very similar to it), which is why many philosophical or scientific works can be studied as literature. The priestly magus must arrange and transform the creatures of fallen, or shattered, or apparently disordered nature into a second nature. He must establish the conditions in which 'transubstantiation', a plain, natural, ordinary miracle can occur—or he must demonstrate the naturalness of what is also strange and wonderful. He must establish some sort of second world: perhaps a green one, perhaps a golden one, perhaps one simpler or more complex than either of these, perhaps what modern scientists call a 'model', but always distanced somehow or somehow clarifying the confused and confusing welter of earthly activity that seems to have no meaning or purpose.

Herrick opens *Hesperides* by defining his aesthetic distance from life's disorder. The 'Argument' is a survey of his epitome, a summary of 'the draft of a draft' that Melville says any significant book must be. Thus, Herrick reveals that he has a critical point of view, that he has selected certain phenomena, which he enumerates, as data from which to generalize a perspective. It is not just the raw data, but a clarification and systematizing of that data. But, like so many works of its time in their willingness to be tentative even as they seek comprehensiveness and completeness, like Burton's or Bacon's for example, it does not appear to have imposed a design. Instead, the design seems to emerge from the data. The argument is a catalogue with no immediately obvious principle of organization. It is a precis of an anatomy, yet one will need to see more of the anatomy before he can discover what is anatomized. As a list it at first seems to be as haphazard as the data collected in preliminary research by various researchers, as haphazard as most readers have found the work it introduces. As a poetic structure it seems to be merely a sequence of couplets that could be longer or shorter than it is without much altering the total effect, just as the listing of natural history data could be endless.

In fact, however, like other perspectives or insights based upon apparently random data (Burton's *Anatomy*, Herbert's *Temple*, Newton's *Principia*), the poem does have a structure and suggests a well-established form, the sonnet. But its form emerges indirectly, after the data have been assembled. To grasp it one needs the older vision, but a new way of seeing also. Without such vision (and the reshaped vocabulary being devised in Herrick's time to describe what one saw) Herrick's constant attention to the perfecting of a 'random' collection of poems, that is, to his 'book', would seem only capricious or wilful. The 'Argument' is not a standard sonnet, but thematic subdivision into both Italian and English patterns seems fairly evident. The 'octave' offers two quatrains describing a landscape of spring and summer, of gaiety and festival, inexhaustible profusion, plenitude captured and held in a vision of an idyllic countryside or ideal garden outside time. Here seedtime and harvest are one, and the culmination of all feasting is marriage. Here 'love and all the world' are ever young, sexuality is Thomas's 'innocent mind and Mayday in girl and boy', 'Adam and maiden'. 'Here Love his golden shaft employs, . . ./Reigns here and revels.' And here the water of life takes myriad forms, preserves Hopkins's 'dearest freshness deep down things', the joy of 'earth's sweet being in the beginning'.

But in the quatrain of the 'sestet' the vision changes. Time and mutability invade the idyll; their dark glory tinges the gold with the russet of decline. What seemed the unalterable present enters history; things are not what they were or appeared to be, and appearance has to be reckoned with as an aspect of experience. Nature is a process of transformation, to be expressed in myths of metamorphosis. As the daylight dims, mysterious beings peer from the shadows. As the semi-sonnet ends in a couplet, one learns the subject of the 'Argument'— and of the book it summarizes. The singer has discovered among the phenomena of earth the lineaments of the earthly paradise and has

F

sought to determine its boundaries. But among those same phenomena he has encountered the gloom and eeriness that may distort or obscure our vision of the place of joy. In the loveliness of earth he has seen vestiges of Creation and of Eden's garden. But, like Bacon, he perceives that 'there is no excellent beauty whereof there is not some strangeness in the proportion.' He cannot combine those vestiges of the unfallen world into an inviolate or pristine vision. He must acknowledge the darkness as well as the light. He must confront things as they are. He finds, therefore, that the subject of any poet (as of any philosopher) who looks at the earth with love or awe is the heaven that terrestrial phenomena never entirely conceal, just as Newton insists. But he also finds that, though he is going to heaven all along, he can get there—as Virgil informs Dante—only by way of hell, which is a part of Earth.

Thus, with greater assurance—or greater daring—than an 'idle singer of an empty day' (the kind of assurance characteristic of the poet-magi), Herrick proclaims that he *has* the power to sing of heaven or hell, to express truth. His book, he says, has ultimately just one theme: the condition of God's 'all-in-allness' that men call heaven. But, like Milton, he recognizes that in some unfathomable way this condition encompasses hell. Hell cannot exist where God is not, for only nonentity can do that, and hell has real existence, at least in the vicissitude of things and in the human depravity to which Herrick devotes so much of his book. Hence, to sing of heaven, one must confront hell.

But, though he experiences the priestly power, the special gift of the Orphic bard and the magus: the ability to derive from life that peculiar combination of joy and terror known as ecstasy, to experience the world as a symbiosis of horror and beauty, he also has the capacity of his time to find the epic cosmos, the stages of heaven and hell, in any blossom or meadow. With his eyes fixed on phenomena, 'the mind's right object', as Cowley says, he recognizes the relationship between the bucolic mode and the epic, the possibility of viewing the former as the embryo of the latter, just as Harvey sees the egg of the chicken embodying the divine Creation. Therefore, as Traherne often does, Herrick writes as though he were a primitive; he approaches great themes, but appears to reduce or to simplify them; he implies amplitude of vision, but veils it, circumscribes it, splits it into manageable fragments; suggests traditional forms, but reworks them, loosens them. He **gives** discipline and control the look and feel of childlike freedom.

For these reasons, *Hesperides*, a book about heaven, a book in its way as intent upon justifying God's ways as *Paradise Lost*, has no obvious pattern. It is highly 'artistic' and 'artificial', the product of an obviously creative intellect, yet it appears to be a miscellaneous gathering of observations made about phenomena. It consists of over fourteen hundred such observations, a variety of types of short poems, many unclassifiable, depicting an ever-lovely, ever-fading domain, its topography and flora, its fauna—human and non-human—their pleasures, pains, griefs, hopes, fears. It is a model of the universe, analogous to the universal natural history Bacon desired—and recognized that only a magian synthesizer can achieve.

For related reasons, the 'Argument' presenting a synopsis of these intimations of epic scope in non-epic form is a non-sonnet, the tight sonnet form sprung apart, or an embryonic sonnet implying much that sonnets have been and are, much that the greatest sonneteers—most of whom have also created models of the world—have concerned themselves with. It implies, too, the sense of much-in-little that Wordsworth describes as a primary attraction of the form to sonneteers, the sense of containing immensity that makes 'hermits . . . contented with their cells'. The 'Argument' thus suggests that readers of the ensuing book may 'see a World in a Grain of Sand,/And a Heaven in a Wild Flower,' a magian, even Faustian aim if there ever was one, and not at all unlike a vision of the world as an artificial man.

It also promises, through its sonnet undertones, the order that most of the great sonneteers have perceived, but in fracturing the sonnet's customary mould it may remind readers how much of that order has been an artistic achievement, an act of creation by which the truth is perceived; and its seemingly random list, anticipating the apparent randomness of the collection to follow, may make readers conscious of the actual disorder with which all sensibilities—and especially the artistic or the scientifically creative sensibility—must constantly grapple. The listing emphasizes the separateness, the discreteness of things and moments perceived, even when the perceptions are organized. The threading of the list through 'octave' and 'sestet' points up the hellish disintegration that mars every image of the earthly paradise, that threatened God's own garden where—in the very heart of the peaceable kingdom—'the Serpent sly/Insinuating . . ./. . . of his fatal guile/Gave proof unheeded . . .'.'

It was, of course, the unfallen Adam and Eve who did not—and later did—heed the serpent. However festive and playful Herrick may be, he knows that the serpent was in the garden before man or woman came. Within the inexplicable and unknowable oneness of God as He has revealed Himself to His creatures, order and disorder are twins, but disorder is the elder: 'in the beginning . . . the earth was without form, . . . and darkness was on the face of the deep.' Disorder is inherent in duality: 'God hates the Duall Number; being known,' Herrick writes, 'the lucklesse number of division.' Division, separation, fragmentation: these are the ineluctable conditions of creation that all must confront. Therefore, despite an unshakable conviction of ultimate unity, Herrick —in his graceful, gentle, sometimes deceptively airy way—seems to share, or even exceed, Donne's awareness of a world 'crumbled out againe to his Atomies'.

Observing it—in its fallen nature, at any rate—'all in pieces, all coherence gone', Herrick, like those of his day interested in things, accepts the fragments as what we have to work with. Like Bacon, he undertakes to work from them and by means of them to a re-achieved wholeness that will be exemplary of their source in the ground of all being,Who is beyond being. Fragmentation, crumbling to atoms, has been the enemy of the Great Idea that is unbroken in the mind of God and for which good science, good philosophy, good poetry search. Proliferation, multiplicity, plenitude have been the agencies whereby that Idea has been manifested to the creatures, and in the creatures. Through their existing as individuals, each conscious creature can perform the imaginative, creative act of recombining, can move towards unity, towards Godhead. This is the creaturely opportunity, a purpose—perhaps *the* purpose—of life: to realize the self as a self, an individual capable of prodigious acts of individuality, but creatively to perceive a greater whole and to surrender the self to that whole, to project the self into it; to see the integrity of each creature, but to recognize its completeness as well, since it is an atom in a complex cosmos, to be defined by both its separateness and its relationship to other pieces, to know and to express the fragile, fearful joy of subsisting in a precarious equilibrium of being and becoming as it undergoes the centrifugal stress of privation.

Of course, Herrick never discursively articulates so deliberate a contemporary approach to phenomena and experience. But his artistry is committed to the struggle against ever-threatening dualism. Poets and new philosophers felt the need for a bridge between the data and the truth, the necessity of imagination, and the activities of each group stimulated and reinforced those of the other. Nearly all felt the pressure to dwindle into over-simplified monism. There were constant pulls towards transcendence only or immanence only, towards deism or pantheism. In a sense Milton's entire imaginative effort is concerned with making immanence as strongly felt as transcendence. His allusion to Comenius in 'Of Education' implies his awareness that some minds tended to settle for the data alone. If that had been its only effect, then the new philosophy would indeed have been fragmenting and destructive in its impact upon both science and poetry.

But, as Harvey seems to have implied when he said that Bacon wrote philosophy like a Lord Chancellor, more was involved than observing or collecting data. Harvey's remark is often treated as though it were contemptuous. It can just as easily mean what Cowley means when he describes Bacon as Lord Chancellor, that is, as interpreter, of both man's and God's laws. Philosophers, scientists, poets: all are concerned with the imaginative leap from the data to meaning. Poetry is the end of the Baconian process of education that Milton describes, but it is also the beginning. The accumulated knowledge has to be put together. The act of imaginative perception is an act of creation; the 'plain magic' of making a poem is the development of an hypothesis about experience; so is formulating a description of the circulation of the blood when one cannot even see the capillaries; and so is stabilizing the chaos of matter in motion in a myth of the creation of society as an artificial man. In each instance what is achieved transcends what the data uncombined would suggest; it even transcends some of the data.

Because there was so much to discover, many men of the time stressed accumulation of knowledge. Burton ingested the thousands of curiosities that fascinated Herrick. Galileo ranged through nearly every art. Donne confessed to an 'immoderate, hydroptique desire' to absorb all profane sciences. But none of them would have been content with *scientia* alone. They wanted *sapientia*, which they saw as the aim of both poetry and 'philosophy'. There could be no other reason for the advancement of learning than the transmutation of fact into value. Bacon treats both poetry and 'philosophy' in his survey because each offers knowledge that becomes power, each contributes to repairing the ruins of our first parents, to relieving man's estate, to conquering the kingdom of darkness. Neither is really possible without the other.

Each is an element in that fully realized *Proairesis* that Milton makes the goal of education.

This similarity of goals is evident in the greatly intensified concern with methodology that characterizes the period. The attention of Descartes and Bacon to this problem is well-known. Although neither Galileo nor Harvey accepts Bacon's inductive system in its entirety, each devotes a good deal of energy to describing his experiments. The best scientific accounts combine the result and the process, just as many of the good poems of the day exemplify the successful solution of the problem of composition which the poems describe. Cowley's 'Of Wit' is such a poem. So is Carew's elegy for Donne. In fact, the number of poems which deal with the problem inherent in their coming into existence is astonishing. A total survey would have to range from Herrick's laments about being deserted by the good demon, through such problems as Marvell poses in 'The Coronet', to *Paradise Lost* itself. A successful scientific experiment bridges the gap between one's knowledge of the consequences of definition and one's knowledge of fact. Poems in the seventeenth century often seem to be similar experiments. A poetic form may be a device (created at need) for organizing fresh images, just as a new form of geometry may serve as an instrument of material investigation.

The intensified self-consciousness of both the artists and philosophers of the period probably contributes to—as it may arise from—the felt necessity of a mediating intellect, the kind of feeling expressed by Traherne that the world of becoming, especially as manifested in microcosmic man, is the necessary, almost the only place in which to discover a Being so wholly other as sometimes to seem inaccessible. The poetic world, the philosophical vision, and the scientific synthesis must resemble one another when seen as the results of such mediating creation. Each is a transformation of brute fact, of the *prima materia* by a capacity that the transformer or maker feels he shares with—at however great a remove—or derives from God. What he makes, then, in some sense becomes an image of God, or—as Milton suggests in *Areopagitica*—an image of the image of God, a reflection of the man who has made the book. It will not be all the truth, but it may be a piece of it, and if it is the work of a master spirit it will have the efficacy of a sacred relic: it will be precious blood 'treasured up to a life beyond life'. It does not seem possible for poetry to acquire more dignity and importance than it acquired by being thus equated with those human creative acts that have borne witness to divine power, that participate in that power. And here Milton is also designating as imaginative writing all books that disturb orthodoxy by seeking truth creatively. Each such work, Milton's metaphor implies, performs the miracle that calls attention to the living spirit in the phenomena. Each such work expresses the poetry of life that Shelley desires for men who wander among the innumerable fragments of truth without the power to imagine what they know. In *Areopagitica* Milton imaginatively considers the same problem by linking the myth of mangled Osiris with the image of the eagle's renewing itself.

For the goal is always a new vision of the Being only partially or vaguely known. His transcendent, terrifying power has been felt in an Old Testament vision of wrath and vengeance. What is His immanence? That is what Moses discovers in the bush not consumed. And this seems to be Cowley's reason for hailing Bacon as the Moses of the new philosophy. To Cowley and to Milton Moses was a poet. But he was also a natural philosopher who provided a new view of nature, an ultimately optimistic one, even if it focused on change within stasis and thereby stressed the tragedy that medieval compartmentalizers such as Chaucer's Monk so vastly oversimplified. For beyond the fall inflicted by Fortuna, goddess of phenomena and change, is the unchanging spirit (human and/or divine) that tragedy affirms. To fix one's eyes upon that great good required a full look at the worst.

Seventeenth-century poetry, like seventeenth-century thought, is exciting because it looks anew and looks hard. If that hard look seems to re-open the dualistic wound, as Descartes' looking does, the process of imaginative perception inherent in the very Cartesian vision finds ways to heal. The art and the thought of the time can be terrifying, because they have the deadly power of Achilles' spear. But, once it had wounded, that spear also had the efficacy attributed in Grail romances to what Herbert calls 'Christ's side-piercing spear'. The universe that harms, heals; spider web stanches blood. Like prayer, an act of creation can simultaneously be an act of destruction. That is what worship is: an act of dying, an act of rebirth. 'Therefore that He may raise the Lord throws down.' Death is absorbed into life. The form appears only in the phenomenon, but then the phenomenon is the window on the form. Platonic thought had been Aristotelianized in the Middle Ages. In the early Renaissance medieval Aristotelianism had been re-Platonized. Now that Platonic theology was being re-Aristotelianized, but this time with a determination in some minds to see the fire and the burning as one by looking hard at the bush, as, for example, melancholy and mirth may be seen, each through the other, in the life and experience of the one who attains to prophetic strain.

Synaesthesia, extremely prevalent in seventeenth-century images of perception, seems to be the psychological equivalent of the oxymoron as an artistic device. The epistemological equivalent, philosophers seem to suggest, is a mathematical formula. A myth—for example, one expressive of simultaneous universes—may integrate all three terms or processes. We get as related performances, then, Traherne's exploration of a world in the water, his new way of seeing, that creative looking he describes in 'On Leaping over the Moon' and 'Walking'; Milton's state of Grace perceived from the perspective of a fallen world; and Hobbes's civilized society overlaid upon a jungle—and presided over by a cannibal chieftain become sovereign, the only demon not exorcized.

The overlaps and parallels among these works are too striking to be merely coincidence. These writers see the world of separateness as also a world of unity, see disorder assimilated into order, see all rebellion moving towards stasis and all rebels turning homeward. Enthusiasts for familiar patterns and systems (and all men of the age have some of that enthusiasm) set up categories such as good and evil, or accept old sub-divisions such as those of faculty psychology. But their experience and their goals keep impelling them to break down the barriers they seek to impose, as the poets keep breaking through the forms. Bacon has a passion for classifying and analysing, but his imagination keeps leaping to synthesis. Descartes refuses to accept the dichotomy he has established, for if not in the pineal gland, then somewhere in what distinguishes life from carrion is the same mystery that differentiates between the melted and the solid beeswax. The locus of that mystery seems to be the result of creativity, the work of the imagination. 'How' and 'why' must be kept separate, say devisers of rigorous methodology, else no great scientific achievement is possible. Kepler and Harvey never manage to learn this lesson. In the abstract, philosophy is certainly distinct from poetry, as Cowley well knew, but in Hobbes's work the dead body comes to life. There is a world of 'appearances' and a world of 'reality', but—as Machiavelli's metaphors of lion and fox suggest—it is virtually impossible to distinguish the one world from the other. Like Montaigne, Sir Thomas Browne so extends the range of the natural that ultimately all monsters may participate in humanity—or divinity. Hobbes insists on the impossibility of being in nature without being in society and, therefore, insists that epic poetry can have no subject but men and manners, but he says so in an essay that makes the imagination very nearly its own place ('herself being all she seeks,' he says of fancy, as he describes in the *Answer to Davenant* her ranging over all experience).

What we are observing, is a deliberate breach in the wall that divides nature from art.[4] The concept is clearly illustrated—not only in the many permutations of the 'fictional' and the 'actual' in *Don Quixote*—but in the implication that 'what I write is me' reflected in Burton's determination to stay healthy by elaborately projecting his melancholy outward, and specifically expressed in Milton's conviction that the poet's life must itself be a true poem. The process appears in most of the poems of Donne in which the poem—and only the poem— is the experience described, for example, in 'A Lecture upon the Shadow' within whose lines alone can the love and the sun stand still; or 'The Canonization', whose speaker, a kind of Devil's Advocate, discovers as he speaks that he accepts the sainthood of the very ordinary lovers, which, because they have never performed the miracles of love required in Petrarchan art, he has begun by challenging (that is, his defence of them as merely people has served as a challenge of them as Petrarchan saints, but he has come to realize that love makes saints out of flawed humanity, that, in fact, the sceptic who defends by challenging *is* the saint).

Dualism is destroyed, defeated, or staved off when such total creation has occurred, when one has created a self, like Montaigne, made one's life a work of art and the work of art one's life (the goal of Milton's 'Of Education', as of Castiglione, with the difference that Milton plunges the embryonic self into extremely mundane activities, such plebeian earthiness as wrestling and scientific field trips). The soul ultimately to be bishop and king over itself in a kingdom of saints, a priesthood of all believers, must begin by absorbing all experience into himself. The threat of fragmented being is opposed when language becomes, not 'poetic', not remote from life, but human; when the word takes on mortality; when one language will serve prose and verse, the goal of Cowley's experiments in both the *Essays* and the *Pindariques*. Such language has a 'plain magic' about it; it can be used by poets and

[4] Here, as elsewhere, my debt to the insight of Joseph Mazzeo is obvious.

by scientists. The magic will consist in *how* it is used. It seeks the naturalness, the completeness of Pindar, the condition and quality of a Faust
who accepts his humanity while feeling his divinity. In 'The Praise of
Pindar' Cowley uses the image of Dedalus, who escaped from the
labyrinth by the power of his own creativity but managed neither to
sink too low nor to soar too high.

The Dedalian ideal is what Cowley, at least, took as the meaning of
aurea mediocritas, an intersection of the truly august and the truly
humble. We might call it 'conversational baroque'. In a variety of
forms it is pursued as the style that will be the man—the whole man.
It is the spirit that lets such lines as 'no fear lest dinner cool' into a
description of life in Paradise. It is the lowly wisdom that accepts a
mistress 'moderately fair' (i.e. as *human* women are) for which Cowley
has been ridiculed by those readers of 'The Wish' who have not noticed
that she is also to be as 'good as guardian angels are'.

Such divine ordinariness, spiritualized matter-of-factness, is one of
the emanations from the astonishing number of creative achievements
in art, science and philosophy in this 'century of genius'. It pervades
the sense of uniqueness given to preserved moments of quite simple
experience. It establishes the sense of eternal *Now*, of truth, that Hobbes
objects to when it is only a word of theologians but that he himself
presents in what his art has compelled millions to experience as an
image or model of reality. This is the reason that his achievement
seems to Cowley to have turned a wasteland into a garden. It sets
forth a living earth. Unlike the false gods, Vulcan for example, of
myth gone dead, Cowley says, the god in Hobbes's living myth—who
is the spirit discoverable in living men, a spirit Hobbes has materialized,
incarnated—creates living beings instead of moving statues. Hobbes's
Answer to Davenant, may scour fairyland, but Hobbes cannot exclude,
does not exclude 'spirit' from the treatment of men and manners.
He hates empty words, but he does not hate the art, by poets often
identified with love, that makes the word take flesh and dwell among
us.

The ego-centric, almost solipsistic, being so prominent in the seventeenth century is impelled to create, to assert his existence by affirming
all existence. Even the most devout, even Herbert, is often lonely,
must re-establish the link each day, for that day 'make a match', until
the morning light 'May both the work and workman show' and the
speaker ascend a sunbeam. Silence must be made to speak, chaos must

be ordered, emptiness must be filled. Phenomena can fill the void, but unless they make a world they are almost more terrifying than nothingness, as Pascal felt. And so, in a sense, one must stretch oneself to infinity. Where have I been all my life, Traherne asks, and he answers that, if he has always been in the mind of God, then he has always, infinitely, been. Such a breathless expansion of consciousness is exhilarating, as Vaughan's 'World' suggests, but the intensified awareness of self that Vaughan describes in 'Regeneration' also intensifies the pressure of other creatures. A stronger awareness of death, because of greater consciousness of mutability, fosters a stronger creative effort. The sense of infinity thus awakened urges one to break through the patterns, as we have noted in discussing Vaughan's rejection of orthodox poetic unity. And such impatience may lead to preoccupation with one's own soul. The temptation becomes very great to achieve the mystical communion, personal totality, here and now, to move towards Godhead.

Descartes finds the evidence of God's existence in himself. Creative perception, making models, bridging worlds, getting to be at home in the world (as their familiarity with phenomena seems to make Herrick or Browne): these are Faustian glories—and Faustian dangers. Giving mystical communion—or even reverence—a local habitation and a name may flirt with the heresy, always threatened by makers of golden worlds, of locating heaven in the life of man, identifying the Muses (who were the patrons of all knowledge, not merely of poetry) with the indwelling spirit, with the mighty dove whose favourite temple, Milton says, is 'th' upright heart and pure', Cowley's active flame, Herbert's 'friend' who whispers against vain pretence. To get God into man's space, as Herbert does when he makes sweeping the floor an act of worship, will seem like blasphemy to some kinds of readers, as Herbert must have recognized in leaving to Ferrar's judgement the preservation or destruction of *The Temple*. To bring heaven to earth always risks exalting the Promethean spirit of Marvell's tragic, heroic 'Unfortunate Lover', who is a figure of the artist; it is to 'knock at a star with [one's] exalted head' like that 'Herculean' candidate for stellification, Robert Herrick. This is to embrace infinity, to experience something very close to apotheosis, to be the 'God-like' poet whom Cowley describes in 'The Muse', 'The Ecstasy', and the *Davideis*. This is to make Faust respectable, as Traherne virtually does when he makes insatiableness the source of creativity and the mode of love. Faustus's lust for knowledge, as Marlowe describes it, begins as a desire to make a better life for his fellows, to help his countrymen. So the impulse to God-head always begins, or appears to begin. Astonishingly, many of the great creators of the seventeenth century seem to have contained their powerful senses of themselves as centres of the world in metaphors of creators of imagined worlds. Their astonishing capacity for harmonization seems usually to have been equal to the blandishments of pride, to have preserved the sense of the mediating intellect as persona, to have maintained the creaturely status of the poetic creator.

But just barely. We have noted that Vaughan does not entirely escape the curse of self-centredness. One needs to read Traherne carefully, noting that his meditations are offered as affectionate aids, gifts of love, to a friend. One must not lose sight of his insistence that *each* soul is the beloved son and that unless *each* can be creator, none can. Creativity has to be set free, so that every structure will equal God's, so that the dream, the thought which is the 'real thing' will be identical with being, so that Bacon's ultimate natural history will be written, and prove to be a history of God—and a history of every soul. Like such devout geniuses as Newton, Milton kept his perspective, despite his consciousness of prodigious personal powers. Because of his capacity to create, he was able to escape from time into a vision of the future and 'a paradise within'. He was able to reach that vision from a simulacrum of divine perspective. He was able to perceive his earth creatively enough to discover and to express its similarity to heaven while recognizing that similarity is not identity.

However, even though he never equates the poet with God—and, in fact, his greatest poet-as-character, Raphael, explicitly emphasizes his role as bridge between heaven and earth, not their maker—Milton is constantly exposed to the occupational disease of great prophets, magi and bards such as Orpheus, the tendency to turn into a god. Both art and science in the seventeenth century claim to offer truth, their visions of the 'true earth'. When their powers are essentially combined, as they are in the work of so many figures of the period, the risk of contracting—or at least carrying—the disease grows. To interpret, or to re-create the scriptures for oneself, to read nature as a scripture, to fuse the two: this is almost to re-create—or to create—the cosmos. ' 'Tis only God can know', says Cowley, whether Hobbes's work matches His own. But ' 'tis so like truth, 'twill serve our turn as well.' He attributes something of this same scriptural quality to Sprat's

History, which sets forth the deeds of those whom Cowley sees as God's prophets and champions, indeed, almost as avatars.

In making a model of the world such as Herrick's or Milton's one transforms the unhappy place into a happy one. One offers an image of the created self, and one views that created self as an image of God. Hence, in a sense, one's justification of God's ways, one's poetic universe, is an image of God. Emulation of His work tends to replace ideal imitation. The line between maker and thing made becomes very thin. The artist, the maker, has a new dignity, as Jonson insists. His priestly role is to participate in an act of transubstantiation, a new sacrament. But, as Browning's Bishop notes, this participation easily comes to seem, to others if not to the poet, a making of God.

It is small wonder that irony and the playfulness often associated with 'metaphysical' wit are so potent in the poetry of the time. The impulse we have examined fostered a sense of almost unlimited human potential. To this corresponds a stronger impulse to Mephistophelean mockery when men fall short of their potential. Poets like Cowley have been accused of not taking poetry seriously. What is really involved is his simultaneous experience of almost identity between the first cause and second causes, especially when imaginatively represented, and of immense distance between them. He sometimes deals with this ambivalent feeling by being very spritely and gay in encompassing phenomena, as in such Anacreontics as 'Sport' or 'Drinking' and in such assignments of all the poetic mistresses in history to himself in 'The Chronicle'. But he can also be profoundly and wittily melancholy when he fuses the august and the homely into his complex perspective. In 'The Wish', for example, creative perception, desire that approaches the inexhaustible divine perspective, focuses on the original garden. Human perspective sees it transformed into Cain's city. The envisioned possibility of the perfect garden is inspired by reverence for the phenomena that could be there. But close attention to the phenomena of earth fosters a sense of discrepancy between the vision and what men do. To reify the garden is to realize the city. Time and space, if not absorbed into eternity and infinity, are at least held in the poetic irony that approaches cosmic joy—and cosmic amusement.

Those who distrusted science were right to distrust poetry as well, for the responsibility and burden of creative power was evident to the poets themselves. Often they turned an ironic or humorous light upon themselves, as Cowley does in his 1656 *Preface* and his dedication of the

Plantarum; or as Herrick does in miniaturizing his immortal and immortalizing creator into a fairyland Hercules, a babe in an enchanted wood whose name is Robin Herrick. But all the while, such poets, stimulated by the new philosophy, were re-enacting and revitalizing an old sense of simultaneous transcendence and immanence that had tended to become sterilized or petrified into unregarded ritual. In 'To the Royal Society' Cowley identifies man's defective knowledge with man's unredeemed self. Whoever rejects the link between things and ideas shuts his eyes to the Incarnation. Without the vision shared by creative poets and philosophers men have to live in the old world of double truth, the two parts of their world separated by a terrifying void. Art can span this void with an image of total life such as the portrait of God in all phenomena of Cowley's 'To Light' or the image of God in man that emerges when *Paradise Lost* is seen as 'the image of God, as it were, in the eye' of its creator.

Such an image has always been terrifying to most men. We have noted the fear or awe among poets themselves. Marvell's Damon can be seen as one who flees from a God-like consciousness of illimitability experienced in meadows to the safety of the ultimate man-made garden, a cemetry. But it is a mistake to conclude that the image terrified all men or that, even if it did, it spoiled poetry in the eighteenth century. The salubrious effect of the new thought was not uniformly evident. There were some retrenchments, some efforts at acclimatization to the heady atmosphere. But the best poetry need not be seen as a shrinking of a great vision. It is just as easy to see it as moving towards the kind of creation acclaimed by Traherne and urged by Hobbes and offered as Michael's vision to Adam—a world full of life, the peopled world that in Cowley's elegy for Harvey comes into being when just one person in it is fully alive. The visionary who perceives only the flash of the divine in the creatures may flee from his consciousness, as Vaughan does in his fear that his expanding, questing soul may spill like a puddle. Ultimately he becomes, perhaps, the most solipsistical of the best poets of the period, the least interested in other men's salvation. But the same impulse in the direction of God-like eccentricity that is reflected in Vaughan's occasionally private imagery (or in Gulliver's pride that withdraws into conversation with horses) may lead from Traherne to Smart (or to the saintly Pedro de Mendez who urges Gulliver to reassume the burden of human love), and on to Blake—to great charity and to great myth-making.

And the great poets of the eighteenth century are great myth-makers. Pope and Swift are just as avid for wholeness, just as strongly creative as Milton. The pressure of technology with its accompanying partial-ness, its specialization, its industrialization of man, its fostering of the 'barbarians' whose proliferation Arnold dreaded: these contributed to the false notion that imaginative creation is incompatible with scientific thought, with experimentation, and with complex modern society. Such a view will not survive a careful reading of Wordsworth's *Preface* or Shelley's *Defence*. And it is preposterous when one re-members Goethe.

The world has always wanted 'the poetry of life'. Those who have feared it or fled it have not belonged to that heroic army for peace and virtue and civilization that Milton sees as an embattled Roman legion amidst the savage chaos of barbarism. Milton would have included Hobbes and Herbert in that legion, despite their differences from him-self. Those who would never join the valiant band were the young men whom a stupid, non-poetic non-scientific education drove pre-maturely into merely commercial pursuits, those who inhabit Pope's vision of Dullness and some of whose descendants lead lives of quiet—or noisy—desperation. That most seventeenth-century poets do not belong in such a vision—and that many poets since have escaped its atmosphere —has surely depended in part, as Sprat foretold it would, upon their having plunged themselves into the world of creatures where men live and work, having felt and expressed their divinity as Faust does when, labouring for and with other men—turning marshes into farms, a wasteland into a garden that can enclose the city of God—he longs for the God-like power that can say to the passing moment: 'Linger a while, thou art so fair.'

SEVENTEENTH-CENTURY LITERATURE AND SCIENTIFIC THOUGHT
Selected Works of the Past Decade

(Many of the books listed include extensive bibliographies.)

Anderson, Fulton H., *Francis Bacon, His Career and Thought* (Columbia, South Carolina, 1963).

Babb, Lawrence, *Sanity in Bedlam: A Study of Robert Burton's 'Anatomy of Melancholy'* (East Lansing, Michigan, 1959).

Beck, Richard J., 'Milton and the Spirit of His Age', *English Studies*, XLII (1961), 288–300.

Bierman, Judah, 'Science and Society in the *New Atlantis* and Other Renaissance Utopias', *Publications of the Modern Language Association*, LXXVIII (1963).

Bierman, Judith, 'The *New Atlantis*, Bacon's Utopia of Science', *Papers on Language and Literature*, III (1967), 327–52.

Brett, Raymond L., 'Thomas Hobbes', in *The English Mind: Studies in the English Moralists presented to Basil Willey*, edited by Hugh Davies and George Watson (Cambridge, 1964), pp. 30–54.

Chambers, Alex B., 'Chaos in *Paradise Lost*', *Journal of the History of Ideas*, XXIV (1963), 55–84.

Cohen, I. Bernard, 'Newton in the Light of Recent Scholarship', *Isis*, LI (1960), 489–514.

Craig, Hardin, *New Lamps for Old: A Sequel to 'The Enchanted Glass'*, (Oxford, 1960).

Crowther, J. G., *Francis Bacon, The First Statesman of Science* (1960).

Davis, Walter R., 'The Imagery of Bacon's Late Work', *Modern Language Quarterly*, XXVII (1966), 162–73.

Debus, Allen G., and Multhauf, Robert P., *Alchemy and Chemistry in the Seventeenth Century: Papers Read at a Clark Library Seminar*, (Los Angeles, 1966).

Donne, John, *The Anniversaries*, edited by Frank Manley (Baltimore and London, 1963).

Eiseley, Loren, *Francis Bacon and the Modern Dilemma* (Lincoln, Nebraska, 1962).

Ellrodt, Robert, 'Scientific Curiosity and Metaphysical Poetry in the Seventeenth Century', *Modern Philology*, LXI (1964), 180–97.

Eurich, Nell P., *Science in Utopia: A Mighty Design: A Study of Scientific Utopias in the Seventeenth Century* (Unpublished Columbia University Dissertation, 1960).

Farrington, B., *Francis Bacon, Philosopher of Industrial Science* (Liverpool, 1964).

Fieler, Frank B., 'The Impact of Bacon and New Science upon Jonson's Critical Thought in *Timber*', *Renaissance Papers* (1958–60), pp. 84–92.

Gilbert, N. W., *Renaissance Concepts of Method* (New York, 1960).

Green, A. Wigfall, *Sir Francis Bacon* (New York, 1966).

Hall, Marie Boas, 'In Defense of Bacon's Views on the Reform of Science', *Person*, XLIV (1963), 437–53.

Hall, Marie Boas, 'Scientific Thought', *Shakespeare Survey*, XVII (1964), 138–51.

Hall, Marie Boas, *Robert Boyle on Natural Philosophy* (Bloomington, Indiana, 1965).

Hamilton, K. G., *The Two Harmonies: Poetry and Prose in the Seventeenth Century* (Oxford, 1963).

Helton, Tinsley, editor, *The Renaissance: A Reconsideration of the Theories and Interpretations of the Age* (Milwaukee, Wisconsin, 1964).

Heninger, S. K., Jr., *A Handbook of Renaissance Meteorology, with Particular Reference to Elizabethan and Jacobean Literature* (Durham, North Carolina, 1960).

Hinman, Robert B., *Abraham Cowley's World of Order* (Cambridge, Mass., 1960).

Hood, F. C., *The Divine Politics of Thomas Hobbes: An Interpretation of 'Leviathan'* (Oxford, 1964).

Jones, Richard F., 'The Rhetoric of Science in England of the Mid-Seventeenth Century', in *Restoration and Eighteenth-Century Literature: Essays in Honor of Alan Dugald McKillop* (Chicago, 1963), pp. 5–24.

Kargon, Robert H., *Science and Atomism in England from Hariot to Newton* (Unpublished Cornell University Dissertation, 1965).

Keele, K. D., *William Harvey: The Man, the Physician, and the Scientist* (New York, 1965).

Keynes, Geoffrey, *The Life of William Harvey* (Oxford, 1966).

Koyré, Alexandre, *Newtonian Studies* (Cambridge, Mass., 1965).

Koyré, Alexandre, *From the Closed World to the Infinite Universe* (Baltimore, 1968).

Larsen, Robert E., 'The Aristotelianism of Bacon's *Novum Organum*', *Journal of the History of Ideas*, XXIII (1962), 435–50.

Manuel, Frank E., *Isaac Newton, Historian* (Cambridge, Mass., 1963).

Margenau, Henry, 'Bacon and Modern Physics: A Confrontation', *Proceedings of the American Philosophical Society*, CV (1961), 487–92.

Marks, Carol L., 'Thomas Traherne and Cambridge Platonism', *Publications of the Modern Language Association*, LXXXI (1966), 521–34.

Marks, Carol L., 'Thomas Traherne and Hermes Trismegistus', *Renaissance News*, XIX (1966), 118–31.

Mazzeo, Joseph A., editor, *Reason and the Imagination* (New York and London, 1962).

Mazzeo, Joseph A., *Renaissance and Seventeenth Century Studies* (New York and London, 1964).

Mazzeo, Joseph A., *Renaissance and Revolution: Backgrounds to Seventeenth-Century English Literature* (New York, 1965, 1967).

Mintz, Samuel I., *The Hunting of Leviathan: Seventeenth Century Reactions to the Materialism and Moral Philosophy of Thomas Hobbes* (Cambridge, 1962).

Mulder, John R., *Literary Scepticism: Montaigne and Sir Thomas Browne* (Unpublished University of Michigan Dissertation, 1964).

Murphey, Murray G., 'The Influence of Science upon Modern Culture', *Proceedings of the American Philosophical Society*, CV (1961), 461–63.

Nauert, C. D., *Agrippa and the Crisis of Renaissance Thought* (Urbana Illinois, 1965).

Nicolson, Marjorie, *Pepys' 'Diary' and the New Science* (Charlottesville, Va., 1965).

Nicolson, Marjorie, 'The Discovery of Space', in *Medieval and Renaissance Studies: Proceedings of the Southeastern Institute of Medieval and Renaissance Studies*, edited by O. B. Hardison (Chapel Hill, North Carolina, 1966), pp. 40–59.

Pelikan, Jaroslav, 'Cosmos and Creation: Science and Theology in Reformation Thought', *Proceedings of the American Philosophical Society*, CV (1961), 464–9.

Plochmann, George K., 'William Harvey and his Methods', *Studies in the Renaissance*, X (1963), 192–210.

Poynter, F. N. L., 'John Donne and William Harvey', *Journal of the History of Medicine*, XV (1960), 233–46.

Price, Martin, *To the Palace of Wisdom: Studies in Order and Energy from Dryden to Blake* (Garden City, N.Y., 1964).

Puever, Marjorie, *The Royal Society: Concept and Creation* (1967).

Rhys, Hedley Howell, editor, *Seventeenth Century Science and the Arts* (Princeton, New Jersey, 1961).

Rossi, P., *Francis Bacon: From Magic to Science*, translated by S. Rabinovitch (1968).

Scoular, Kitty W., *Natural Magic: Studies in the Presentation of Nature in English Poetry from Spenser to Marvell* (Oxford, 1965).

Sessions, W. A., *The Hunt for Pan: A Study in Bacon's Use of the*

Imagination (Unpublished Columbia University Dissertation, 1966).

Steadman, John M., 'Mimesis and Idea: *Paradise Lost* and the Seventeenth-Century World-View', *Emory University Quarterly*, XX (1964), 67–80.

Stempel, Daniel, '*The Garden*: Marvell's Cartesian Ecstasy', *Journal of the History of Ideas*, XXVIII (1967), 99–114.

Tayler, Edward, *Nature and Art in Renaissance Literature* (New York, 1964).

Taylor, E. G., 'Rousseau's Debt to Hobbes', in *Currents of Thought in French Literature*, edited by J. C. Ireson (Oxford, 1965), 277–302.

Traherne, Thomas, *Meditations on the Six Days of Creation* (1717), edited by George R. Guffey (Los Angeles, 1966).

Turbayne, Colin M., *The Myth of Metaphor* (New Haven, Conn., 1962).

Vickers, Brian, *Francis Bacon and Renaissance Prose* (Cambridge, 1968).

Webber, Joan, *Contrary Music: The Prose Style of John Donne* (Madison, Wisconsin, 1963).

Webber, Joan, *The Eloquent 'I': Style and Self in Seventeenth Century Prose* (Madison, Wisconsin, 1968).

West, Robert, 'Milton as Philosophical Poet', in *Th' Upright Heart and Pure: Essays on John Milton*, edited by Amadeus Fiore (Pittsburgh, Pennsylvania, 1967).

Yates, Francis A., *Giordano Bruno and the Hermetic Tradition* (1964).

Note

Editions
The standard edition of Marvell's poems is H. M. Margoliouth's *The Poems and Letters* (2 vols., Oxford, 1927; 2nd edition, 1952), from which I quote throughout. A. B. Grosart's *The Complete Works* (Fuller Worthies' Library, 4 vols., 1872 1875) is still the most recent full edition of the prose. Dennis Davison edited a selection from the prose and poetry (1952). Other recent selected editions of the poetry include those by Hugh Macdonald (London and Cambridge, Mass., 1952), Joseph H. Summers (New York, 1961) and Frank Kermode (New York and London, 1967). *The Latin Poetry of Andrew Marvell*, edited by William A. McQueen and Kiffin A. Rockwell (Chapel Hill, 1964), includes useful English translations *en face*. In his edition Margoliouth expressed reservations concerning the attribution of most of the later satires which he printed as possibly by Marvell. In *Poems on Affairs of State, Vol. I: 1660–1678* (New Haven and London, 1963), George deF. Lord included those satires, printing a number of them as anonymous and one as by John Ayloffe; he also printed 'The Second' and 'The Third Advice to a Painter' as by Marvell. Accepting *Bodleian MS. Eng. poet. d. 49* as prime authority, Mr. Lord prints the latter poems in his edition of *Andrew Marvell: Complete Poetry* (New York, 1968), omits 'A Dialogue between the Two Horses' and a few others, and prints 'A Dialogue between Thyrsis and Dorinda', 'Tom May's Death', and 'On the Victory obtained by Blake' as 'Poems of Doubtful Authorship'.

Criticism. T. S. Eliot's famous essay on Marvell was first printed in the volume of tercentenary essays edited by W. H. Bagguley (1922). The pioneer biographical and critical study was Pierre Legouis's massive *André Marvell: Poète, Puritain, Patriote* (Paris and London, 1928); Legouis condensed it and brought the annotations up to date for an English version, *Andrew Marvell: Poet, Puritain, Patriot* (Oxford, 1965). Marvell was treated in most of the many volumes concerned with the 'Metaphysical' poets or poetry or with the 'Donne revival'. A number of the important essays concerning Marvell and that revival are available in *Seventeenth-Century English Poetry: Modern Essays in Criticism*, edited by William R. Keast (1962). Other volumes containing treatments of Marvell's poetry include Ruth Wallerstein's *Studies in Seventeenth-Century Poetic* (Madison, 1950), Maren-Sofie Røstvig's *The Happy Man*, Vol. I (Oslo, 1954), Christopher Hill's *Puritanism and Liberty* (1958), Don Cameron Allen's *Image and Meaning* (Baltimore, 1960), Kitty Scoular's *Natural Magic* (Oxford, 1965), George Williamson's *Milton & Others* (1965), and Stanley Stewart's *The Enclosed Garden* (Madison, 1966). Volumes published after 1928 which are wholly devoted to Marvell include those by V. Sackville-West (1929), M. C. Bradbrook and M. G. Lloyd Thomas (Cambridge, 1940), John Press (1958), Lawrence W. Hyman (New York, 1964) and Harold Toliver (New Haven, 1965). George deF. Lord's *Andrew Marvell: A Collection of Critical Essays* (Englewood Cliffs, N.J., 1968) emphasizes essays of the nineteen sixties.

VII

Andrew Marvell:
Private Taste and Public Judgement

JOSEPH H. SUMMERS

★

T. S. ELIOT's tercentenary essay of 1921 provided the major impetus and a number of the key formulations for the modern critical revival of Andrew Marvell's poetry, a movement that shows no signs at all of waning. We owe Eliot's essay and the subsequent criticism and scholarship an enormous debt, but I do not wish to dwell on that debt here or to add to the mass of commentary on the best known poems. Instead, I shall risk the charge of ingratitude by concentrating on what I consider some of the mistakes and limitations associated with that revival. I do so in an attempt to understand the larger body of Marvell's work, and with the hope that such an understanding may help us to return to the more familiar poems with some freshness of view.

The larger number of Marvell's modern admirers, I believe, have come to the poems with the assumption that the relatively short, supposedly 'private' poem, uncommitted to cause or action, is the most desirable or highest kind of poetry, and they seem to assume that Marvell must have agreed with them. But a number of Marvell's poems, when we consider them closely, may shock us with their kind

---

Both C. V. Wedgewood's *Poetry and Politics under the Stuarts* (Cambridge, 1960) and Ruth Nevo's *The Dial of Virtue* (Princeton, 1963) consider Marvell's political poetry along with his contemporaries'. The fullest consideration of the political poems within their historical settings is John M. Wallace's *Destiny His Choice: The Loyalism of Andrew Marvell* (Cambridge, 1968). J. B. Leishman's posthumously published *The Art of Marvell's Poetry* (1966) is both critically suggestive and the most thorough consideration of Marvell's uses of past and contemporary poets. Rosalie Colie's forthcoming '*My Echoing Song*': *Andrew Marvell's Poetry of Criticism* promises to be the most stimulating treatment yet of the lyrics and 'Upon Appleton House'.

of 'privacy'. However modern Marvell may seem in his apparently self-conscious and experimental aestheticism, he is very much a representative of the Renaissance amateur gentleman in writing so many of his poems, in so far as we can tell, with no thought whatsoever of having them printed. Most of them seem not even to have circulated in manuscript, and the posthumous publication of the bulk of the poetry in 1681 was occasioned only by a complicated legal and financial manœuvre on the part of some business acquaintances who neither recognized nor cared about the poem's literary qualities. I may be forgetting obvious instances, but I cannot think of a poet after Marvell who wrote poetry in English of the first rank without at least considering its publication or distribution. (One thinks of Emily Dickinson, but by her early submission of a few poems, she showed that she could at least imagine her 'private' lyrics being printed.) Although some moderns can hardly imagine how anyone might write good poetry without intending publication or, short of personal or public disaster, how anyone might quit writing magnificent 'private' poetry after he had shown that he could do so, there were advantages to Marvell's old-fashioned position. At least he never seems to have anticipated the peculiar difficulties of some modern poets who assume both that valuable poetry should be essentially 'private' and inward in subject and style, and also that the poet must be 'dedicated' and 'professional', since only his identity as a poet (a special form of 'the artist') provides a justification for his existence. Sometimes these assumptions almost appear to be a formula for self-destruction. Should the poet fail to keep up, in both quantity and quality, his production of 'private' poems, he may think he has provided public evidence of personal and spiritual failure. As a result, he is subjected to extraordinary tensions and strains, including a pressure to exploit ruthlessly his private experience. Marvell never seems to have imagined that his personal salvation depended upon his continued production of poetic masterpieces. I do not believe it ever occurred to him to worry about how he could write a *second* 'To his Coy Mistress' or 'The Garden'; the attitudes and anxieties which such a concern imply might well have made it impossible for him to write the first ones.

But if these poems are in one way more 'private' than anything we can easily imagine today, they also use the rhetorical devices of an age supremely conscious of the powers and problems of the social, and particularly the persuasive, uses of language. The mistress may be anonymous if not imaginary, but she is addressed most formally and even syllogistically. The speaking voice pretends to speak only to his mistress, or to Quiet and Innocence and the Fair Trees, or to God, or to mediate or to define according to recognizable and circumspect patterns. Even in the most 'private' poems we can never safely assume that the main import of the poem is simply some shadowy urge for 'self-expression', for almost every one of them assumes an immediate rhetorical object of address as well as the possibility of a larger group of 'overhearers', however difficult either may be to define precisely. (We shall, incidentally, read 'The Definition of Love' very differently depending on whether we assume its immediate rhetorical audience to be a lady who glories in an ideal and unconsummated love, a lady who has hoped for a more ordinary love, or even the Resolved Soul.[1]) And nearly all of the most 'private' poems represent or imitate at least a momentary decision or judgement related to the rival claims of the retired and the active lives.

But these poems do seem most 'private' in comparison with the ones in which Marvell celebrates or derides public men and events. Until recently the conventional opinion has been clear about the contrast: Marvell's good poems were the 'private' ones, and the public poems, with the exception of 'An Horatian Ode', were bad. Marvell could even serve as the prime exemplary proof for the 'cultural break', the 'dissociation of sensibility' which set in at 1660· before that date, supposedly, Marvell wrote the poems which we all admire; afterwards, he was the victim of politics, satire and an age (the beginning of our modern one) when thought and 'feeling' (it was rarely clear whether 'feeling' meant sensation or emotion) were hopelessly split apart. I think it remarkable that an age which saw some of the finest work of Milton, Dryden, Rochester, Traherne, Congreve, Swift, Pope and Gay could for long have been lamented as marking the onset of poetic or literary darkness. One can understand that readers who admire most the relatively short, supposedly 'private', tightly organized poem which uses low or middle diction and dramatizes emotional choices, may view the new age with a sense of loss. But they should be careful that in their defence of private and personal values they do not attribute too much to abstract and hazily apprehended social or historical forces. Actually, few of the most interesting poets of the earlier seventeenth

[1] For the latter, see Ann E. Berthoff, 'The Allegorical Metaphor: Marvell's "The Definition of Love"', *Review of English Studies*, XVII (1966), pp. 16–29.

century wrote such poems for long; and the dates when they ceased, like their reasons for ceasing, differed widely. Is the fact that Donne wrote remarkably few poems, secular or religious, during the last twenty years of his life really to be attributed to the unsatisfactory cultural climate between 1611 and 1631? Can anyone seriously maintain that Henry Vaughan's failure of inspiration after the second part of *Silex Scintillans* in 1655 is directly related to the notable social or political or aesthetic changes in Brecknockshire immediately after that date? Like a number of the others, Marvell seems to have been a gentleman who for a time wrote a kind of poetry that we have come to admire greatly. Although he was, with Jonson and Milton, one of the most 'literary' poets of the century, unlike them he conceived of himself neither as a professional nor as a dedicated poet. When the inspiration or the occasion for a particular kind of verse was past, his choice seems to have been either to quit writing verse altogether or to turn to a new kind of poetry.

I do not mean to deny that there were significant changes during the seventeenth century—social, religious and political, economic, philosophical and linguistic, as well as literary—to the point that it is possible, by means of selected passages of prose or poetry, to demonstrate what seem to be two different 'worlds', an Elizabethan one at the beginning and a modern one at the end. I am only objecting to the tendency to exaggerate the changes (it is also possible by means of other selected passages of poetry and prose to demonstrate a number of continuities), to localize them precisely in one year or even decade, and to attribute all the literary changes to large, impersonal 'movements'—as if all talented writers were hapless victims of an age rather than, literarily at least, among the creators of it.

From fairly early in the seventeenth century a number of the poets began to cultivate intensely the Jonsonian part of their inheritance. There were probably manifold reasons. Fashions have a way of changing even faster than manners, and both 'strong lines' and attempts at bluff persuasions and arguments could quickly come to seem tiresomely old-fashioned. Smoothness and polish might easily be preferred to roughness and 'strength'. The very ideal of the passionate and markedly individual (if not eccentric) voice might come to be viewed with suspicion and some distaste. The period heard a large number of such voices, in political and religious controversies as well as in literature, voices immensely concerned with important issues and strongly committed to specific public and private positions. It would certainly be understandable if, both before and after bloodshed and revolutions, many men came to prefer voices which attempted, or at least pretended to, a measured and balanced tone appropriate to rational and compromising public judgements.

As nearly as we can tell, Marvell's practice differed from the normal responses of his age chiefly in agility and elegance. But we really have remarkably little evidence for dating most of Marvell's best poems. Although it is sensible to assume that 'The Garden' and the Mower poems are probably associated with 'Upon Appleton House' and Marvell's residence with Lord Fairfax from 1651 to about 1653, and also that the poems concerning love are those of a relatively young man (dating roughly from the same period or earlier), we have no way of knowing. And Marvell's concern with traditions and genres seems so intense and in some ways so modern that I am haunted by the thought that he might have found himself in a position resembling André Malraux's description of the modern painter's: possessed of an imaginary museum filled with the works of all ages and cultures, and therefore capable both of imitating anything and of concentrating on what he thinks the essence of art (rather than on art within its normal contexts and functions), quite apart from the usual chronologies. Is it possible that Marvell's interior anthology of the Latin, English, and French poems which he had mastered served him as an ever-present reminder of the aesthetic possibilities of past forms and genres, and that he might have written some of his most admired lyrics, perhaps with a good deal of nostalgia, shortly before his death in 1678? It is a mischievous question, calculated to disturb our assumptions of historical certainty, and I am sorry that I do not really think an affirmative answer to it is likely. Still, we might remember that few literary historians or critics thought it likely that anything resembling Thomas Traherne's poetry could have been written during the Restoration before some of Traherne's manuscripts were discovered and his first volume of poetry published in 1903. (We cannot dodge the latter embarrassment simply by assuming that Traherne was a provincial recluse, unaware of his times. He may have begun humbly enough in Hereford, but he took three degrees at Oxford; he had read his Hobbes as well as the Cambridge- and neo-Platonists; and he was chaplain to Sir Orlando Bridgeman, the Lord Keeper.) And what about Edward Taylor?

Certainly, the poems of Marvell that we can date do not support the thesis that the fine lyric poet was suddenly changed into a writer of political poems and satires. One of the earliest of Marvell's datable poems was the rather brutal, if funny, satire on 'Fleckno'. 'An Horatian Ode', his finest poem on public affairs, was written in the early summer of 1650, before the poems associated with Appleton House. Both the lovely 'Bermudas' and the comic political libel 'The Character of Holland' seem to have been written in 1653; the two long Cromwell poems belong to 1654 and 1658; and the elegant 'On Mr. Milton's *Paradise Lost*' comes in 1674, *after* Marvell's longest political satire, 'The Last Instructions to a Painter' and just before the 'Statue poems' —assuming that Marvell wrote the latter. Unless we can learn a great deal more about the composition and dating of Marvell's poems than it seems likely we ever shall, any attempt to present a precisely detailed account of Marvell's psychological or aesthetic development is doomed to depend on more than usually random hunches or abstracting fictions.

If the prevalent notions about seventeenth-century literary history and Marvell's development have not always proved helpful, the attempts to place Marvell in a specific 'school' of poetry have also occasionally misled or perplexed. A student who has learned that Marvell belongs to the 'School of Donne' may be disconcerted when he discovers Marvell's concern for euphony, his usual rejection of impatient or impassioned speakers, and his preference for simple metrical schemes and Jonsonian diction. If he has learned that Marvell was a 'Metaphysical Poet' and that 'metaphysical poets' were either Anglo- or Roman Catholic, what can he make of Marvell's open hostility to both? In his effort to preserve the teaching that 'metaphysical poets' were partisans of Charles and enemies of Cromwell, a bright student may try to read 'An Horatian Ode' as a poem that expresses primary allegiance to Charles, but what can he do with the other two Cromwell poems?

But of course many of the best readers have not been primarily concerned with such matters. There are many interesting ways of looking at Marvell's poems, and many questions or 'approaches' which close readings suggest. Recently a number of scholarly critics (most notably the late J. B. Leishman) have been profitably engaged in bringing to light the rich complexity of Marvell's literary heritage. It now appears that few other seventeenth-century poets of significance owed so much to so many English contemporaries as Marvell did: he delighted in considering the meanings and overtones of another poet's phrases or images and in bending them to new and often surprising uses. When one comes to recognize some of the things Marvell took from Donne, Jonson, Lovelace, Suckling, Carew, George Herbert, Cowley, Crashaw, Waller, Cleveland, Davenant, Dryden, Milton, as well as Mildmay Fane, Lord Fairfax, Thomas Randolph and Thomas Stanley, Marvell's lines may come to seem strewn with words and phrases so redolent of other contexts that they should properly be printed in italics—if not precisely the same italics so widely used in the *Poems* of 1681. And this is the same poet whom Eliot called the most Latin of all the seventeenth-century poets, and also the one whose debt to French poetry seems unusually large: to Théophile de Viau and Saint-Amant for more than themes and *libertin* poses and the uses of eight-syllable lines, and perhaps too to Tristan L'Hermite and Georges de Scudéry—and he translated into Latin four lines from Georges de Brébeuf. But if Marvell is something of a ventriloquist who momentarily catches any number of voices, he is also even more of an alchemist who mysteriously transmutes almost everything he touches to a gold stamped with his individual hallmark. As with some other notable poetic magpies, the remarkable thing is not how much he borrowed or stole, but how confidently he brought 'the booty home' and made it his own.

That ability is related to the fact that Marvell's interest in the proprieties and possibilities of literary forms and genres seems as intense as some later poets' interest in their own personalities. Something of the scope of Marvell's art can be seen in the range of his rhetorical and poetic forms: meditations, complaints, persuasions, 'praises' or encomiums, satires or libels, descriptions of figures or landscapes, a definition, an epitaph, an heroic ode, dialogues or debates, a framed monologue, songs with or without frames, and 'Upon Appleton House', that extraordinary poem in which, under the disguise of a traditional 'country house poem' that compliments a man or family by means of a description of the owner's house (articulated within the general framework of a guided tour of the house and grounds), Marvell managed to include all his major themes as well as a dazzling display of his rhetorical inventions and transformations—even to touches of the masque and the heroic.

Readers who find the continued contemplation of such matters dazzling or distracting may wish to consider the poems in terms of a smaller, more comfortable number of categories. If they are historically minded and remember Hobbes, they may see that most of Marvell's poetry falls within a sort of pastoral grouping (extended to include the Mower poems and the garden and countryhouse poems), more than most readers recognize within the satiric or 'scommatic', and that a kind of heroic is used consistently in the Cromwell poems and intermittently in the Fairfax poems. Probably a larger number of readers will find it more natural to consider the poems in terms of their general subjects. It is surprising to discover how many can be described as predominantly concerned with love, or religion, or politics. (In Marvell's verse the ethical is usually associated with one of those three.) Some of the poems are notable for the odd relations they assume or suggest between love and religion, religion and politics, or even between politics and love. The must popular of Marvell's poems today either clearly fit into one of the categories or mark the transitions from one to another: 'To his Coy Mistress', 'The Definition of Love', 'The Garden', 'The Coronet', 'On a Drop of Dew', 'Bermudas', 'An Horatian Ode upon Cromwell's Return from Ireland', perhaps even 'The Picture of Little T. C. in a Prospect of Flowers'.

★   ★   ★

It probably does not matter much how one classifies the poems for critical or historical or mnemonic purposes. But whatever one's method, the increase in Marvell's reputation during this century makes an additional caution advisable. The words 'great' and 'major' have been introduced in connection with the poetry, and a 'great' or 'major' poet today is sometimes thought to be a *magister vitae* in a fairly simple sense, perhaps even the possessor of a single message or system. He is assumed to be 'moral' in the implications of his verse if not conventionally in his personal life. Since Marvell used bits of most of the systems known to his time, a number of intelligent readers with something like these assumptions have spent an extraordinary amount of effort in the attempt to demonstrate that among the aptly titled *Miscellaneous Poems* there is a respectable central pattern of doctrine or belief, Platonic, Christian, Romantic, or modern. The results have sometimes been formidably learned, but often seem to have little to do with the Marvell whom nearly all of his contemporaries remembered as witty. It is difficult to read Marvell sympathetically if one assumes that idleness is always reprehensible, the contemplation or pursuit of pleasure always trivial or immoral, elegance socially suspect.

The best readers surely will be among those who recognize that artifice and the 'artificial' can be delightful.

Frank Warnke has recently remarked that a large number of Marvell's lines or poems are literally playful.[2] J. B. Leishman was making a related point when he described Marvell's characteristic effects as those of 'humorous gravity', 'measured hyperbole', and 'serious burlesque'. T. S. Eliot's memorable phrase about 'a tough reasonableness beneath the slight lyric grace', like Thomas Fuller's description of Marvell's father, that moderately Puritan conforming clergyman, as 'Most *facetious* in his *discourse*, yet *grave* in his *carriage*', may suggest that subtlety and nimbleness of movement, mental, physical, or aural, are usually associated with such effects:

> The Grave's a fine and private place,
> But none I think do there embrace.

> Society is all but rude,
> To this delicious Solitude.

> My Love is of a birth as rare
> As 'tis for object strange and high:
> It was begotten by despair
> Upon Impossibility.

A reader who comes to Marvell's poetry with such possibilities in mind will probably also bring an unusual alertness to matters of argument, shape and balance. If he pays a good deal of attention to precisely those formal matters which advocates of spontaneous or confessional poetry sometimes dismiss as unimportant, he may find that a large number of the supposed problems concerning the poems either never arise or are fairly easily resolved.

Two lines from 'On a Drop of Dew' can serve as an emblem of the way in which many of the poems work:

> Moving but on a point below,
> It all about does upwards bend.

In those lines Marvell was describing, by analogy with the movement of a drop of dew within a rose, the appearance and movement of the soul glimpsed within the body on earth; but that description of nimble

[2] 'Play and Metamorphosis in Marvell's Poetry', *Studies in English Literature*, V (1965), pp. 23–30.

movement and delicate balance, along with the suggested 'shaping' from the 'point below' to a higher realm might be applied to a number of the poems which move nimbly and subtly around a central point of balance and also suggest applications to 'higher' realms of discourse or meaning. One can take 'To his Coy Mistress' as a fairly simple example. Almost everyone has noticed the structure of the poem in which the traditional plea to give up coyness and to seize the day for love is given a syllogistic form: 'Had we but World enough, and Time'; 'But at my back I alwaies hear . . .'; 'Now therefore . . .' The three divisions are precisely weighted. The speaker's generous willingness to practice almost eternal gallantry is emphasized by the twenty lines that it requires, but the necessities of time and morality neatly overbalance that movement in only twelve lines. The final fourteen lines of the resolution both prove firmly conclusive for the immediate moment and also suggest costs and values beyond that moment.

Often the 'point' on which a Marvell poem moves is very fine indeed, and despite the casual, gentlemanly surface, the balance is mathematical. There is nothing very remarkable in the notion that if one wishes to praise both a lady's beauty of person and of voice, one may well choose a three-stanza form and emphasize the double triumph of love; but Marvell's 'The Fair Singer' is remarkable both in its beauty of movement and in the way it relates the victory of Love to the highest senses and elements in each of its three stanzas:

> To make a final conquest of all me,
> Love did compose so sweet an Enemy,
> In whom both Beauties to my death agree,
> Joyning themselves in fatal Harmony;
> That while she with her Eyes my Heart does bind,
> She with her Voice might captivate my Mind.
>
> I could have fled from One but singly fair:
> My dis-intangled Soul it self might save,
> Breaking the curlèd trammels of her hair.
> But how should I avoid to be her Slave,
> Whose subtile Art invisibly can wreath
> My Fetters of the very Air I breathe?
>
> It had been easie fighting in some plain,
> Where Victory might hang in equal choice,

But all resistance against her is vain,
Who has th'advantage both of Eyes and Voice,
And all my Forces needs must be undone,
She having gainèd both the Wind and Sun.

The fact that 'On a Drop of Dew' is one of the subtlest and most lovely in movement of English irregular (or 'Cowleyan') odes may obscure the precisely mathematical balance upon which it rests. The poem's descriptions of the drop of dew and the soul are given exactly eighteen lines each. At the end of line 36, the platonic analogy and the balance are exact: the last four lines concerning the manna and the 'Almighty Sun' introduce a surprising and unmistakably Christian development and conclusion.[3] 'The Coronet' also uses the resources of irregular verse to suggest the winding and the wreaths, but its sense of refined and yet firm conclusion owes a great deal to the balance of its rhetorical elements: an initial sixteen lines of narrative, divided neatly into eight lines in an ordinary conditional ('When ... I seek ... I gather flowers') concerning the speaker's desire to construct a garland for his Saviour and eight in a more immediate conditional (dramatized by the 'now' of line 9) concerning the discovery of the entwined Serpent; a two-line apostrophe, an expostulation of moral judgement by a voice that comments on the narrative from a point of resolution beyond the narrator's ('Ah, foolish Man, that would'st debase with them,/And mortal Glory, Heavens Diadem!'); and an eight-line prayer that concludes the poem. That intrusive two-line apostrophe which breaks the perfect and abstract symmetry is essential for the poem's form to reflect accurately its meaning.

One can find this sort of thing almost everywhere. Arithmetic reflects or supports meaning again and again. It is the third stanza of the five-stanza 'The Picture of Little T. C. in a Prospect of Flowers' which focuses the difficulties of the subject and the prospect. The central 'song' of praise of 'Bermudas' is neatly framed by four-line passages of narration and description in the past tense, passages which help to make us conscious of what is, structurally, a hymn of four

[3] The elegaics of the Latin poem *Ros* neither attempt to imitate the irregular movements nor to preserve the balance: the poem gives twenty-two lines to the drop of dew and only twenty to the soul. And although the last four lines of the Latin are close to the English, its plural '*Solibus ... benignis*' does not suggest the almost inevitable English seventeenth-century pun on 'Almighty Sun'.

eight-line verses. Some of the readers who have found 'A Dialogue between the Resolved Soul, and Created Pleasure' a dull poem have probably failed to note a number of the details: that the opening lines are spoken, supposedly privately, to the soul by its human 'possessor', a voice not at all to be confused with that of the later chorus, made up of something resembling All Angels and Saints; that, after Pleasure's initial two-line welcome, the Soul usually takes only two lines to answer Pleasure's four-line temptations, and in so doing demonstrates not Puritan surliness but witty economy—and the claim that it already possesses the truly valuable essences of the sensuous pleasures as well as those 'higher' and more complex appeals to all beauty and love united in feminine beauty, gold and all worldly possessions, complete military and civic power and glory, and absolute knowledge. The Resolved Soul implies, therefore, that in offering such objects as final and exclusive goals, Created Pleasure is only offering false appearances. On the one occasion when the Soul does require four lines instead of two, it is in response to music's temptation to the sense of hearing, a sense which Marvell, a poet enchanted with sounds and rhythms, placed higher than sight:[4]

> Had I but any time to lose,
> On this I would it all dispose.
> Cease Tempter. None can chain a mind
> Whom this sweet Chordage cannot bind.

Since the famous 'central' stanzas V–VII of 'The Garden' are framed by stanzas that are witty distortions of classical myth and the biblical account of Eden, I have come to believe that the chief formal problem of the poem concerns how the three introductory stanzas (those which claim that the garden contains a truer fame, quiet, innocence and amorousness than the world outside) are balanced or 'concluded' by the single final stanza concerning the gardener, the floral sundial and the industrious bee.[5]

I think that attention to the arithmetic is essential if we are to under-

[4] In *From Shadowy Types to Truth: Studies in Milton's Symbolism* (New Haven and London, 1968), pp. 155–66, William Madsen sketches the differing traditions for identifying hearing or sight as the noblest sense.

[5] See my 'Reading Marvell's "Garden"', *The Centennial Review*, XIII (Winter, 1969), pp. 18–37.

stand 'A Dialogue between the Soul and Body'. Frank Kermode notes in his recent edition of the poems that there is an undated manuscript notation in the Bodleian copy of *1681* to the effect that the poem may be incomplete. I should think that whoever wrote the note recognized that with the first forty lines the debate is at a stalemate, and that the Body's additional four lines at the end give it at least a quantitative victory. Perhaps pious expectations were shocked. But the poem strikes me as fully and beautifully complete. The Bodleian reader may not have been familiar enough with Marvell's delight in using conventional materials in fresh (if not topsy-turvy) ways. But the formal emphasis of the poem is also perfectly justifiable along the most orthodox lines. The issue of debate is not, after all, whether the body or the soul is more valuable or nearer the divine. Instead, Marvell has wittily personified the Body and the Soul as totally separate (or at least separable) personalities, each intent on exonerating himself and blaming the other for all the sufferings, frustrations, or mere discomforts of human life. Of course it is a fiction: the body cannot even formulate the intellectual objections apart from the soul; and the human soul does not and cannot, in ordinary human experience, speak or acquire experience apart from the body and its sensory aids—as George Herbert noted in 'In Angelos' (*Lucus*, xxiv), that marks the prime difference between the knowledge of men and the knowledge of angels. But granted the temporary suspension of disbelief necessary for the fiction, the Body must win at least a Pyrrhic victory in Marvell's poem. The Body's four last lines indicate the victory clearly:

> What but a Soul could have the wit
> To build me up for Sin so fit?
> So Architects do square and hew,
> Green Trees that in the Forest grew.

Of course the Body could not sin or suffer metaphysical anguish apart from the Soul. The animals are sinless. But the final two lines underline the limitations of that judgement. The Body speaks as a seventeenth-century child of nature, hostile to all architects who hew and shape the growths of nature for the uses of man. But the witty ingenuity of Marvell's poem should prepare its readers to see the other side: in charging that only the Soul could have the 'wit' to build as the human architect, the Body has also implied that only the Soul could have

G

'built' up man's possibilities for creativity, glory and godlike conversation as well as for sin. Although the Body has clearly won the debate
as to who is most responsible for man's suffering, only a confirmed
Grill could conclude that it has also established its own superior importance or value.

Rosalie Colie has suggested that Marvell's preference for the eight-
line stanza in octosyllabics owes something to the notion that it is a
'perfect' form, perhaps a *carmina quadrata*, and I think she is probably
right. But I do not believe that Marvell ordinarily paid much attention
to the more rarified matters of numerology or mystical significances.
In addition to his nimble intelligence, Marvell possessed a strong
measure of scepticism, and he usually had little patience with the
portentous. Within the poems he often took consciously wayward or
elaborately negligent stances, and if one tries to describe that side of
his dramatized sensibility, one can probably not do better than Montaigne's *ondoyant*. But the structural mathematics often dramatize the
movements towards decision or judgement which underlie the poems.
Rival claims are fully weighed, and the judgements are made with full
knowledge. Almost every poem 'presents a precise stance, an unique
position and a decision taken at one moment with a full consciousness
of all the costs. The costs are counted, but not mourned; the position
is taken, the poem is written, with gaiety.'[6] The 'numbers' help to
make clear the nature and the humanity of the judgements. In describing the modestly unpretentious 'lines' of Fairfax's house at Nun
Appleton, Marvell wittily emphasized the human significance of a
certain kind of mathematics:

> *Humility* alone designs
> Those short but admirable Lines,
> By which, ungirt and unconstrain'd,
> Things greater are in less contain'd.
> Let others vainly strive t'immure
> The *Circle* in the *Quadrature*!
> These *holy Mathematicks* can
> In ev'ry Figure equal Man.
>   ('Upon Appleton House', ll. 41–8)

Although I believe Marvell would have rejected the adjective 'holy'
from any description of his own poetic mathematics, I think he would

---

[6] 'Marvell's "Nature" ', *English Literary History*, XX (1953), p. 134.

have conceded that the rest of the passage might apply to part of what he was after in his poems.

*   *   *

Along with the unusually 'private' poems, Marvell wrote a number of semi-private ones, poems intended directly for specific readers but not for publication. Both 'Upon the Hill and Grove at Bill-borow' and 'Upon Appleton House' are subtitled, the first 'To the Lord Fairfax' and the second 'To my Lord Fairfax'. (The 'my' correctly indicates the greater degree of intimacy of the second.) Although neither poem addresses Fairfax openly, each is obviously written for his eyes as well as in his honour. Yet each seems much more 'private' than the usual seventeenth-century poem addressed to a famous public man; both of them reflect, I believe, Marvell's special status as a member of the household (the tutor of Fairfax's daughter), and although one can imagine either the poet's or Fairfax's sharing them privately with friends, I do not think one can imagine either having them published. Perhaps this special semi-private quality partly accounts for the apparent freedom and fancifulness of 'Upon Appleton House', the most interesting long poem that I know between *The Faerie Queene* and *Paradise Lost*. 'Music's Empire', with what seems the compliment in its final lines to Fairfax, probably belongs roughly to the same group, and the sung pastoral dialogues that Marvell wrote for the marriage of Cromwell's daughter also have a tone of personal commendation and seem created for a larger but still a semi-private audience.[7] The original version of 'On the Victory obtained by Blake' appears to be intended privately for the eyes of Cromwell. It may just be possible that 'An Horatian Ode', with its dramatic shift to direct address in line 113 ('But thou the Wars and Fortunes Son/March indefatigably on'), may also be conceived as a semi-private commendation to Cromwell; if so, the poem is even more daring than most scholars and critics have imagined.

[7] The other pastoral dialogues may also have been conceived for public musical performances. William Lawes (d. 1645), John Gamble and Matthew Locke all set 'A Dialogue between Thyrsis and Dorinda'. Almost anyone who listens to Locke's setting (available on Westminster Records XWN-19082) will be struck by the different effects (and the different questions one asks) when one hears that poem as a musical performance rather than as a 'privately' written dialogue.

A much less unusual group of poems is formed by the public encomiums which Marvell wrote, in his own person and with his name
attached, for publication in volumes by or in honour of the men he
praised. They include the poem to Lovelace, Marvell's contribution to
the volume on the death of Lord Hastings, the one on *Paradise Lost*,
and the one 'To his Worthy Friend Doctor Witty upon his Translation
of the Popular Errors'. The latter contains some of Marvell's sharpest
literary criticism. Its description of the faults of translators should be
better known than it is:

> Some in this task
> Take off the Cypress vail, but leave a mask,
> Changing the Latine, but do more obscure
> That sence in *English* which was bright and pure.
> So of Translators they are Authors grown,
> For ill Translators make the Book their own.
> Others do strive with words and forcèd phrase
> To add such lustre, and so many rayes,
> That but to make the Vessel shining, they
> Much of the precious Metal rub away.
> He is Translations thief that addeth more,
> As much as he that taketh from the Store
> Of the first Author. Here he maketh blots
> That mends; and added beauties are but spots.

Although the genre is a conventional one, there is nothing tamely
conventional about Marvell's handling of it. I shall return to the
Paradise Lost poem.

The least and probably the most poorly read of Marvell's poems
today are the fully public ones which Marvell wrote for anonymous
publication and with which he meant to influence public opinion.
They include 'The Character of Holland', 'The First Anniversary of
the Government under O. C.' and the satires of the Restoration.
Related to them if not actually included are 'An Horatian Ode', 'Tom
May's Death' and 'On the Victory obtained by Blake'. Marvell
obviously intended 'A Poem upon the Death of O. C.' to be fully
political, but I think it fails of his intention precisely because it presents
the poet's sorrow and near despair so frankly that it undercuts its final
attempt to build political support for Richard Cromwell. The later
satires, both the few about which we can feel fairly sure and the many
which were attributed to him, reflect the fact that after his election to

Parliament in 1659, Marvell devoted his major energies to public matters—and numbers of people knew it. I do not find it at all self-evident that we always have the right to regret it when a poet becomes so concerned with public affairs that he either devotes his poetry to them or gives it up. Milton's is, of course, one of the most startling examples; but even had Milton died before completing *Paradise Lost*, I think we should have had no just right (though excuse enough) to lament the political pamphlets and the Latin Secretaryship. There was hardly for Milton a possible choice between either the poetry or the public career, since he believed that he could not write heroic poetry unless he was willing to sacrifice his private ambition when he thought public duty required him to do so. In Marvell's case, it is almost impossible to imagine a poet so intelligent, so witty, and so constant in his attendance on the parliaments of Charles II who could resist the promise—and the satisfactions—of verse satire.

Some readers' difficulties with Marvell's political poetry may stem from a critical assumption quite widespread a few years ago that the most 'mature' (and therefore literarily desirable) human attitude is an ironic embracement of all contradictory impulses—a condition of complete paralysis costing not less than everything. One can certainly understand, too, the temptation in our age to identify the serious poet as precisely the person who is not selling anything, and to assume that any poet must compromise his private standards if he attempts to influence public action. Still, such notions are seriously anachronistic; moreover, they are not likely to prove very helpful for our reading of most panegyrics and satires. Probably making for more immediate difficulties with Marvell's poetry is the prevalence among scholars and critics of a sentimental Royalism. (Americans are often particularly subject to it: there are supposedly more chapels dedicated to Blessed Charles King and Martyr in the state of Texas than in all the British Isles.) Many sensitive and learned readers would rather not be reminded of Marvell's poems in praise of Cromwell, and some of them have spent a good deal of ingenuity on attempts to read 'An Horatian Ode' as a covertly Cavalier poem. A number have accepted the attribution to Marvell of the bloodthirstily royalist 'An Elegy upon the Death of my Lord Francis Villiers', a poem which it seems most unlikely that Marvell wrote.[8]

[8] Margoliouth printed the poem in an appendix with a long note by C. H. Wilkinson pressing its claims (I, pp. 329-34), but he did not state his own

John M. Wallace's volume, *Destiny His Choice: The Loyalism of Andrew Marvell*, contains some of the most interesting recent pages on the political poems. Rather than beginning with the questions, 'What does the poem mean to me, privately?' Wallace has tended to ask two other questions, 'What was the poem's immediate political context?' and 'What is the poem's rhetorical structure?' Among other things, his readings demonstrate that the range of possible political positions at any one moment in Marvell's career was a good deal wider than modern readers are likely to assume. I am indebted to Mr. Wallace in my following attempt to sketch the workings of two of those poems, 'The First Anniversary of the Government under O. C.' and 'The Last Instructions to a Painter', Marvell's longest and most sustained examples of political celebration and political satire. (The latter is also one of the few Restoration satires of which the attribution to Marvell has never been seriously questioned.) Both poems show that Marvell was an intelligent and witty poet who knew what he was doing and thoroughly enjoyed doing it. In neither is there any ambiguity at all about the central attitudes: the first praises Cromwell as a 'Prince' who has surpassed all former and present kings and has miraculously created a strong and just England out of what had been remarkably near chaos; the second satirizes unmercifully the political events and personalities of 1666–7, and argues that Charles II must summon new advisers if he and England are to survive. Readers interested in history and in Marvell will probably be interested in those arguments in themselves. But the literary effectiveness of the poems depends chiefly on how the positions

---

acceptance of the attribution. A single copy of the poem was left by George Clarke (1660–1736) to the Library of Worcester College, Oxford, and the donor's manuscript notation, 'by Andrew Marvell', is the sole evidence for attribution. Although Clarke was a careful collector whose attributions are valuable for works of the late seventeenth and eighteenth centuries, there seems to be no other case in which they are at all significant for works written before his birth in 1660. I find it difficult to believe that the same poet could have written the poem on Lovelace in February of 1648 and the poem on Hastings in June of 1649 and, between the two, in July of 1648, also have written the sort of *verse* found in the elegy upon Villiers. Moreover, the fact that the elegy's final lines (beginning, 'And we hereafter to his honour will/Not write so many, but so many kill') seem to imply that their author was fighting with the royalist forces, makes most improbable their attribution to a notorious non-participant in the war.

are managed: whether we are shown and made to feel the reality, in the first poem, of a governor and a government worthy of being preserved; and, in the second, of a public situation so hopelessly venal and inefficient that, while we laugh, we recognize with the poet that it must be changed.

'The First Anniversary', written for December of 1654 and published anonymously shortly thereafter, begins with the contrast between the usual triumph of time over mortal man and the fate of Cromwell:

> Like the vain Curlings of the Wat'ry maze,
> Which in smooth streams a sinking Weight does raise;
> So Man, declining alwayes, disappears
> In the weak Circles of increasing Years;
> And his short Tumults of themselves Compose,
> While flowing Time above his Head does close.
>   *Cromwell* alone with greater Vigour runs,
> (Sun-like) the Stages of succeeding Suns:
> And still the Day which he doth next restore,
> Is the just Wonder of the Day before.
> *Cromwell* alone doth with new Lustre spring,
> And shines the Jewel of the yearly Ring.

The first section of the poem celebrates what Cromwell is and what he has done. What we have thought of him before is, supposedly, irrelevant: the imaginatively contrasted paragraphs proceed 'objectively' in the third person. In the rapid sequence of witty, mythic images of Cromwell (as the sun who triumphs over time, as the miraculous musician-architect who surpasses Amphion, as the Archimedes who has found a place for his foot and 'hurls' the world about him), Marvell created a vision of a dynamic force, both part of and superior to ordinary nature, which cannot fail to interest his readers. The section ends with the wish that the benighted Princes would recognize Cromwell as the leader capable of achieving 'The Great Designes kept for the latter Dayes'.

At this point the objective narration ceases with an apostrophe to the 'Unhappy Princes'. Then the speculations of the 'I' create the 'we' for the rest of the poem:

> Hence oft *I* think, if in some happy Hour
> High Grace should meet in one with highest Pow'r,
> And then a seasonable People still

Should bend to his, as he to Heavens will,
What *we* might hope . . .   (131–5; my italics)

But although we can know of the 'great Designes', we cannot know of their times: ''tis the most which we determine can,/If these the Times, then this must be the Man.'

Only after the 'objective' description of Cromwell and his creation, and after the personal statement which anticipates and re-directs the arguments of the Millenarian opposition in such a way that 'we' must join, does the poem turn to address Cromwell directly: 'And thou, great *Cromwell* . . .' The implications of the 'thou' and the new 'we' are largely sustained in the rhetorical inventions which move us swiftly to the conclusion. Despite Cromwell's birth, virtue and miraculous escapes from death, 'Our Sins endanger, and shall one day kill' him. His recent coaching accident provides the evidence. At the thought of his possible death there, 'We only mourn'd our selves', for Cromwell, like Elijah, would have ascended. Cromwell had already given up 'all delight of Life' when he became 'the headstrong Peoples Charioteer': he was the cloud which brought plenty to the thirsty land, the Gideon who conquered and yet refused to be 'Lord', the olive which only 'in just time didst aw' 'Th'ambitious Shrubs'. The simile of the 'lusty Mate' who saved the ship of state when the 'artless' Barebones parliamentarians were about to wreck it provides the occasion for the poem's definition of freedom and of Cromwell as the Father:

'Tis not a Freedome, that where All command;
Nor Tyranny, where One does them withstand:
But who of both the Bounders knows to lay
Him as their Father must the State obey.   (279–82)

Cromwell is the Noah who has survived the Flood and established a new world. The 'Chammish issue' have hoped he would be killed, but Cromwell, 'returning yet alive/Does with himself all that is good revive.' At the thought of his death, we were like the first man who, experiencing the first sunset and night, followed the fallen sun in despair: 'When streight the Sun behind him he descry'd,/Smiling serenely from the further side.' The hostile princes, startled by that sun, give the ultimate praise to the revived nation and to the might of the English navy, but it is Cromwell, the 'soul' of that nation, whom they fear most. When the single speaker interrupts their unwilling praise, he

addresses Cromwell at last as 'great Prince'. Yet, although that title may
have been intended to have profound political significance outside the
poem, within it, it seems almost incidental, since the poem itself has
'proved' that as sun, architect, musician, creator, prophet, soldier,
great captain, father, day, star and soul of the nation, Cromwell *is*
greater far 'Then ought below, or yet above a King'. If the hostile
monarchs want him to take the title of king only to prove his common
mortality with them, then we, of course, do not wish it. Cromwell is
semi-deified and the great anniversary fully celebrated; yet time has
not stopped. The poet will no longer contend for the prize of praising
Cromwell properly *while* Cromwell raises his 'venerable' head 'As far
above their Malice as my Praise', and while 'the *Angel* of our Common-
weal,/Troubling the Waters, yearly mak'st them Heal.' The conclusion both completes the praise and makes clearly evident the relation of this anniversary to the uncertain future, when, with the ultimate
disturbance of the waters by his death, Cromwell will no longer be
living to heal them. Politically, the poem not only praises Cromwell
and rallies support for him, but it also emphasizes the pressing importance of some solution to the problem of the succession.

'Upon the First Anniversary' can still be remarkably effective as a
whole. 'The Last Instructions to a Painter' is likely as a whole to
remain the preserve of the specialists. Written in the early fall of 1667,
it surveys the political events and court scandals of the preceding year
so fully (in almost a thousand lines) that it inevitably has some of the
obscurity of any detailed annal centuries later, when the personalities
and the events are forgotten. Yet the surprising thing about the poem
is not how much of it may seem dead, but how much, even at the
most cursory reading, still seems alive.

Only the year before, in 1666, Edmund Waller had published
'Instructions to a Painter, For the Drawing of the Posture and Progress
of His Majesty's Forces at Sea, Under the command of His Highness
Royal, Together with The Battle and Victory obtained over the Dutch,
June 3, 1665.' He thereby became, quite unintentionally, the English
father of an entire satirical genre. For in his fulsome praise of the Duke
of York for the 'great victory' of Lowestoft, Waller failed to mention
the facts that after the battle the Dutch fleet was allowed to escape
because the Duke was taking a nap and that subsequent events were not
generally considered cause for English rejoicing. The satirical possibilities were seized upon by a number of writers. Despite its title, Marvell's

poem was by no means the last of the 'Advice to a Painter' poems which derived from Waller's panegyric, but it is the best.

Marvell's 'Instructions' should discourage the painter from the start. No one medium will serve to paint the monstrous 'Confusion, folly, treach'ry, fear, neglect' which characterize 'Our Lady State':

> After two sittings, now our *Lady State*,
> To end her Picture, does the third time wait.
> But er'e thou fal'st to work, first *Painter* see
> It be'nt too slight grown, or too hard for thee.
> Canst thou paint without Colours? Then 'tis right:
> For so we too without a Fleet can fight.
> Or canst thou dawb a Sign-post, and that ill?
> 'Twill suit our great debauch and little skill.
> Or hast thou mark't how antique Masters limn
> The aly roof, with snuff of Candle dimn,
> Sketching in shady smoke prodigious tools?
> 'Twill serve this race of Drunkards, Pimps, and Fools.
> But if to match our Crimes thy skill presumes,
> As th'*Indians*, draw our Luxury in Plumes.
> Or if to score out our compendious Fame,
> With *Hook* then, through the *microscope* take aim. . . .
>   (1–16)

Without such resources, the painter shall 'oft' curse his 'guiltless Pencil' and 'Stamp on' his 'Pallat'; and these gestures of rage may prove the most effective strokes of all:

> So may'st thou perfect, by a lucky blow,
> What all thy softest touches cannot do.   (27–8)

For the task at hand the poet and painter will need the resources of savage indignation as well as of artful disdain.

The poet invites the painter to paint a number of horrendous portraits; he may also paint a trick-track board (with the dice deciding fate) as an image of the House of Commons, and a large battle piece to represent the debate over the Excise Bill. But most of the time the painter must 'rest' and observe 'With what small Arts the publick game they play'; he cannot possibly paint a single comprehensive canvas since 'Our Lady State' at this time has neither centre nor coherence. The poet finally bids the painter adieu; Charles, now that he has dismissed Clarendon, will surely become both poet and painter and sit for himself. The envoy begs Charles to dismiss the false courtiers who, 'where all *England* serves, themselves would reign', to summon a true court, and to 'rule without a *Guard*'. With the idea of a restoration of natural order, an 'ideal' poem and picture become again possible.

In the meantime, there is the problem of this poem: how *does* one construct an admonitory picture of chaos?[9] Historical 'order' may be far from ideal, but at least it exists; and Marvell, after his portraits of St. Albans, the Duchess of York and the Countess Castlemaine (all sexually depraved and all with past or future designs upon the crown), turns largely to episodic narrative of the parliamentary, military and diplomatic events: the struggle over the Excise, which is neither a decent backgammon game nor a proper battle; the absurd and self-righteous diplomacy with the Dutch and French; the ironic pastoral triumph of de Ruyter and the Dutch fleet as they rape the Thames and Medway; the one example of mythic integrity and suffering in the death of Douglas, the 'Valiant Scot'; the renewed intrigue with the prospect of peace. But with all the variety and disorder, the concept of sovereignty—the poem's 'picture' of those who really rule, or wish to rule, or attempt or pretend to rule—provides more unity than we at first suspect. It is Clarendon who 'Reigns in his new Palace' and 'sits in State Divine' after the House is prorogued; it is Louis and the Dutch who possess real civil and military power; it is de Ruyter who truly rules the ocean, the English rivers and later the English navy (the gallants, who came 'To be Spectators safe of the *new Play*', flee in comic disorder when the dramatic issues of sovereignty become actual); it is 'brave Douglas' who will rule in legend as hero—the court can only coin a new farthing with the image of the Duchess of Richmond as Britannia ruling '*the four Seas*'; the court wishes to isolate Parliament from any share in ruling, and a corrupt Speaker rules Parliament; it is Charles who must, as King *in* Parliament, begin to rule.

And throughout the poem is Marvell's wit. The court party chose Peter Pett, Commissioner of the Navy at Chatham, as the scapegoat for the entire naval disaster; we do not have to know anything about the historical realities to respond to those sixteen lines for which *Pett*

[9] In 'The "Poetic Picture, Painted Poetry" of *The Last Instructions to a Painter*', *Modern Philology*, LXIII (1966), pp. 288–94, Earl Miner has explored the ways Marvell uses the conventions of the Painter poems to give unity.

supplies the rhymes and to delight in the climactic unmasking of the absurdity:

> Who all our Ships expos'd in *Chathams* Net?
> Who should it be but the *Phanatick Pett.*
> *Pett*, the Sea Architect, in making Ships,
> Was the first cause of all these Naval slips:
> Had he not built, none of these faults had bin;
> If no Creation, there had been no Sin.   (783–8)

It was an inspiration to imagine that if, during the year, Charles II had been visited by a nude female vision of distressed England or the Peace, his response would have been erotic rather than political; yet in his Envoy to Charles, Marvell makes one of the last moving appeals to the older idea of the English royal commonwealth.

If we are to read most of Marvell's political poems intelligently and with pleasure, we need to know more than we do. But even a glance at 'The First Anniversary' and 'The Last Instructions' suggests a number of points which scholars and critics might keep in mind while they attempt to increase our knowledge. Marvell used and mastered more than one style. When he wrote occasional poems, he was aware of a potential public audience and of immediate political possibilities. (He would surely have considered the unintentional admission into either a panegyric or a satire of an individual poet's private misgivings, an example not of 'honesty' but of incompetence.) And he seems to have realized that political poems, like other poems, are less immediately effective and less ultimately interesting if the poet assumes that he is merely voicing common sentiment, formulated before his poem is written—or read. Whether panegyrist or satirist, the poet must appropriate, undermine, or destroy those visions and attitudes in the external world which oppose or differ from the central visions and judgements of his poem.

If we recognize these things, the other political and quasi-political poems may become less problematic and more interesting. We may be able to read 'The Character of Holland' as a cheerful libel on the Dutch people and culture, more humane in its playful exaggeration and a great deal funnier than the war-time propaganda we are used to. We may see that 'On the Victory obtained by Blake', in the midst of its rhetorical congratulations, takes full advantage of the prophetic possibilities offered by the fact that the Spanish gold (instrument of oppression and future wars) was sent to the bottom of the sea in the Canary Islands—a setting, like the Bermudas, which offered an Edenic image of the political possibilities ahead for Cromwell and England. We might find Shakespearean analogies for 'An Horatian Ode' in *Richard II* and *Henry IV* rather than in *Macbeth*, and see the Charles of the poem as tragic because, like Richard, he only achieves nobility and fully acts his role as king when he forfeits his crown and his life to a 'greater Spirit'. And we might consider the possibility that Marvell makes the ghost of Ben Jonson so denunciatory in 'Tom May's Death', not because of Marvell's fervent royalism, but because, whatever the politics, he despised the pettiness, the venality, the hypocrisy and the broken faith that he thought May had shown.[10] In attempting to judge the authenticity of the later satires, we might hold on to the fact that Marvell is rarely dull or awkward; but we might not rule out the possibility that, when political conditions become desperate and his verse had to go underground, a poet of his skill *could* have used the popular, galloping accentual verse for rough and devastating effects.

When we read Marvell's political writings, we get an impression of integrity that implies more than the poet's mastery of rhetoric. Marvell was committed to the greatness of England and to freedom of conscience, and he was seriously engaged with the major political personalities as well as issues of his time. Except for the poems on the birth of Princess Anne (written when he was sixteen), Marvell never wrote a poem to Charles I which praised him; nor did he ever denigrate him: even in the most violent of the later satires, he presented Charles as primarily benighted and betrayed by his own supporters rather than as the betrayer. Marvell did not welcome Charles II with a panegyric after composing a funeral ode for Cromwell, nor during his long

---

[10] Among other things, May had given a fulsome description of Charles as 'A King in Virtue and in Royalty' in 1633, just twelve years before he had written an introduction to *The King's Cabinet Opened*, a publication of the letters taken from the King as Naseby, which included the canting remark: 'the drawing of this curtain may be as fatal to popery, and all antichristian heresy here now, as the rending of the veil was to the Jewish ceremonies in Judea at the expiration of our Saviour' (see A. G. Chester, *Thomas May: Man of Letters*, Philadelphia, 1932, pp. 167, 174). Among all the other charges I know of none to the effect that May was personally concerned about religion.

career in Restoration politics did he ever slander the Cromwell he had
so much praised. Except for the pleading conclusion of 'The Last Instructions', he never wrote anything resembling panegyric verse to
Charles II. In a century when the shifts of most poets who attempted
political poetry are occasionally embarrassing to their admirers, Marvell's principles and practice remained remarkably consistent.

Marvell's political maturity occurred during a revolution and a
counter-revolution. Such times make simple traditionalism and con-
stitutionalism intellectually impossible: they pose the fearful questions
about what could and should happen when the traditions contradict
each other, when the constitutions break down. One can heartily agree
that it is probably better to have no interesting political poems than
to experience such times, and still recognize that the possibility or
reality or memory of such occasions is likely, along with the brutal,
to give rise to the most interesting political poetry. For if the poet
writes anything beyond battle cries and curses, such times prevent his
relapsing thoughtlessly into the formulae of conventional wisdom. He
must re-examine his inheritance and the present and create an image
of order which, however much it owes to the past, is something
new.

★   ★   ★

Although he continued until the year of his death to write his witty
prose attacks on various men and subjects associated with religious
intolerance and strict Calvinist determinism, Marvell seems to have
written his last verse satire in 1675. Just the year before, he published
'On Mr. Milton's *Paradise Lost*' as prefatory to the second edition.
Marvell's poem is, I think, the only rival of Carew's Elegy on Donne
as the seventeenth-century poem which most effectively turns literary
criticism into poetry; it dramatizes beautifully the process by which
private hesitancies and discriminations can be transformed into clear
and powerful public judgements.

Marvell's association with Milton had been long: he had admired
and used Milton's early verse soon after it was published; Milton had
recommended him as his assistant as Latin Secretary; and the two men
had become friends. According to contemporary report, Marvell
helped save Milton's life after the Restoration, and he defended him
both in the House of Commons and in print. With the publication of

Paradise Lost, Marvell may have recognized that, despite his use of Jonson's lyrics in his earlier poems, Milton was the first major poet after Donne and Jonson who was not primarily an heir of either. If Milton had a single important English ancestor, it was, of course, Spenser. Good classicist that Marvell was (I sometimes think of him as playing Horace to Milton's Vergil), Marvell must have particularly responded to the way in which for the first time a man of his own world had successfully undertaken a role not merely as an imitator but as a competitor of the ancient epic poets.

Marvell lets no trace of personal intimacy show in his poem, but, properly for its occasion, makes it a fully public encomium. He begins with three paragraphs (totalling twenty-two lines) concerning his initial suspicions of, and fears for, *Paradise Lost.* First, the vast subject (and Marvell's summary of it is splendid) made him fear that 'sacred Truths' might be 'ruined' 'to Fable and old Song', and even that Milton may have intended so 'overwhelming' 'the World' as revenge for his blindness. Then, acknowledging the poet's admirable intentions, he feared that he might not succeed in fulfilling them, but would only 'perplex' or 'render vain' religious events and truths. And even if Milton succeeded, his example might lead others to imitate him who would cheapen the sacred subjects. (Here, a particular shaft is aimed at Marvell's *bête noire,* John Dryden, and his plan for *The State of Innocence.*)

Only after describing the doubts and fears does the poet address Milton directly and resolve the misgivings (in reverse order) with three more paragraphs summarizing the evidence of Milton's poem: it is so good as to defy imitators; its majesty preserves both the sacred truths and the poet; it owes its inspiration not to revenge (like Samson's) but to Heaven's consolatory inspiration (like Tiresias's). These paragraphs of unequal length, like the first three, total twenty-two lines: characteristically, underneath the apparent casualness the balance is precise:

> Pardon me, *mighty Poet,* nor despise
> My causeless, yet not impious, surmise.
> But I am now convinc'd, and none will dare
> Within thy Labours to pretend a Share.
> Thou hast not miss'd one thought that could be fit,
> And all that was improper dost omit:

So that no room is here for Writers left,
But to detect their Ignorance or Theft.
    That Majesty which through thy Work doth Reign
Draws the Devout, deterring the Profane.
And things divine thou treatst of in such state
As them preserves, and Thee inviolate.
At once delight and horrour on us seize,
Thou singst with so much gravity and ease;
And above humane flight dost soar aloft,
With Plume so strong, so equal, and so soft.
The *Bird* nam'd from that *Paradise* you sing
So never Flags, but alwaies keeps on Wing.
    Where couldst thou Words of such a compass find?
Whence furnish such a vast expense of Mind?
Just Heav'n Thee, like *Tiresias*, to requite,
Rewards with *Prophesie* thy loss of Sight.   (23-44)

I doubt that Marvell's description of the 'majesty' of *Paradise Lost* has
ever been bettered. Then, separating his own discourse from the described grandeur of Milton's, Marvell adds a stylish coda, focusing on
the chief technical novelty of the poem (the non-dramatic blank verse)
and including another swat at Dryden and a distinction between the
poems which need rhyme and those which do not:

Well mightst thou scorn thy Readers to allure
With tinkling Rhime, of thy own Sense secure;
While the *Town-Bays* writes all the while and spells,
And like a Pack-Horse tires without his Bells.
Their Fancies like our bushy Points appear,
The Poets tag them; we for fashion wear.
I too transported by the *Mode* offend,
And while I meant to *Praise* thee, must Commend.
Thy verse created like thy *Theme* sublime,
In Number, Weight, and Measure, needs not *Rhime*.

Marvell clearly recognized and admired the miracle of *Paradise Lost*,
but, except in a few lines, he did not imitate it. Perhaps he recognized
that Milton's combination of blank verse and high style, divorced from
greatness of subject and greatness of spirit, was likely to result merely
in windiness or bombast. And Marvell, ostentatiously staying with the
couplets that had served him so well, correctly reflected the mode of
1674 and anticipated the most promising manner of the immediate

future. The best poets of the next half-century would prove to be only more remote heirs of Jonson as they further developed a verse that, subjecting private taste to rational examination, moved towards a balanced and witty poetry of public judgement.

Note

Modern Editions

The satires on the Duke of Buckingham are collected in *Poems and Songs Relating to George Villiers, Duke of Buckingham*, by F. W. Fairholt, Percy Society (1850). Donne's satires are in Grierson's *Works* (1912); Hall (1949) and Marston (1960) have been edited by Arnold Davenport for the Liverpool University Press. *The Shorter Poems of Ralph Knevet* are edited by Amy C. Charles (Ohio State University Press, 1966). Cleveland's prose has never been edited or collected, but for the poetry see *The Poems of John Cleveland*, edited by Morris and Withington (Oxford, 1967). The *Songs and other Poems* (1661) of Alexander Brome have not been reprinted since 1668. Milton's contributions to the 'Smectymnuus' war are in *The Complete Prose Works of John Milton*, published by Yale University Press (1953–   ). Neither Suckling nor Cowley have been edited recently, and the standard texts are still *The Works of Sir John Suckling*, edited by A. H. Thompson (1910), and *The English Writings of Abraham Cowley*, edited by A. R. Waller (1905–6). There is a fine edition of *The Poetical Works of Denham*, by T. H. Banks (1928). Butler's minor satires and notebooks are in *The Collected Works of Samuel Butler*, edited by A. R. Waller and R. Lamar (1905–8), and *Hudibras* is edited by John Wilders (Oxford, 1967). Although Rochester's work falls outside the scope of this essay the introduction and notes to David M. Vieth's *Complete Poems of John Wilmot, Earl of Rochester* (1968) are invaluable on the background of the period. The definitive edition of Marvell is Margoliouth's *Poems and Letters* (second edition 1952), though there is new information in *Poems on Affairs of State*, vol. i, edited by George deF. Lord (1963).

Scholarship and Criticism. A general conspectus is given in James Sutherland's *English Satire* (1958); the most detailed study of the period is Ruth Nevo's *The Dial of Virtue* (1963); the scholarly background is available in Douglas Bush's *English Literature in the Earlier Seventeenth Century* (1945). The poetical miscellanies are described and listed in A. E. Case, *A Bibliography of English Poetical Miscellanies* (1935) (though many additions might be made), and there is a useful check-list in Norman Ault's *Seventeenth Century Lyrics* (second edition, 1950). The authorship of the poems in *The Rump* is discussed by H. F. Brooks, in *Rump Songs* (Papers of the Oxford Bibliographical Society, 1939). Many of the poems of the period are discussed from a special viewpoint in George Kitchin's *Burlesque and Parody in English* (1931). Restoration satire is best approached through J. H. Wilson's *The Court Wits of the Restoration* (1948), and its coterie quality is seen in David M. Vieth's *Attribution in Restoration Poetry* (1963). On the theory of satire there can be few better things than Alvin Kernan's two books, *The Cankered Muse* (1959) and *The Plot of Satire* (1965).

VIII

Satire from Donne to Marvell

BRIAN MORRIS

★

> . . . a warlike, various, and a tragical age is best to *write of*,
> but worst to *write in*. (Cowley)

LIKE the lonely North Atlantic island of Rockall the satires on the life
and death of George Villiers, Duke of Buckingham, protrude un-
accountably in the year 1628. Although books of epigrams and satires
continued to be published in the early years of the seventeenth century
in total disregard of the Order of 1599 forbidding their appearance, it
seems as if that Order had the unintended effect of redirecting the
satiric impulse into channels other than the formal ones in which, in
1598, it had found such memorable expression. The first problem is to
descry and account for the new directions which satire took between
the death of Queen Elizabeth and the outbreak of the Civil War.

The poems on the Duke of Buckingham written before 1628 have
an unnervingly proleptic quality; they point out his likely end:

> GEORGIVS DVX BVCKINGAMIAE. MDCXVVVIII.
> Laeto jam saeclo tandem sol pertulit annum;
> Noni non videat, quaesumus, Alme, diem.
> Thy numerous name with this yeare doth agree,
> But twenty-nyne God graunte thou never see.

Another, 'Upon the D. of B.', in *Sloane MS. 826*, after elaborating the
analogy 'Of Brittish beasts the Buck is king' ends with the couplet:

> A beast shall perish; but a man shall dye,
> As pleasures fade. This bee thy destinie.

The brooding foretaste of assassination was triumphantly fulfilled when
the Duke was murdered at Portsmouth by John Felton, on 23 August,

1628. It is uncommon, as Fairholt points out, to find 'laudations of a murderer like Felton proceeding not from the rabble but from the educated and the poetic classes'. Yet the case is clear. In manuscripts inhabited by the poems of gentlemen lines like these are boldly written:

> By Felton's hand God wrought his overthrowe.
> What shall wee say? was it God's will or noe,
> That one sinner should kill another soe?

And in a poem ascribed to 'Jo. Heape' the following bitter lines are spoken by Buckingham's ghost:

> I that my countrey did betray,
> Undid that king that let mee sway
> His sceptre as I pleas'd; brought downe
> The glorie of the English crowne;
> The courtiers' bane, the countries' hate,
> An agent for the Spanish state;
> The Romists' frend, the gospells' foe,
> The Church and kingdomes overthrowe;
> Heere a damned carcase dwell,
> 'Till my soule returne from hell.
> With Judas then I shall inherit,
> Such portion as all traytors meritt.
> If heaven admitt of treason, pride, and lust,
> Expect my spotted soule among the iust.

The life and death of 'Steenie' Buckingham, the king's favourite and the people's scorn, aroused a hostility which found passionate expression in satire and invective quite unlike anything which had gone before.

The interest shown by Elizabethan poets in Juvenal and Persius, together with the more recent example of Erasmus' *Encomium Moriae*, suggested to them certain models, and certain ways of distinguishing 'satire' from the other recognized 'kinds'. The best-known and most obvious characteristic is the 'difficulty and obscurity' necessary because the word *satire* was thought to have been derived from the Greek *satyr*, and because these were the qualities they discerned in Persius. Hall, who fell too easily into simplicity and sense, screws himself up to the recommended obscurity in the first satire of Book IV of his *Virgidemiarum*:

Who dares vpbraid these open rimes of mine
With blindfold *Aquines*, or darke *Venusine*?
Or rough-hew'ne *Teretismes* writ in th'antique vain
Like an old *Satyre*, and new *Flaccian*?

Marston, in Satire II of *The Scourge of Villainie*, elaborates Juvenal's
'difficile est Satyram non scribere' when he describes himself as 'a
sharpe fangd Satyrist' wielding 'Satyres knottie rod', and making his
'shamefac'd Muse a scold'; and Donne, to take only the last ten lines
of his fifth satire, brings together Urim and Thummim, the great
Carricks Pepper, Haman's Antiquities, Aesop's fables and a swimming
dog, to create a procession of images whose meaning is almost impenetrable. In each case the effect is powerful. The satires published in
1598 present a close family likeness; they have the same lineage. The
immediate impression of obscurity, allusiveness, violent rhythms,
articulate outrage is supported by the recognition of their place in an
identifiable tradition, and their conformity to a general theory of satire.
They represent a conscious attempt to recast satire into a classical
mould, which failed because the native English strain emanating from
Langland and Chaucer and Skelton proved too strong; each satirist
made his own private treaty with the 'satyr-figure', the goatish *persona*
who acts as the presenter of the subject-matter; and, despite the personal
scurrilities and backbiting in which they engaged with one another, the
poems they wrote are general rather than particular, typical rather than
individual, and ethical before they are social.

The importance of this quality of impersonality must be securely
seen. When Marston rails against the sexual licentiousness of his age he
never accuses any known man of adultery; when Donne writes about
religion no living prelate, priest or reformer is permitted in the poem.
The protagonists have names like Mirreus, Crantz and Graccus, and
the true religion is sought 'at Rome', 'at Geneva' or 'at home here'.
For all their violence and allusiveness these satires are abstractions from
contemporary life and their judgements of the human situation are
made in ethical categories. Their indirections, lashing the vice but
sparing the name, are in the tradition of Spenser's oblique attack on
Archbishop Grindal in *The Shepherd's Calendar*, where the asperities
are veiled in a decent allegory. It would have been impossible to
predict, in 1598, that the life and death of a public figure thirty years
later would be treated as it was. The attacks on Buckingham, alive and

dead, are public, personal and political. The judgements offered are unequivocal:

> . . . then, Felton, did the land
> Receive a speedie cure by thy iust hand.

There is the same grim quality in the lines 'Upon the Duke's Death':

> The pale horse of the Revelation
> Hath unhorst the horseman of our nation,
> And given him such a kick on his side
> (At Portesmouth) that he sware, and dy'd.

Even Waller, who never satirized anything, saw the event in personal terms when he wrote 'Of His Majesty's receiving the News of the Duke of Buckingham's Death', though there is a certain ambivalence in the 'best pattern' he can select for the event—Achilles' grief over the death of Patroclus.

The satiric impulse in Donne is not exhausted in his formal Satires. It appears strongly in the Elegies, and frequently in the Songs and Sonets. 'The Will', for example, is in the tradition of the medieval 'Will and Testament' poems, and lines like

> My constancie I to the planets give;
> My truth to them, who at the Court doe live;
> Mine ingenuity and opennesse,
> To Jesuites. . . .

will later find echoes in Oldham. But although Donne is everywhere dramatic, he is always dramatizing himself. He never creates fully realized characters and subdues himself to them. To this extent Donne's satire is an end, not a beginning, and it is left to Marston to extend the satiric impulse into the theatre and give it a more personal context of judgement. James Sutherland writes:

> The more usual Elizabethan idea of satire is to be found in such misanthropic characters as Shakespeare's Thersites and Apemantus who rail and snarl so bitterly in the contemporary drama; rough-tongued, honest, sardonic fellows who mouth their 'taunting gyrds, and glikes and gibes' with all the appearance, to use a modern colloquialism, of 'putting on an act'.

This is true, so far as it goes, but Thersites' is not the only voice, and it is not difficult to discriminate among the chorus. Marston's Malevole, whose speech is described as 'halter-worthy at all hours', lacerates the corrupt court in Thersites' vein, but he commands a far wider range of satiric utterance than any of Shakespeare's Greeks. He can 'rail and snarl' when required, but he has a more subtle attitude to the world:

> . . . I'll live lazily, rail upon authority, deny kings' supremacy in things indifferent, and be a pope in mine own parish.   (II. v)

Marston has developed from the formality of his verse satires through the freedom offered by the dramatic mode. Malevole is no longer the simple passive figure railing against the human state; he has become the critic involved in his society, the mask for Altofronto in a community where everyone is disguised. Marston's other satiric characters vary this theme. Hercules, in *The Fawn*, abandons the role of the 'rough-tongued, honest, sardonic fellow' altogether, and makes the satiric point by blatantly practising the vices he is concerned to expose. In *The Dutch Courtesan* there is no trace of the 'satyr figure' at all; the criticism is pervasive and relational, clear enough in the gulling of Mulligrub, but with less obvious moral bearings in the figure of Franceschina, the whore. The freedom afforded by the dramatic method is fully exploited in the diversification of the critical spirit, especially in the variations played upon the theme of the critic in society. Yet although the possibilities for invective and personal abuse are given free rein in each of Marston's 'comicall satyres', the one element common to each satirist's stance is the sceptical attitude adopted towards mankind in general. The attack is non-specific. The plays are set among the civilities of the town, or in the courts of princes, in places where men act out their most sophisticated rituals, and yet Malevole makes the secure, central judgement when he says:

> Man is the slime of this dung-pit, and princes are the governors of these men; for, for our souls, they are as free as emperors, all of one piece; there goes but a pair of shears betwixt an emperor and the son of a bagpiper. . . .   (IV. v)

This note is often sounded in the first decade of the seventeenth century. It is Hamlet's vision of the world as 'a foul and pestilent congregation of vapours', his picture of man as 'this quintessence of dust', his realization that

> Imperious Caesar, dead and turn'd to clay,
> Might stop a hole to keep the wind away.

Man delights them not, no, nor woman neither, for Bosola describes
humanity to the Duchess of Malfi just before her murder:

> Thou art but a box of worm seed, at best, but a salvatory of green
> mummy: what's this flesh? a little cruded milk, fantastical puff-
> paste . . .   (IV. ii)

The satire is directed against human pretensions, and it takes its fine
edge from its setting in princes' palaces, and from the fact that the
satirists are themselves functional members of the grand society.

But satire feeds not only upon kings. Beaumont, Dekker and especially Middleton show how middle-class and 'citizen' values and qualities
are constantly the objects of the sceptic's scrutiny. Yet the greatest of
these is Jonson. The sustained acts of the creative imagination in which
he develops his critique of the acquisitive society are the closest we can
get in scale and in vision to the worlds of Horace and Juvenal. *Volpone*
opens with the fully ironic presentation of its crucial image:

> Good morning to the day; and, next, my gold!
> Open the shrine, that I may see my saint.

And the play never relaxes its ironic grasp. The stricture upon greed is
developed through the formal devices of the plot, through the language, even through the rich ambiguities of the characters' names. Similarly the basic image of *The Alchemist*, the metaphor of change, is
elaborated through its mercantile, social and religious mutations.
Subtle's description of Mammon, 'If his dream last, he'll turn the age
to gold', is satiric in a fully dramatic way, in that it permits the validity
of the paradisal vision while stressing its practical unattainability—the
audience realize full well that the resonant line is a fake alchemist's
ironic jibe at a foolish knight. The power and complexity of Jonson's
dramatic satire can be gauged by comparing the plays with his more
formal verse satires and epigrams. In these Jonson is writing in the
tradition of the Elizabethan satirists, and the criticism is usually maintained at a level of generality which castigates the folly of a type.
Epigram XV, 'On Court-worme' is representative:

> All men are wormes: but this no man. In silke
> 'Twas brought to court first wrapt, and white as milke;
> Where, afterwards, it grew a butter-flye: ·
> Which was a cater-piller. So t'will dye.

Even in the most virulent of his poems, 'An Execration upon Vulcan', Jonson maintains the air of patrician impartiality. But in the plays the satiric persona is liberated by the dramatic character, though Jonson's stage-figures are not 'characters' in the obvious sense of the word. Volpone, Mosca, Surly, Mammon, Subtle, they are all delicate compromises between realism and abstraction. It is only within the walls of Lovewit's house that Subtle and Face have any existence; they are simply not credible in any other society. Jonsonian dramatic satire represents a forward movement from the type-dominated poems of Marston, Hall and Donne because in the plays the concept of individualized character is permitted to develop. Jonson's art maintains a universal dimension because his people are more than unique individuals, and his criticism of society has the benefit of both worlds; but the new direction in which the satiric impulse was moving was beginning to focus attention on the unrepeatable quality of human personality, and the ultimate responsibility of every man for his own deeds.

Jonson's dramatic satire encompassed most aspects of social life, but it remained resolutely non-political. It may be that the swift retribution which followed the satire on the Scots in *Eastward Ho!* had a deterrent effect upon its authors, but the fact remains that it was not until 1624 that Middleton's *A Game at Chess* brought contemporary politics squarely on to the public stage. The play ran for nine days, the first long run in English theatrical history, and only after thousands had seen it did the authorities close it down and issue a warrant for Middleton's arrest. Among other things the play commented fairly boldly on the rash visit of Prince Charles and the Duke of Buckingham to Madrid, in 1623, an event which Richard Corbett had written in on in 'A Letter to the Duke of Buckingham, being with the Prince in Spaine', a piece of place-seeking servility which many of his contemporaries reproved. The play and the poem are evidence of the unpopularity of Buckingham's policies, but they also illustrate the two distinct kinds of political poetry which developed side by side throughout the seventeenth century. Ruth Nevo has pointed out that political verse is generally thought of as being confined to satire, but this is only one side of the coin:

The finding of ways to write serious verse about political events, personalities, or issues was a highly complex, even complicated task. Great difficulties were encountered when such literary traditions as were available were applied to contemporary material; and these difficulties were aggravated by the connection, found in practice to be inevitable, between two such opposing impulses and such opposing styles as the panegyrical and the satiric.

Panegyric is not our present concern, but its presence must not be overlooked, and its growing importance is evidence of the new quality of satirical writing. Satire is no longer a fashionable academic exercise, re-enacting the gestures of the classical poets. It becomes part of a dialectical search for truth, and, as such, it must 'respond to the stresses and pressures of actual events in a political context'. New directions were not quickly established, no single commanding voice emerged to set the tone, and in the years between the death of Buckingham and the outbreak of the Civil War there are many subjects and many styles. The vagaries of satire may be illustrated from the work of a minor, uninfluential writer, Ralph Knevet. His *Stratiotikon*, a poem of some two thousand lines, was published in 1628. It is concerned, like Ascham's *Toxophilus* (1545) and Barnabe Rich's *Alarme to England* (1578), with the need for military training in England, stressing the importance of constant vigilance and a well-prepared militia. In satirizing the lily livers of his countrymen Knevet's lines recall Tudor values, and appeal to the standards of the classical age:

> Great evils, with great honours be combin'd
> And march like Pikes, with Muskets interlin'd
> Our Postures are French conges, and few can
> Know Mounsieur, from an English Gentleman:
> So like are we to them, so frenchify'd
> In garbes and garment: but great God forbid,
> That our newfangled change should ere declare
> Such sad events, as did the Scimitar
> Of King *Darius*. . . .   (504–12)

This is simple, drum and trumpet patriotism, lit from behind by the glories of the past. Three years later, in 1631, Knevet is concerned to satirize the expediency and amorality of contemporary politics in a more oblique, sophisticated way in his play *Rhodon and Iris*. In Act V, scene ii, Martagon rebukes Cynosbatus:

> Thou art too ceremonious for a politician,
> And too superstitious: our duties 'tis to judge
> Of the effect as it concernes the state of our affaires,
> And not to looke backe on the meanes by which 'twas wrought.

He is unfit to rule a Civill state
That knowes not how in some respects to favour
Murther, or treason, or any other sinne
Which that subtill animall, call'd man,
Doth openly protest against, for this end,
That he may more freely act it in private,
As his occasions shall invite him to't.   (1511–21)

The thought is as modern as *Il Principe*, the voice almost the voice of Webster's Flamineo.

The increasing pressure and urgency of political events brought about the rapid diversification of satire. At the turn of the century the chief vehicles were the formal verse 'satire', modelled on Horace, Juvenal or Persius, and the epigram, whose mentor was Martial. By the time of the Civil War the range was extended to include the prose 'Character', the diurnall, the political ballad and even the newspaper editorial. Satire was immediate, localized, personal, and its effect was gauged for the moment, not for all time. There was less agonized exploration of the eternal verities, more concern with specific social issues. As Douglas Bush puts it, there was a 'sense of security . . . attained partly by turning back from the troubled explorations of the individual soul to the accepted sententiousness of public occasions and general experience'. But the public occasions were almost always seen in terms of the public figure, men were appraised not *sub specie aeternitatis* but by their functions and their performance. This is clear from the mixed nature of the 'characters' in a collection like Sir Francis Wortley's *Characters and Elegies* (1646), where 'The Character of His Royall Majestie' and 'The Character of the Queen' appear alongside the more traditional pictures of 'A True English Protestant', 'A Jesuit' and 'A Sharking Committee-man'. But, as Ruth Nevo points out, the first of the 'characters' to be adapted to purely political purposes was Cleveland's *The Character of a London-Diurnall* which appeared in 1644, and was afterwards included in most editions of his poems. One of the most striking characteristics of this prose piece is the cryptic quality of its imagery, 'wit stenographied', which places it immediately in the tradition of the 'strong-lined', 'metaphysical' poets, and shows how, quite suddenly, political satire has found an appropriate utterance:

A *Diurnall* is a puny Chronicle, scarce pin-feather'd with the wings of time: It is an History in *Sippets*; the English *Iliads* in a Nut-shell;

the *Apocryphal* Parliaments booke of *Maccabees* in single sheets. It would tire a Welch pedigree, to reckon how many aps 'tis remov'd from an Annal: For it is of that Extract; onely of the younger House, like a Shrimp to a Lobster.

The power of such writing is obvious, its refusal to make concessions to the slow-witted or the uninformed, its arrogant assumption of the right to make contemptuous judgements, establish an invincible tone for the Royalist pamphleteers. Its effect was immediate. It was reprinted several times within a year or so, it provoked a number of furious replies from Parliamentarian journalists, and it was flattered by a host of imitations. At the centre of the piece, and probably the real reason for it, stands the jeering 'character' of Cromwell. Cleveland had long been his enemy. The Preface to the 1677 edition, *Clievelandi Vindiciae*, reports that he had strongly opposed Cromwell's election as Burgess for the town of Cambridge, and when the vote was passed 'he said with much passionate Zeal, That single Vote had ruined both Church and Kingdom.' In *The Character of a London-Diurnall* he expands upon the sentiment:

> This *Cromwell* is never so valorous, as when he is making Speeches for the Association, which neverthelesse he doth somewhat ominously, with his neck awry, holding up his eare, as if he expected *Mahomets Pidgeon* to come, and prompt him: He should be a Bird of prey too, by his bloody beake: his nose is able to try a young Eagle, whether she be lawfully begotten. But all is not Gold that glisters: What we wonder at in the rest of them, is naturall to him; to kill without Blood-shed: For most of his Trophees are in a Church-Window; when a Looking-Glasse would shew him more Superstitition: He is so perfect a hater of Images, that he hath defaced Gods in his owne Countenance: If he deale with Men, it is when he takes them napping in an old Monument: Then downe goes dust and ashes. And the stoutest Cavalier is no better. O brave *Oliver!* Times voyder, Subsizer to the Wormes; in whom Death, that formerly devoured our Ancestors, now chewes the Cud. . . .

Anthony à Wood praised Cleveland for his 'high panegyrics and smart satyrs', and it is important to realize that the obverse of his phillipic against Cromwell is his praise of Prince Rupert:

> Where providence and valour meet in one,
> Courage so poiz'd with circumspection,

That he revives the quarrell once againe
Of the Soules throne, whether in heart or braine;
And leaves it a drawn match. . . .

Both 'characters' are hyperbolic assaults, ruthlessly personal judgements, carried through upon waves of imagery, buoyed up on
allusions which may be commonplace or recondite. Every point is
directed relentlessly at the target. From the facts of his biography it is
quite likely that Cleveland met Cromwell, and that he was acquainted
with Prince Rupert, yet there is no sense in either the 'character' or the
poem of a specifically personal assessment or engagement. Cleveland's
attitude is detached, observant, judicial, but if we examine his satires
in chronological order it is possible to see how a particular satirical
persona asserts itself, and is then gradually altered by the pressure of
the political, wartime events. Cleveland begins as the notable defender
of authority and order, and ends as the snarling critic of mob-rule.
In the early poems, 'A Dialogue between two Zealots', and 'Smectymnuus' the tone is one of easy, assured authority, condescending to the
follies of the rabble in phrases they could not possibly understand:

> Smectymnuus? The Goblin makes me start:
> I'th'Name of Rabbi *Abraham*, what art?
> *Syriac?* or *Arabick?* or *Welsh?* what skilt?
> Ap all the Bricklayers that *Babell* built.
> Some Conjurer translate, and let me know it:
> Till then 'tis fit for a West-Saxon Poet.

There is no danger in this monster, it is an amusing aberration, a fair-
ground freak:

> Next *Sturbridge-Faire* is *Smec's*; for loe his side
> Into a five fold *Lazar's* multipli'd.

The members of the Westminster Assembly, characterized by Cleveland as a 'fleabitten Synod' in 'The Mixt Assembly', are subjected to
the same haughty contempt:

> Oh that they were in chalk and charcole drawne!
> The Misselany Satyr, and the Fawne,
> And all th' Adulteries of twisted nature
> But faintly represent this ridling feature.

The attack is the same in the later prose piece, 'The Character of a Country Committee-man', where the very real object of hatred is festooned with grotesque allusion to render him harmless:

> He is one of *Mars* his Lay-Elders, he shares in the Government, though a *Non*-conformist to his bleeding Rubrick. He is the like Sectary in Arms, as the Platonick is in Love; keeps a fluttering in Discourse, but proves a Haggard in the Action.

But the changes in the Royalist fortunes bring about a change in Cleveland's tone. The earlier satires, for all their curt wit, for all their lofty allusion to a world of certain values in which the Parliamentarians were interlopers, have a strong element of playfulness, and are based on a sure assumption that folly will eventually destroy itself. When events made it clear that this faith would not be fulfilled both the satirist's role and his style underwent painful change. He could no longer pose as, in Edward Phillips' phrase, 'the first, if not only, Eminent Champion in Verse against the Presbyterian Party', and arrogant contempt is disarmed by defeat. Alexander Brome chronicled the collapse of the Royalist cause in a series of increasingly sad little drinking songs, which even the Restoration could not sweeten:

> We have ventur'd our estates,
> And our liberties and lives,
> For our Master and his mates,
> And been toss'd by cruel fates. . . .

Cleveland went the clean contrary way. As the scene grew darker his verse became more cryptic, more impenetrable, as if only the strongest-twisted threads of bitter burlesque could match the tragic absurdity of the times. When King Charles escaped from Oxford disguised as a servant, on 27 April, 1646, Cleveland could no longer sustain the scourger's role. His poem 'The King's Disguise', although he twice revised it later, was probably written very soon after the event, and the unrevised version makes poignantly clear the agony of the poet's position, forced to record the satirist's judgement upon the King who has betrayed his sovereignty:

> And why a Tenant to this vile disguise,
> Which who but sees blasphemes thee with his eyes?
> My twins of light within their pent-house shrinke,
> And hold it their Allegeance to winke.

Oh for a State-distinction to arraigne
Charles of high Treason 'gainst my Soveraigne.   (1–6)

The poem lurches on, through a long series of tortured catachreses,
to a final, hideously apt, Old Testament analogy:

But oh! he goes to *Gibeon*, and renewes
A league with mouldy bread, and clouted shooes.

The detached, judicial observer has disappeared, one has only to
compare Cleveland's poem with Vaughan's on the same subject to
enforce the point. So far as we can tell Cleveland was silent on the
subject of the King's execution. Many poems were written about it,
and several were attributed to him, but none is likely to be genuine. It
is what one would expect. The latest of his satires, 'The Hue and Cry
after Sir John Presbyter', was probably written between 1647 and 1649,
and it shows the final stage of his retreat into barbed obscurity, armed
at every point against the new hierarchy of handicrafts:

This stating *Prelacy*, the *Classick* Rout,
That spake it often, ere it spake it out.
 So by an Abbyes Scheleton of late,
 I heard an Eccho supererogate
 Through imperfection, and the voice restore
 As if she had the hicop or'e and or'e.
Since they our mixt Diocesans combine
Thus to ride double in their Discipline,
That Paul's shall to the Consistory *call*
A Deane *and* Chapter *out of* Weavers-Hall,
Each at the Ordinance for to assist
With the five thumbs *of his* groat-changing *Fist.*

Some of the methods of the early satires are still discernible: the
reductive comparison of the 'hicop', the recondite frame of allusion, the
contempt, but the five-thumbed monster of the Classick Rout is a
very different beast from Smectymnuus. Cleveland can no longer
render it harmless by describing it as grotesque. In 'The Mixt Assembly'
he could display the absurdity of the rebels by evoking allusively the
richnesses of the world of order and decorum which they threatened,
but in 'The Hue and Cry' the point of comparison is a ruined abbey,
and the only opposing voice is an echo.

Cleveland's is a poetry of defiance and defeat, but his verse has unmistakable power. Part of his strength derives from his allegiance to the metaphysical manner (though he burlesques that manner superbly in 'A Hecatomb to His Mistresse'). He writes for a selected, educated, coterie audience, and he would have approved Jasper Mayne's remark 'We are thought wits, when 'tis understood.' Cleveland's achievement was to raise the status of satire by giving it both a new personal directness of attack and an allusive mode which permitted sophistication and a strenuous intelligence to prosper.

In a period of such political urgency Cleveland's manner found many imitators. There were some who adopted his attitudes, like John Quarles, who wrote in 'The Authors Farewell to England', published in *Regale Lectum Miseriae*, 1649, lines which have Cleveland's hauteur with none of his wit:

> . . . I cannot stoop so low,
> To be subordinate to *them*, I know
> Are but *inferiors*, though they have of late
> Converted *Monarchy* into a *State*.

Others, many others, took over his image-ridden style, and loaded every rift with allusion. Prominent among these is the mysterious R. Fletcher, who published *Ex Otio Negotium* in 1656, and about whom almost nothing is known. Sometimes the imitation is craven, as when he writes on that well-worn satirical theme 'The Publick Faith':

> Stand off my Masters: 'Tis your pence a piece,
> *Jason*, *Medea*, and the golden Fleece;
> What side the line, good Sir? *Tygris*, or *Po!*
> *Lybia? Japan? Whisk?* or *Tradinktido?*
> *St. Kits!* St. *Omer;* or St. *Margaret's* Bay?
> *Presto* begon? or come aloft? What way?

This is an absurd exaggeration of Cleveland's 'Upon Sir Thomas Martin', but Fletcher can write more trenchantly in Cleveland's vein. The Committees which proliferated under the Commonwealth are shrewdly observed in his poem 'A Committee':

> Cast *Knaves* my *Masters*, Fortune guide the chance,
> No packing I beseech you, no by-glance
> To mingle Pairs, but fairly shake the Bag,
> Cheats in their Spheres like subtil spirits wag.

But Fletcher is only one amongst a host. The satires in Thomas Weaver's *Songs and Poems of Love and Drollery*, 1654, include one on

John Williams, Archbishop of York, which was long taken to be Cleveland's, and with good reason. Thomas Jordan's *A Royal Arbor of Loyal Poesie*, published in 1664 but containing poems written much earlier, is clearly indebted to Cleveland; and the section of Satires in Robert Heath's *Clarastella*, 1650, betrays his influence time after time. All these poets write openly and virulently on public, political events, they name names, and they attack living targets. The satirists of the Civil War and the Commonwealth period are not interested in chastising vice and folly in general or typical terms; they pillory 'King Oliver' or 'King Pym'.

The Parliamentarians and the leaders of the Commonwealth found few satirists to champion their cause. There were some like the notorious Payne Fisher, known as 'Cromwell's Poet Laureate', and one of the most shameless turncoats of his age, who would attack anything for money, but they were few and uninfluential. There were plenty of prose pamphleteers ready with invective against the vacillations and inanities of King Charles, but only one poet wrote satire of any stature in the republican cause: John Milton. He announces a theory of satire in 1642 in the *Apology for Smectymnuus*. It is important to remind ourselves that this pamphlet has no connection with Cleveland's poem, but is a direct confrontation with Joseph Hall, who began the pamphlet war over Smectymnuus and had published the (by now) outdated *Virgidemiarum . . . The first three books of tooth-lesse Satyrs, the three last Bookes of byting Satyres*, in 1598. Milton claims high authority for satiric writing. Jesus Christ, he points out, had many ways of teaching, and spoke sometimes 'with bitter and ireful rebukes, if not teaching, yet leaving excuseless those his wilful impugners'—a good point, which seems to have eluded other theorists like Sidney, and Casaubon and Ben Jonson. Following the divine exemplar Milton concludes that 'there may be a sanctified bitterness against the enemies of truth', and adds Aristotle to his authorities when he claims:

> For a satire as it was born out of a tragedy, so ought to resemble his parentage, to strike high, and adventure dangerously at the most eminent vices among the greatest persons, and not to creep into every blind tap-house, that fears a constable more than a satire.

He goes on to address himself directly to Hall's satires, and to demolish the distinction of the title-page:

> But that such a poem should be toothless, I still affirm it to be a bull [i.e. blunder], taking away the essence of that which it calls itself.

H

For if it bite neither the persons nor the vices, how is it a satire? And if it bite either, how is it toothless? So that toothless satires are as much as if he had said toothless teeth.

The majority of Milton's own satire is located in the prose pamphlets, and in general it lives up to the ideas expressed in the *Apology*, especially in its bitter and ireful rebukes. It is easy to pay too much attention to Milton's command of colloquial and vulgar language in these 'occasional' pieces, and to overlook the high seriousness of his subjects. He does indeed 'strike high', and his tone can be proportionately lofty. In the fourth chapter of *Eikonoklastes*, he rails delicately against that part of the so-called 'King's Book', *Eikon Basilike*, which deals with tumults:

> We have here, I must confess, a neat and well-couched invective against tumults, expressing a true fear of them in the author; but yet so handsomely composed, and withal so feelingly, that, to make a royal comparison, I believe Rehoboam the son of Solomon could not have composed it better.

Rehoboam, we may recall, sent his servant Adoram to reduce his rebellious people to reason, but the people killed Adoram and attacked the king, who promptly fled with his attendants to Jerusalem. Earlier in *Eikonoklastes* Milton had dealt brilliantly with the relationship between King Charles and his servant, Strafford. Milton's few satires in verse, 'On the New Forcers of Conscience' and the two sonnets on *Tetrachordon*, are well-known and appreciated, but the range, the subtlety, and the power of his satirical prose still awaits proper recognition.

To focus attention upon the figures of Cleveland and Milton is, of course, to ignore others. There is a great deal of fine satirical writing to be found in the work of Suckling; Cowley's 'The Puritan and the Papist' and 'Poem on the Late Civil War' contain stringent and witty criticism of contemporary events; and Denham, in 'A Western Wonder' or 'News from Colchester', looks with a cheerful, mocking eye on the excesses of his time. Despite Saintsbury's edition of his poems in the third volume of *Minor Poets of the Caroline Period* the achievement of Nathaniel Whiting, as an anticipator of the mock-heroic mode, has gone largely unregarded, and his *Albino and Bellama* is still unread. Whiting's concern is with the exploitable absurdities of the heroic-romantic epic, and his manner recalls the elegance of

Marlowe's *Hero and Leander* just as it looks forward to Byron's *Don Juan*. Don Fuco, the rejected suitor, exclaims against those heroes who risked their lives for love:

> The Thracian harper was a silly ass,
> That for his wife passed through the Stygian stench,
> The clubman's foolery did his surpass,
> That spun and carded for a Lydian wench.
> The Greeks were fools that for a light-skirt strumpet
> Chang'd the still viol to a loud-mouth'd trumpet.

Yet Whiting is criticizing the follies of literature, while Suckling, Cowley and Denham are only part-time satirists; they lack the comprehensive vision, the commitment to a cause, that characterizes the work of Milton and Cleveland. They write about politics only incidentally, and the whole development of the satirical impulse in this period is towards engagement with the dire events which were breaking an old world and labouring to create a new.

Perhaps the most unexplored area of seventeenth-century literature is the territory of the poetical miscellany. Scores of them appeared in the first half of the century, ranging from the severely academic productions of the universities, written to celebrate some such sociopolitical event as the birth of another royal child, or the king's happy return from a journey, and as often written in Latin and Greek as in English, to the cheerful collections of occasional, erotic and simply amusing poems like *Wit and Drollery*, 1656, *Witts Recreations*, 1640, or *Parnassus Biceps*, 1656. Before the Civil War poems on political themes appear regularly in many of these collections, but under the Commonwealth, not surprisingly, political comment went underground, and the satires upon the government were usually printed (if they were printed at all) as broadsheets. In the sixteen fifties the miscellanies tend to have titles like *Sportive Wit*, 1656, or *Wit Restor'd*, 1658, and to exclude poems like Sir John Birkenhead's hilarious 'The Four-Legg'd Elder', which appeared as a broadside in 1647, and was not reprinted until thirty years later. But satires, burlesques, invective and lampoon continued to flourish, and at the Restoration we are faced with an outburst of political poetry: on the one hand, the loyal panegyrics written in 1660 to celebrate the monarch's return, and on the other, the satires against the Parliamentarians composed during the previous twenty years, which could now enjoy a peaceful and profitable market. The best of these poems were published in 1662 under the title *Rump: Or an Exact Collection of the Choycest Poems and Songs relating to the Late Times. By the most Eminent Wits from Anno 1639 to Anno 1661.* The Preface to the Reader begins:

> Thou hast here a Bundle of Rodds; not like those of the Roman Consulls, for these are signes of a No-Government.

And it goes on to give reasons for the anonymity of the contents:

> You have many Songs here, which were never before in Print: We need not tell you whose they are; but we have not subjoyned any Authors Names; heretofore it was unsafe, and now the Gentlemen conceive it not so proper.

The titles alone give a fair indication of the matter: 'Pym's Juncto. 1640', 'The Parliaments Pedigree', 'Englands Woe', 'Pym's Anarchy', 'The Publique Faith', 'Cromwell's Panegyric' and so on. There are ballads, songs and several exercises in stock themes like the mock-Litany, and the Petition of the Poets. Denham, Cleveland and Fletcher are among the authors represented, and the attacks are relentlessly personal. It is not ideas that are wrong but men who are fools and knaves. *The Rump* reprints one of the many poems on the fart let in the Parliament House, a subject which gives wide scope for the naming of names:

> Quoth Sir *Henry Poole* 'twas an audacious trick
> To fart in the face of the Body Politick.
> Sir *Jerome* in Folio swore by the Mass
> This Fart was enough to have blown a Glass:
> Quoth then Sir *Jerome* the Lesser, such an Abuse
> Was never offer'd in *Poland* nor *Pruce*.

Such writing eschews all ethical concerns, and leaves the moral earnestness of Juvenal far behind. The satirist's task is to discredit and destroy living men, to frustrate their politics, and to cast a-down the proud.

    There are other retrospective collections of the period's political verse, and among the most important are *The Posthumous Works of Mr. Samuel Butler*, 1715–17, and *The Genuine Remains in Verse and Prose of Mr. Samuel Butler*, 1759. The former contains a great deal of verse which is not by Butler, but, significantly, has been attached to his name. Some poems, in the *Posthumous Works* especially, are more savage than anything *The Rump* printed. 'Upon the Storm at the Death of Oliver Cromwell', for example, opens with unusual violence:

> Then take him devil! hell his soul doth claim,
> In storms as loud as his king-murthering fame.
> His cheating groans and tears has shak'd this Isle,
> Cleft *Britain's* oak, for *Britain's* funeral pile.

In the seventeenth century any poem might be fathered on to an author whose name might give it a chance of survival—the 1653 edition of the poems of Beaumont is the *locus classicus*—but it is still ironic that a poem of such bitterness and violence should have been attributed to the author of *Hudibras*. Butler's great poem has been much misunderstood. As recently as 1931 George Kitchin described it as an 'immortal burlesque' and claimed that it 'belongs to the same school of burlesque as *The Knight of the Burning Pestle*'. It is far more than this. John Wilders, in the brilliant introduction to his edition of *Hudibras*, emphasizes the complexity of Butler's satirical attitude:

> . . . the age itself induced in him the distinctive tensions of the satirist: a sense of the opposition between the ideal and the actual, between what ought to be and what is. Hence he was impelled, like most satirists, to reveal the reality which he believed to lie behind traditional opinion and popular superstition. In *Hudibras* he attempted to show that scholarship was often no more than futile pedantry, that religion was commonly a pretext for the acquisition of power or wealth, that romantic love was generally a cover for self-interest, and that military honour was the reward for barbarism. . . . He applies to the objects of his satire the same sceptical attitude which pervades the notebooks. . . .

The key word is 'sceptical', and it is his scepticism which divides Butler from the satirists who preceded him. He sees as much proneness to error and delusion in the experimental science of Bacon as in the medieval, religious world-view; his allegiances are with Davenant and Hobbes. Almost the only positive quality which emerges from *Hudibras* is the sense that the Christian faith is essentially a reasonable and unenthusiastic belief, delicately poised because easily perverted by the churches, sects and mysticisms it so easily breeds. In its literary form *Hudibras* is an attack on the epic and the heroic tradition of conduct which the epics upholds. In this sense it is parasitic upon *The Faerie Queen*, questioning the relevance of chivalry and the sufficiency of

H*

'honour'. The strength of the poem lies in its superb gallery of portraits, and in the rigorous sustaining of the unique sceptical viewpoint.
The Pyrrhonic eye remains marvellously undeceived by the profusion
of the narrative. Yet this very profusion is also a source of weakness.
Hudibras is a rambling poem, striving to include in its vision all the
multifarious possibilities of human error. The proliferation of incident,
idea and comment becomes eventually uncontrollable. Any analysis of
the three parts makes it clear that Part I is more successful than the
other two, and this is partly due to the fact that in Part I the objects of
attack are comparatively simple, uncomplicated by anything that has
gone before. The 'characters' are presented in firm, vigorous portraits.
The description of Hudibras's faith is an example:

> For his *Religion* it was fit
> To match his Learning and his Wit:
> 'Twas *Presbyterian* true blew,
> For he was of that stubborn Crew
> Of Errant Saints, whom all men grant
> To be the true Church *Militant*:
> Such as do build their Faith upon
> The holy Text of *Pike* and *Gun*;
> Decide all Controversies by
> Infallible *Artillery*;
> And prove their Doctrine Orthodox
> By Apostolick *Blows* and *Knocks*.

The qualities described in the man are developed in the action. His
learning leads him instantly astray, his stubborness lands him in the
stocks, his militancy is the cause of his intolerant interventions, and all
his arguments are of the knock-down variety. But whereas Butler can
sustain a narrator's scepticism he cannot develop his concept of character over the full length of the three parts. By the first canto of Part
Three the knight is no longer a living personality; he has become simply
a lay figure, and his controlling part in the action shrinks accordingly
while other matters assume control. The ultimate failure of *Hudibras*
is a failure of dramatic art. The poet dominates his creatures; the Knight
and his Squire cannot develop lives of their own. *Hudibras* was written
over a long period, probably between 1658 and 1677, and in a sense it
stands apart from the development of satire in those twenty years.
Butler is a spectator at the political arena, and seems unaware of the
way the religious issues of the age become entangled with, and

eventually merge into, the secular policies. He is not sufficiently a disciple of Hobbes to see how pervasive his master's influence had become in a very short time. To chart the distance between Butler and Hobbes we need only compare Hobbes's ideas on speech in Part I, chapter iv, of *Leviathan* with a passage in *Hudibras*, I. iii, where Butler is indebted in almost every phrase to Cleveland—who died in the very year in which the poem was probably begun:

> Lay-elder, *Simeon* to *Levi*,
> Whose little finger is as heavy
> As loyns of Patriarchs, Prince-Prelate,
> And Bishop-secular. This Zelot
> Is of a mungrel, diverse kind,
> *Clerick* before, and *Lay* behind;
> A Lawless *linsie-woolsie brother*,
> Half of one Order, half another.

The language is taken over from an age of certitudes, and Butler's scepticism can offer no emotional substitute for faith.

The panegyric chorus at the Restoration was soon muted by events. The defeats of the Dutch Wars, and their climax in the ignominious burning of the English ships at Chatham, the unpopular legislation embodied in the Corporation Act, the Conventicle Act, the Five-Mile Act, the affront to Puritan sensibilities offered by court profligacy, the uneasy and uncertain rule of Charles's chief minister, Edward Hyde, Earl of Clarendon, all these were swiftly depressive to the panegyric tone. But the malaise had a deeper seat. The image of 'the King restored' was soon seen to be insufficient to explain the political situation. The court had returned, but the old court culture was dead. The Acts and Ordinances of the last years of Charles I and the Commonwealth effectively limited the new King's prerogative, and prevented monarchical rule. Parliament had been restored, after Cromwell's various constitutional experiments, and it was a powerful force. The Church of England had been restored, but much of its glory (and its confidence) departed with the Puritan secession. John Freke looked back at this period in his 'History of Insipids', 1676, and summarized the disillusion:

> Chast, pious, prudent, *Charles* the Second,
> The Miracle of thy Restauration,
> May like to that of *Quails* be reckon'd

Rain'd on the Israelitick Nation;
The wisht for Blessing from Heav'n sent,
Became their Curse and Punishment.

It is to this period of disenchantment and national gloom that the satires of Andrew Marvell belong. It seldom seems possible that these poems should have been written by the author of 'On a Drop of Dew' or 'The Garden', but to say that Marvell's satires are undeviatingly mundane is to say nothing to their discredit. They are the work of the Member of Parliament for Hull, and a glance at Margoliouth's edition of the *Letters* shows how completely Marvell subdued himself to the demands of his job. A letter to Mayor Lambert, in 1668, is typical:

> *Gentlemen my very worthy friends*
> The Bill of 300000ˡˡ upon wines proceeds still but many publick businesses intervening we shall be much straitned neither do I belieue we can finish it and the rest within the time limited us by his Majesty. To day the Bill for the City of London was committed which contains further directions for the building, large powers to be invested in the mayor & Aldermen to that purpose, and more years then formerly allotted for that worke. . . .

And so on. The letters are almost a diary of the day-by-day business of the House, but a diary with very little comment or judgement; they report the events which the satires were written to evaluate. Since the Yale University Press began to publish the editions of *Poems on Affairs of State* it has been possible to open a much deeper perspective for the study of Marvell's satires, and to see that they belong to a genre of political poetry which includes the work of men like Dryden, Rochester and Oldham on the one hand, and Buckingham, Mulgrave, Sedley, Etherege and Savile on the other. The majority of these poets had a personal concern in the practical affairs of government; they were capable of making political decisions and (in various ways) influencing the conduct of affairs. And since politics is the science of the possible, the moral course of early Restoration satire is set in the direction of expediency rather than idealism. Dryden alone transcended the boundaries, but *Absalom and Achitophel* was not published until 1681. Marvell's most significant contributions to the genre lie in his development of the idea of a 'character', and in what Ruth Nevo calls 'a serious epic intention' in poems like 'Last Instructions to a Painter'.

The period of Marvell's satires coincided with the most mature work of the greatest of the Restoration portrait painters, Sir Peter Lely. Lely's rival, Samuel Cooper, tended to work either in small portraits, or, more usually, in miniatures, but the first striking thing about Lely's pictures is their size. The life-size scale carried with it a heroic attitude; indeed, the sonorous use of colour, the rich movement, and the noble poses of his subjects are often heroic fictions, as a comparison of his portrait of the Duke of Lauderdale (c. 1672) with those of Gennari or John Riley will show. Marvell matches this heroic assertion in his 'character' of Douglas, the captain burnt to death on his ship at Chatham, in 'The Loyall Scot':

> Like a glad lover the fierce Flames hee meets
> And tries his first Imbraces in their sheets.
> His shape Exact which the bright flames enfold
> Like the sun's Statue stands of burnisht Gold:
> Round the Transparent fire about him Glowes
> As the clear Amber on the bee doth Close;
> And as on Angells head their Glories shine
> His burning Locks Adorn his face divine.

Marvell uses the heroic concept of character to turn the disaster at Chatham into an immolation, almost an apotheosis, for patriotic and political purposes:

> Noe more discourse of Scotch or English Race
> Nor chaunt the fabulous hunt of Chivy Chase:
> Mixt in Corinthian Mettall at thy Flame
> Our nations Melting thy Colossus Frame,
> Shall fix a foot on either neighbouring Shore
> And Joyn those Lands that seemed to part before.

We may take this gilded and ennobled character as a point of comparison for Marvell's fully satiric and reductive portraits. In 'Third Advice to a Painter' (which I accept as Marvell's) an anti-heroic spirit is at work. The poem recounts the disastrous naval battle of 1–4 June, 1666, and at least part of the blame is fixed upon the commander, George Monck, Duke of Albemarle. Pepys records, 'The Duke himself had a little hurt in his thigh, but signified little'; Marvell curtails the episode of any hint of heroic nobility:

> . . . But most with story of his hand or thumb
> Conceal (as Honor would) his Grace's bum,
> When the rude bullet a large collop tore

> Out of that buttock never turn'd before.
> Fortune, it seem'd, would give him by that lash
> Gentle correction for his fight so rash,
> But should the Rump perceiv't, they'd say that Mars
> Had now reveng'd them upon Aumarle's arse.

The military disaster is seen in intensely personal terms. The satiric persona which Marvell adopts here sees man stripped of his brief authority and the trappings of his office; the aristocratic assertion of 'Honor', 'His Grace', 'Fortune' and 'Mars' is literally undercut. But it is in his 'judicial' study of character that Marvell foreshadows the achievement of Dryden. He turns from the prosecutor to the judge when, in 'Last Instructions to a Painter' he develops the character of a diplomat, politician and gambler, Henry Jermyn:

> Paint then St. Albans full of soup and gold,
> The new court's pattern, stallion of the old.
> Him neither wit nor courage did exalt,
> But Fortune chose him for her pleasure salt.
> Paint him with drayman's shoulders, butcher's mien,
> Member'd like mules, with elephantine chine.
> Well he the title of St. Albans bore,
> For Bacon never studi'd nature more.
> But age, allaying now that youthful heat,
> Fits him in France to play at cards and treat.

This is magisterial comment, and 'Last Instructions' is undoubtedly Marvell's most serious and extensive exploration of the satiric mode. It records England's part in the Second Dutch War, together with the parliamentary and court affairs between September 1666 and the fall of Clarendon in the following autumn. As George deF. Lord points out 'Although it amounts to a massive indictment of Clarendon's administration and the Court party in the House of Commons, the record is in the main remarkably faithful to the facts in so far as they can be determined from other sources'. The achievement of the poem is its sustained, comprehensive vision, and the way in which it sees the political events in terms of personalities. The superb portraits of Clarendon, Sir William Coventry, the Duke of York and his Duchess, and, above all, Charles's hated mistress the Countess of Castlemaine, are set into a double framework: the narrative account of political events and the 'instructions' to an imaginary painter. The range of tone and reference brings competing worlds into court: the portrait of the politically ineffective Earl of St. Albans is balanced by the picture of Anne Hyde, Duchess of York:

> She perfected that engine, oft assay'd,
> How after childbirth to renew a maid,
> And found how royal heirs might be matur'd
> In fewer months than mothers once endur'd.

The lecherous Countess of Castlemaine immediately precedes the picture of Parliament:

> Draw next a pair of tables op'ning, then
> The House of Commons clatt'ring like the men.
> Describe the Court and Country, both set right
> On opposite points, the black against the white.
> Those having lost the nation at trick-track,
> These now advent'ring how to win it back.

Yet all these details subserve the general theme of political indictment. An alert reading of the poem requires a great deal of factual information, but this in no way disables it as an outstanding satiric achievement, raising the level of satire close to that of epic, and enforcing Marvell's insight that the political and the personal judgements cannot be divorced.

In *Measure for Measure* the Duke says to his deputy:

> Angelo,
> There is a kind of character in thy life,
> That to the observer doth thy history
> Fully unfold. . . .
> Heaven doth with us as we with torches do,
> Not light them for themselves: for if our virtues
> Did not go forth of us, 'twere all alike
> As if we had them not.

This is precisely the discovery which the satires written in the first half of the century make. The obsession with politics is determined by the pressure of historical events, but the interest in character, individual character, derives from the growing belief that the individual personality uniquely influences public events. It is a move away from the view of man as dominated by humours, or stars, or heavenly intervention, towards the realization that we are responsible for our own actions, and answerable for them.

Note

Students of the social situation of poetry will be aware that books on the subject are rare, and for the seventeenth century rarer than for the sixteenth and eighteenth, which have received relatively more attention. Foundation information about the book trade is charted well enough in handbooks like *A Dictionary of Printers and Booksellers in England, Scotland and Ireland, 1557–1640*, edited by R. B. McKerrow (1910); *A Short-Title Catalogue of Books, 1475–1640*, edited by A. W. Pollard and G. R. Redgrave (1926); *A Short-Title Catalogue of Books, 1641–1700*, edited by Donald Wing (1945–51); W. W. Greg, *Some Aspects and Problems of London Publishing between 1550 and 1650* (1956); H. R. Plomer, *A Dictionary of Printers and Booksellers, 1668–1725* (1922). A good starting-point on the general picture is provided readably by Marjorie Plant, *The English Book Trade* (1939), which is now available in a new edition (1966). Similarly, there are some excellent studies of particular genres of literature and the social circumstances of their origin, including Walter Graham, *The Beginnings of English Literary Periodicals, 1665–1715* (1926); D. A. Stauffer, *English Biography before 1700* (1930); Ian Watt, *The Rise of the Novel* (1957); R. S. Crane and F. B. Kaye, *A Census of British Newspapers and Periodicals* (1927); L. C. Knights, *Drama and Society in the Age of Jonson* (1937); Leslie Hotson, *The Commonwealth and Restoration Stage* (1928).

It is more difficult to fill the general framework with accurate information about the attitudes and habits of writers in their social contexts: in general, scholars have been much more interested in content than in context. Phoebe Sheavyn's *The Literary Profession in the Elizabethan Age* (1909) contains much information that is relevant to 1600–40, and I have produced a revised edition (1967). Chapters III–VI of my own *The Profession of English Letters* (1964) refer to the seventeenth century. I have also tried a contextual analysis of one particular author in 'Milton, Diomede and Amaryllis', *A Journal of English Literary History* (December 1955). The best starting-point is still F. W. Bateson's *English Poetry* (1950): see particularly chapters I–IV, VII–VIII.

Individual biographies ought to be a good source of information about social situations, but are usually disappointing, largely because until recently biographers do not seem to have found interesting the questions most fundamental to the social contextualist: which friends read what? what earnings derive from what? how much money did he live on per year? Few have the curiosity of David Masson: *The Life of Milton* (1859–94). But near-contemporary biographies should not be neglected: John Aubrey, Izaak Walton, Gerard Langbaine, Anthony à Wood. Other primary sources, like prefaces to books, familiar letters, etc., are strongly recommended to the patient sleuth.

For the rest, I can only recommend books and articles I have personally found illuminating, studies which, in pursuit of another object, unearthed significant

IX

The Social Situation of Seventeenth-
Century Poetry

J. W. SAUNDERS

★

It is the misfortune of one kind of thinking to see the seventeenth century as a transition period of total conflict sandwiched between two opposed ages of relative clarity and stability, so that its social phenomena may be rationalized as developments en route between the starting-point and an end venue of a completely different kind. The social situation of Tudor poetry is so very clear. The scene was set by Wyatt, Surrey, Bryan, Vaux and the other importers and creators of courtly values in the time of Henry VIII, and after the brief and reactionary interregnum of Mary, it was established by Sidney, Raleigh, Dyer and Greville under Elizabeth's blessing, and upon its stage Shakespeare, Spenser and dozens of fine poets flourished. This was the great age of the courtly amateurs. Because of the need to centralize all forms of social power, to organize a nationalistic and patriotic state as a kind of solar system round the person of the monarch, to create a rich and lively vernacular language and literature which would stand up to continental comparisons, the writers came into London from Stratford or Canterbury or wherever and attached themselves in some way to the court—tutor, secretary, agent, chaplain, groom, lawyer and so on. The man with the gift of golden words travelled the *carrière*

information about specific social situations: A. Alvarez, *The School of Donne* (1961); R. C. Bald, *Donne and the Drurys* (1959); I. A. Shapiro, 'The "Mermaid Club" ', *Modern Language Review* (1950); C. V. Wedgwood, *Poetry and Politics under the Stuarts* (1960); W. R. Mueller, *The Anatomy of Burton's England* (1952); Marchette Chute, *Ben Jonson of Westminster* (1954). In the last analysis, the student of the social situation of poetry finds himself, inevitably, an avid reader of any good index of any book written about the period, an Autolycus snapping up what to many other scholars are 'unconsider'd trifles'.

ouverte aux talents towards social promotion and success. There were
all kinds of difficulties, and personal disaster lurked on every sidewalk,
but writers had no alternatives. The printed-book trade was in its
infancy and subject to strict limits, both political and economic, and
could not support a profession in *belles-lettres*. The public playhouses,
potentially the only viable centres of an independent profession, were
also circumscribed, and part of the courtly system. Poetry was predominantly amateur, was circulated in manuscript within the circle of
friends, and was not committed to authorized print except under
special safeguards. And the qualities of Tudor poetry are those de-
manded by the brilliant courtly society: we find it notably personal,
erotic, egocentric and indeed self-dramatizing, lyrical and gracious,
and above all metaphorical. These poets were essentially actors, playing
out their antic dispositions by hypothesis and make-believe in 'highly-
conceited' verses. Socially, poetry was a grace, an essential part of
courtly converse, a civilized accomplishment and skill; individually, it
was a sense-maker, a way of discussing and fathoming and thinking
about the mysterious phenomena of inconstant experience. It was
natural to civilized and sophisticated Man, in a way that inanimate
Nature could never match. Sidney was emphatic:

> Nature never set foorth the earth in so rich Tapistry as diverse Poets
> have done, neither with so pleasaunt rivers, fruitfull trees, sweete
> smelling flowers, nor whatsoever els may make the too much loved
> earth more lovely: her world is brasen, the Poets only deliver a
> golden.[1]

And this is one end of the seventeenth century.[2]

At the other end of the century, from 1688 through to certainly the
seventeen forties, the equally stable era of the Augustan squirearchy.
Here the scene was set by Waller, the later Milton and Dryden, the
poets recognized in their own day as pioneering a new order, and it
was established by Pope and his generation of contemporaries. Poetry
was now apparently decentralized: no longer dependent exclusively
upon the court and its ramifications, it flourished in every library of
every country home, wherever it might be in the wide countryside,
for the squire needed the poets to assert his cultured civilizedness, as he
needed the Palladian architects and the portrait painters and splendid

[1] *Defence of Poesie*, edited by A. Feuillerat (1923), pp. 8–9.
[2] *Vide* my *Profession of English Letters* (1964), chapters III–V.

composers like Handel. Poetry was also now national and public; the neo-classicists had won their battles about the status of literature, and it was generally recognized that, as in Augustan Rome, the nation esteemed itself by the quality of certain kinds of its writing, among them the high poetry of epic, panegyric, commemoration and cleansing satire. Print was now the normal medium of communication, as was proper for a culture widely disseminated: handsome print in folio and quarto for the armorial bookplates of the squires, and less expensive editions for a widening circle of readers in commerce and the professions. The individual patronage of the sixteenth century has been replaced by corporate patronage, often through the medium of the subscription edition which brought national recognition to Milton, and in addition substantial prosperity to writers like Pope and Prior. In the sixteenth century it would have been considered impertinent and irrelevant for a poet to write for fame and posterity; now fame is the spur and poetry a national duty for all serious writers. And the poetry reflects the values of an age committed to both an aristocracy and an enlightened rationalism: it is well dressed with gentility and punctilio, it has the majesty and dignity of the organ, and it is committed to the qualities of succinctness, clarity and perspicuity, and the figures of reason rather than emotion—paradox, oxymoron, zeugma, antithesis rather than metaphor, simile, symbol, anagogy.

One of the simpler misreadings here of the transit from A to B is to see the Civil Wars as the great divide and catalyst, the means whereby decentralization, dissemination and professionalization became first possible and then proper. On this reading the reign of Charles I is a prelude of deepening conflict between two rival cultures, the reign of Charles II a brief reaction against the irresistible tide, and 1688 the final dateline for the values of the English Renaissance. In point of fact the run of events cannot with truth be so simplified.

It is salutary to note how many things the mannered Tudors and the mannered Augustans had in common: *plus ça change, plus c'est la même chose*. Sidney would have been more at home at Drury Lane watching Addison's *Cato* than at the Globe with *Antony and Cleopatra*, and Spenser would have been a happy member of the court of Pope, approving even the publication of 'familiar letters' and perhaps of juvenilia too. The Renaissance claim for a *divine vis* in poetry would have shocked the medievals; but it was essential in the neo-classic view of poetry shared by the Augustans, and further modified and extended, beyond Dryden and Pope, by Shelley's assumption that poets were 'unacknowledged legislators' and the whole Romantic concept that poets were seers and prophets. There is a steady extension of Sidney's dictum through to the times of Tennyson and Browning, and finding its last expression in Yeats, T. S. Eliot and Dylan Thomas; it is only in our own times that there has been anything like a revolution in the way people think of poets, and it is certainly true that no fundamental change of attitude occurred in the seventeenth century. Moreover, if one looks closely at the professionalization and decentralization of poetry that appears to be the outstanding trend of change after Elizabeth, the more questionable both these terms seem. The court itself, by stages, certainly lost its primacy, but culture remained very much the monopoly of the metropolis right through to our own times, and, *mutatis mutandis*, the system of poet-audience relationships was very similar. London and poetry were really inseparable, partly because the major printing presses and publishing firms stayed in London, for economic now rather than political reasons, and partly because no provincial centre could rival London's attractiveness for the artist. Locations changed within London: the Elizabethans congregated at the great houses, at the Inns of Court, at the playhouses and taverns; the Augustans congregated at the town houses of gentry, at the coffee houses and clubs, and at the playhouses and taverns. There were many more 'centres' and literate people, but the audiences remained organized in metropolitan coteries. Outside London, it is difficult to identify any increase in importance of role and context gained by the country houses of the eighteenth century. The writers who were supported and encouraged at Penshurst by the Sidneys, at Wilton by the Herberts, at Kenilworth by the Dudleys, at Harefield by the Egertons, would have found equivalent centres, but with fellow-writers, with Pope at Twickenham, with Swift in Dublin, with Sterne at Shandy Hall, rather than with noblemen. The identity of the patron, the centres of patronage, have changed, but the function of the intimate circle of colleagues-cum-patrons has remained essentially the same. And the tradition of the amateur died hard. For all Waller's revolutionary work with language and metre, he remained, what Douglas Bush has rightly called him, 'a fluent trifler, the rhymer of a court gazette'; his 1664 publisher says that he wrote 'only to please himself, and such particular persons to whom they were directed'. Swift did not want money for his work, though he would help others capitalize their talents, and saw his poems as 'the product of rage or raillery, whereof some few escape to give offence, or mirth, and the rest are burnt.' Prior saw himself as a 'poet only by accident', and modelled himself on Sedley and Rochester rather than on 'drudge Dryden'. And the attitude of the dilettante is dominant in the careers of later poets like Gray, Collins and Goldsmith.

None of this denies that Augustan poetry was radically different from Tudor poetry; rather, it underlines the need to be quite precise about the particular deficiencies in the Tudor fabric which required change and which indeed begin to change with the poets of 1600 to 1660. And it seems to be the case that the chief fault found in what were ultimately regarded as rather barbarous times was *not* that poetry had been too closely confined to minorities but that, on the whole, it had not been confined enough. At the beginning of the century, there is a curious protest from Michael Drayton, in the preface to *Polyolbion*, published in 1605:

> There is this great disadvantage against me, that it commeth out at this time, when Verses are wholly deduc't to Chambers, and nothing esteem'd in this lunatique Age, but what is kept in Cabinets and must only passe by Transcription.[3]

Drayton was a typical courtly satellite of his time. Of Warwickshire yeoman stock, he served Sir Henry Goodyere and Lucy, Countess of Bedford, and had many patrons in the Midlands, including Anthony Cooke, lord of the manor of Hartshill, and Robert Dudley, the son of Leicester. When Sir Walter Aston was made Knight of the Bath in 1603, for the coronation of James I, he made Drayton an esquire, and the poet sported the title in printed books from 1605, taking up a whole line of print for it. He writes affectionately of the 'shepherds and shepherdesses' with whom he lived on intimate terms in the great country houses, particularly Polesworth in Arden, home of the Goodyeres. But his career went sour on him. Though second only to Spenser in the number of times quoted by Robert Allot in *England's Parnassus* (1600), that most useful barometer of public opinion at the turn of the century, he did not gain the promotion he wanted and died in some penury. He was a sober man, sober enough to be singled out as an exception from the general rule, in *2 Return from Parnassus*,[4] and

---

[3] *Works*, edited by J. W. Hebel (1933), IV. v.
[4] *Three Parnassus Plays*, edited by J. B. Leishman (1949), p. 240.

a man discreet enough to be employed as a secret agent; but he was rebuffed by James, when like Spenser with Elizabeth he sought for substantial recognition, and must have been regarded with some suspicion, to judge from the refusal of a licence for his unexceptionable metrical psalter and from the fact that *Polyolbion* required, it would seem, four licensers. The best evidence we have about the reasons for his failure lie in what he says himself about his literary ambitions, and from these we can see that he was a misfit. For what they were worth to him, he enjoyed all the social contexts of the day: quite apart from his intimacy with courtly life, he was luckier than most with the publishers, finding print on many occasions, for instance for his *Heroical Epistles*, in five editions between 1597 and 1603, and for a collected edition, in five editions between 1605 and 1613; and he was connected with the public playhouse, writing for the Rose between 1597 and 1602. The point seems to be that he wanted a social context *which did not exist at the time.*

He rejected equally the notion that poetry should be 'incloistered' 'in private chambers' 'and by transcription daintly must goe', and the low tastes of the printed-book public. He has a professional contempt for 'private pieces' and does not account them worthy of notice in any account of the age.[5] On the other hand, he has the courtier's contempt for popular printed poetry:

> Base baladry is so belov'd and sought,
> And those brave numbers are put by for naught,
> Which rarely read, were able to awake
> Bodyes from graves . . .
>   . . . but I know, insuing ages shall,
> Raise her againe, who now is in her fall;
> And out of dust reduce our scattered rimes,
> Th'rejected jewels of these slothfull times.[6]

It infuriated him that printed-book readers did not seem to want his beloved *Polyolbion*: they bought 'beastly and abominable Trash (a shame both to our Language and Nation)' and rejected the poetic topography of England—so 'outlandish' and 'unnaturall' were they—on the grounds that 'there is nothing in this Island worth studying

---

[5] *Epistle to Henry Reynolds. Works,* edited by J. W. Hebel (1933), III, pp. 230-1.
[6] *To Master George Sandys. ibid.,* III, p. 208.

for.'[7] 'Soul blinded sots,' he calls them

> . . . that creepe
> In durt, and never saw the wonders of the Deepe.[8]

His view of literature and its worth and dignity was like Spenser's, and he too rested his hopes upon posterity. All the audiences (even the ladies!) saw poetry as ephemeral and lyrical; for the long grave poem, which would last through the generations, there was no audience, or at best a very inadequate and unrewarding one.

Drayton's discontent was very similar to Samuel Daniel's. Daniel complains a good deal: about the carelessness of patrons, about the unscrupulousness of pirate printers, about political restrictions, but he has even fewer real grounds for complaint than Drayton. He occupied an honoured position at court, as Groom of the Chamber, and was accepted as a friend and intimate in so many noble families, with the Herberts, Cliffords, Wriothesleys, Egertons and so on; he had a good and conscientious publisher in Simon Waterson; he did not care much for the public theatre, but he held at one time the key position of Licenser of the Revels. Like Drayton, then, he was connected with the three main audiences of the time. But again he was very unhappy about the context in which longer, graver works might flourish. He seems confident the ladies would read his *Civil Wars*, which is more than Drayton felt about them and *Polyolbion*; but in general people 'neglect, distaste, uncomprehend, disdain'. He was sure about his professional dedication:

> The love I beare unto this holy skill:
> This is the thing that I was borne to doo,
> This is my Scene, this part must I fulfill.[9]

Therefore, though his audience be few, 'that few, is all the world.' One understanding reader is to him 'a Theater large enow'. He too had faith in posterity. Above all he saw the need to extend outwards towards an international audience:

> And who, in time, knowes whither we may vent
> The treasure of our tongue, to what strange shores
> This gaine of our best glory shall be sent,
> T'inrich unknowing Nations with our stores?[10]

---

[7] *ibid.*, IV, p. 391.
[8] *ibid.*, IV, p. 199. [9] *Musophilus* (1599), 949–60, 556–79. [10] *ibid.*

Poets as serious as Spenser, Drayton and Daniel were perhaps in a minority in the early seventeenth century. But it was to this persuasion that Milton belonged, and it was Milton who ultimately set about creating the very audience they lacked. Here was another poet blessed with the best contexts, but who also reached elsewhere.

> Alas! What boots it with uncessant care
> To tend the homely slighted Shepherds trade,
> And strictly meditate the thankles Muse,
> Were it not better don as others use,
> To sport with *Amaryllis* in the shade
> Or with the tangles of *Neaera*'s hair?[11]

The death of Edward King, the overt subject of *Lycidas*, faced Milton with a disillusioning thought: was it really worth while to spend decades preparing himself for his 'trade'; was it not better to follow the courtly fashion and play with poetry for the ladies? The symbolic Amaryllis, Alice Spencer, later the Countess Dowager of Derby, for whom he wrote *Arcades* and for whose grandchildren he wrote *Comus*, and Neaera, another famous patron, Elizabeth Sheffield, wife of the tenth Earl of Ormonde, offered immediate rewards in a life which Milton found not uncongenial: he could play the courtly game as well as any, was a good swordsman, loved plays, knew how to attend a lady and turn a sonnet. He had preferred to withdraw from the court and to embark on a programme of encyclopedic learning which one day would equip him to write the serious poetry he had in him.

> . . . he who would not be frustrate of his hope to write well here-after in laudable things, ought him selfe to bee a true Poem, that is, a composition and patterne of the best and honourablest things; not presuming to sing high praises of heroick men, or famous Cities, unlesse he have in himselfe the experience and the practice of all that which is praise-worthy.[12]

He was not interested in writing for the printed-book market or the public playhouse, any more than he fancied a political career under Charles or an ecclesiastical career under Laud. In the first twenty nine years of his life his only poems to reach print were the Latin lines, *Naturam non pati senium*, privately and anonymously printed at Cam-

[11] *Lycidas*, 64–9.
[12] *An Apology*, (1642). *Life Records of John Milton*, edited by J. M. French, vol. I (1949), pp. 207–8.

bridge for the Commencement of 1628, and the epitaph *On Shake-speare*, prefixed without a name or even initials to the 1632 folio. Henry Lawes persuaded him to have *Comus* published in 1637, but the poem was 'not openly acknowledg'd by the Author' and in the absence of any need for tact, the printers bound up some copies of it with the *Poems* of Thomas Randolph. As with the publication of *Lycidas* in the following year, in a memorial volume, Milton's chief benefit from it was the facility to send copies to friends like Sir Henry Wotton and thus to avoid 'the often Copying of it' in manuscript.

When he visited Italy in the early sixteen forties, Milton was delighted to discover an excitingly new context for writers. At this time every Italian professional man of any note—the civil servants, churchmen, lawyers, doctors, scientists, geographers, philosophers, antiquarians and all kinds of writer including poets—belonged to one or other of the learned academies of *literari*. In Rome alone there were over fifteen such 'clubs', including in their membership over four hundred and fifty writers. The Italians had never heard of this brilliant young Englishman but they invited him to their meetings, and among Gaddi's *Svogliati* and Coltellini's *Apotisti* Milton recited from memory, and to their applause, some of his Latin compositions. He found that thinking men, literary men, were highly respected in their communities, and was flattered to be introduced to Galileo, Grotius, Manso, Frescobaldi, Benmattei, Holstenius and John Diodati. Not only did he now firmly decide to write a British epic, but he began on his return to England to look about for a fit audience, as literary and as committed as the confraternity of writers he had met abroad. By this time the theological quarrels which preceded the Civil Wars were well under way, and Milton became involved in his stream of prose pamphlets, at first anonymously but within very few years openly printing his name. What is more important, the audience he conceived for these pamphlets was not a popular one at all, but an aristocracy of the best minds, at home and abroad:

> I feel myself not as if in a forum or law-court, surrounded only by one people, whether Roman or Athenian, but as if, with nearly all Europe listening, and as it were seated together before and criticising . . . an aggregate of all the meetings and conventions of the gravest men, cities and nations.[13]

[13] *Defensio Secunda* (1654).

He sent out complimentary copies 'ex dono authoris' (Milton was the first writer to prize offprints). He made use of his friends on travels as postmen, Marvell delivering a copy to Bradshaw, Oldenburg taking off a supply overseas. He made sure that copies were sent to Patrick Young, Keeper of the King's Library at St. James's, and to John Rous, Bodley's Librarian, to ensure that his writings were preserved for posterity in 'a temple of perpetual memory'.

And it is much the same intellectual 'academy' he had in mind for his poetry, a new literary audience which was very much what Drayton and Daniel had been looking for. He found a publisher in Humphrey Moseley, who had made a name for himself printing editions of genteel authors like Waller, Davenant, Crashaw, Shirley and Carew. With this help he produced a collected edition in 1645, prefaced by a portrait of the author (not uncommon procedure if the author were dead, but an extremely rare innovation for a living author). And it is clear from the Latin work published, as well as prefatory letters in Latin from Italian friends, that the book is aimed primarily at an educated public, complete with commendation from Wotton, the whole demonstrating without shame or modesty that Milton had a high reputation among 'the learnedst *Academicks*, both domestick and forrein'. When *Paradise Lost* was finally published in 1667, Milton reached an agreement with the publisher, Samuel Simmons, that with each of the first three impressions thirteen hundred copies were to be 'retail'd off to particular reading Customers' (even this general sale seems highly selective), while two hundred were to be made available to the author for personal distribution. Milton was thus reaching forward to the system of subscription patronage used by the Augustans. Indeed the fourth edition of *Paradise Lost*, Jacob Tonson's in 1688, was one of the first subscription editions recorded. From the list of over five hundred subscribers, we have some idea of the identity of the 'academy', 'fit audience, though few', Milton hoped to address —along with the noblemen, leading intellectuals like Atterbury, Betterton, Dryden, L'Estrange, Southerne, Waller. By then the poet was dead, but there is plenty of evidence that he found in his own lifetime the special audience of educated, cultured people, at home and abroad, which he needed. Secure in his context, like Pope many years later, he unearthed old manuscripts and published everything he could lay his hands on: an *Accedence Commenc't Grammar*, a *History of Britain*, the treatise *Artis Logicae*, and even juvenilia preserved for forty two years, and personal correspondence. It is in these latter years, after achieving his own revolution, that he feels free to criticize the idols of his youth, rejecting them along with whole Tudor system, and we find hard comments from him about rhyme, sonnets, Sidney, Shakespeare and even Spenser.

Milton's chief contribution to the professionalization of poetry was thus the identification and achievement of an elite audience within the printed-book public. The important thing is that this is a literary elite rather than a social, and a literary elite whose tastes the nobility followed. In earlier times the *litterateurs* had had the worst of the argument. The row between Thomas Nashe and Gabriel Harvey was based upon Harvey's attempt to claim respect for one of his 'standinge in the Universitye and profession abroade' and to anathematize 'the Beacheroule of Inglish Rimers'.[14] It was unfair to class Nashe with the rednose fiddlers: there was a third group, the skilled courtly writers with the gift of golden speech who put in the shade both the pedants and the balladists. Ultimately, Nashe could rest his case on Sidney's dictum 'I have found in divers smal learned Courtiers, a more sound stile, then in some professors of learning.'[15] Unfortunately, Nashe as a writer for print placed himself with the popular entertainers and lost his claim to superiority, in the eyes of Harvey and nearly everybody else. In those days a social superiority implied a literary superiority, and the printed-book audience had no class at all. The printers knew very well that among their audience were the satellite gentry of the universities and Inns of Court, and many printed books were specifically addressed to this special public; but as yet this was a small public and in the sixteenth century such addresses and claims to gentility were primarily catchpenny with the general public, as we can see from the many books which were designed for tradesmen and their apprentices and wives but which are dressed up as if for courtly folk. Spenser's difficulty (and Drayton's and Daniel's) was that he was tied to a social elite. He added to the published *Faerie Queene* sixteen dedicatory sonnets, seeking out particular Privy Councillors or gracious ladies, but the multiple dedication, which was a method adopted by several poets—including Thomas Churchyard, Joshua Sylvester, Michael Drayton, Thomas Drant, Gervase Markham, Barnabe Barnes, John

[14] *Letter-Book of Gabriel Harvey*, 1573–80, edited by E. J. L. Scott (Camden Society, 1884), pp. 59 60.
[15] *Defence of Poesie*, edited by A. Feuillerat (1923), p. 43.

Davies of Hereford and Henry Lok—was merely a development within the system of patronage, like the early subscription editions by John Foxe and John Taylor, the Water Poet, and the private editions by such as Samuel Daniel. Milton's development was of a different order altogether. At a time of social revolution, when the traditional social elite became the enemy of the Commonwealth he advocated, he had to look for a new and literary aristocracy.

Before Milton, Ben Jonson, rather than Spenser, is the poet who concerns himself most with literary elites. For all the complaints of 'poore Ben', he was luckier than most with his social context. At different times he had good patrons: Lord d'Aubigny, with whom he lodged five years, Sir Walter Raleigh, Sir Robert Townshend, the Countesses of Rutland, Bedford and Derby, and Charles I whom he served as king's poet with an annuity. After Shakespeare, he was the most successful man of the theatre of the day: actor, playwright and masque-writer, earning about twenty five pounds a year throughout his career in the theatre alone (having connections not only with the public and private playhouses, but with the Revels and the children's companies). He had a connection with the City of London, serving for a time as chronologer, one of the few really important antiquarians of the time. And he had a good publisher in Edward Blount. He suffered the usual trials of rough times: imprisonment for *Eastward Ho!*, censorship with other plays, trial for murder and popery. But he won a kind of proud independence for himself. And it is plain he had no respect for the empty-headed, whatever social class they belonged to. He refused to write down in the theatre for the 'grounded judgments' fit only for sweeping up the stage and gathering the broken apples for the bears within. His 'well-thought-out plays' were not for the groundlings who wanted 'Jigges and Dances': indeed no other writer is so overtly neo-classical and contemptuous of the muddles of the public playhouses. The bright young university men win all the battles in his plots. He wrote as he pleased and told the audience 'By —— 'tis good, and if you like't you may.'[16] 'I have here set it down whole: and doe heartily forgive their ignorance whom it chanceth not to please.'[17] On the other hand, there were times when he welcomed an ignorant audience: 'If thou can'st but spell, and join my sense, there is more

[16] *Cynthia's Revels*, epilogue. *Ben Jonson*, edited by C. H. Herford, and P. and E. Simpson, Vol. IV (1932), p. 183.
[17] *Hymenaei. Ben Jonson, op. cit.*, Vol. VII (1941), p. 225.

hope of thee than of a hundred fastidious impertinents.'[18] He was irritated by courtly fashions, both inside the theatre and out of it: he loathed writing that was 'imbrodered' and 'painted', 'writh'd and tortur'd', and growled 'Nothing is fashionable, till it bee deform'd: and this is to write like a *Gentleman*. All must bee . . . affected, and preposterous.'[19] He detested the pretentious ill manners of the stage gallants. And as a dedicated writer, he had little sympathy with the amateurisms of his age:

> Poetry in this latter Age hath prov'd but a mean *Mistresse*, to such as have wholly addicted themselves to her, or given their names up to her family. They who have but saluted her on the by, and now and then tendred their visits, shee hath done much for, and advanced in the way of their owne professions (both the *Law*, and the *Gospel*) beyond all they could have hoped, or done for themselves, without her favour.[20]

Jonson was the first poet who elevated intellectuality above court-liness. He produced an *English Grammar* and other scholarly disserta-tions. He lectured on rhetoric. He accepted honours offered to his high intellectual status: a burgess-ship at Edinburgh, an honorary degree at Oxford. He insisted on scrutinizing his plays through the press. He published his collected poems and prose in 1616 as 'Workes'. He set up at the Mermaid 'the right worshipfull Fraternitie of Sirenaical Gentle-men', a fanciful title for what was primarily a seriously intellectual club concerned with establishing a literary elite. His chief friends, and manuscript audience, consisted in the main of fellow-scholars—Sir Robert Cotton the antiquarian, whose fine library was used by Bacon, Camden, Selden and many other scholars; Hugh Holland, Queen's Scholar at Westminster and Fellow of Trinity College, Cambridge; Inigo Jones, the architect and art-collector; John Selden the jurist; and younger 'wits' like Francis Beaumont and Sir Kenelm Digby. Groups of friends, listening to, criticizing and planning literature together, were integral parts of the courtly system: long before Sidney's 'Areo-pagus', groups existed in all kinds of centres—country homes, Inns of Court, universities, acting companies, the Revels Office. Jonson's group is different for three reasons: it is devoted to the publication of

[18] *New Inn*, Address to the Reader.
[19] *Discoveries. Ben Jonson, op. cit.*, Vol. VIII (1947), p. 581.
[20] *ibid.*, p. 583.

I

scholarly works in print; it cuts across social distinctions and is primarily literary; and it is formalized as a club with a habitat and a name.

The difference becomes clearer if we compare Jonson with Donne. Donne took no interest in print until the years round about 1610, when he published the *Anniversaries*, the *Elegy on Prince Henry*, and his theological prose, *Pseudo-Martyr* and *Ignatius his Conclave*. This was a period when Donne was poor, and needed money; when he was a nobody and needed help to be 'incorporated into the body of the world'; and when he was in acute distress about whether or not to accept a career in the Church, and needed to rehearse his part to satisfy himself of his worthiness. He applied for the posts of Secretary in Virginia and Clerk to the Privy Council, but the direct result of his publications was to convince James, and himself, that he had 'the abilities of a learned Divine; and will prove a powerful Preacher'. He used print, as Shakespeare did with *Venus and Adonis*, to advertise his talents and to extend his patronage. He began to publish his sermons and devotions in the last nine years of his life; but most of these, and all his other poems, remained out of print during his lifetime. As we learn from his letters to Sir Henry Goodyere, he regretted very much 'to have descended to print anything in verse', and cannot pardon himself.[21] He was fundamentally the courtly satellite whose poetry was essential to his private life and thinking, but whose primary ambition was non-literary and who therefore saw no justification in making poetry public. And the circle of friends who comprised his manuscript audience were associates from politics and the Inns of Court: their function for him was only partially literary. They included other writers whose ambitions lay outside writing—men like Sir Henry Wotton, diplomat, Provost of Eton and Member of Parliament; Sir John Davies, attorney-general, serjeant-at-law and Member of Parliament; John Hoskyns, serjeant-at-law, justice and Member of Parliament. Jonson would have regarded them for all their intellectual earnestness as amateurs and would have been utterly contemptuous of the kind of attitude voiced by Hoskyns, for instance:

> . . . we study according to the predominancy of courtly inclinations: whilst mathematics were in requests, all our similitudes came from lines, circles and angles; whilst moral philosophy is now a while spoken of, it is rudeness not to be sententious. And for my part

[21] Edmund Gosse, *Life and Letters of John Donne* (1899), Vol, I, pp. 303–4.

I'll make one. I have used and outworn six several styles since I was first Fellow of New College, and am yet able to bear the fashion of the writing company.[22]

One can hear Jonson growl 'fastidious impertinent'.

Yet most people were like Donne and Hoskyns rather than Jonson and Milton. If one lists the major poets of 1600–60, the scene has changed very little from the Elizabethan. Very nearly all the poets earn their major living in courtly service: poetry is important in their private lives, and within their own circles of friends, but they are those whom Jonson would describe as saluting poetry 'on the by', and now and then tendering their visits. There are leading courtiers, like Sir William Davenant, Sir John Davies (at one time Lord Chief Justice), Sir John Denham (Surveyor General of Works), Edward, Lord Herbert of Cherbury or Sir Henry Wotton. Then there are their major satellites, men like Thomas Carew (Sewer to Charles I and Gentleman of the Privy Chamber), Abraham Cowley (Secretary to Queen Henrietta Maria), and others like Richard Lovelace, Andrew Marvell, George Sandys, Sir John Suckling and Edmund Waller. On the fringes of the court, but still very much part of the system, were William Browne, tutor to the Herberts, Thomas Campion the musician, Francis Quarles the secretary and Robert Herrick. Herrick is an interesting example of a 'failed' courtier, a poet who stayed in the system too long for his own good. Like many others, he was in no hurry to enter the Church, his most obvious career (he delayed his M.A. until 1620 and his ordination until 1629), because he looked for political preferment which was denied. His life at Dean Prior was second-best for him, and deprived of London, we find him manufacturing for himself a local circle of genteel *litterateurs*.

There are very few independent of the court, notably the physician Henry Vaughan, and country gentlemen with landed estates, like William Drummond of Hawthornden (but he was related to the Scottish royal family), Sir Edward Fairfax and William Habington, one or two 'journalists' like George Wither, and some churchmen— George Herbert (but he had 'court-hope' and his brother was Lord Herbert), Richard Crashaw (but he had connections with the court in exile and was a protegé of Queen Henrietta Maria), and the two Fletchers, Giles the Younger, and Phineas. The court thus remained

[22] *Directions for Speech and Style*, edited by H. H. Hudson (1935), p. 39.

predominant in the lives of poets, and this primacy was retained and intensified at the Restoration, for the great majority of poets, and indeed dramatists, in the last four decades of the century were directly attached to the court: in poetry, Denham and Davenant were joined by younger men like the Earl of Rochester, the Earl of Dorset, Sir Charles Sedley, Shadwell, Godolphin and Dryden; and in drama, the leading writers were the Earl of Orrery, Sir George Etherege, William Wycherley, Sir John Vanbrugh and William Congreve, all of whose careers were founded upon the court. The point does not need to be laboured: for all the reaching forward of Milton and Jonson, there is very little difference between 1580 and 1620 and 1680 in the social contexts of poetry.

What *is* remarkable with all these writers, as with Jonson and Milton, is a rapidly changing attitude to print. With each decade the Elizabethan stigma of print fades, until after 1640 there is very little of it left though the phrases of apology linger on as clichés, fashionable expressions of modesty. Donne's attitude in 1610 was soon to be old-fashioned. Some poets, it is true, continue to avoid print in their own lifetimes, or at least until the year or two before their death—Beaumont, Carew, Crashaw, the Herberts, Suckling, Traherne, Wotton. But the majority now find themselves compelled to publish. In the following list of representative poets, the first date is that of their first authorized edition (never their only published volume, in most cases the first of several) and the second date is that of their death:

William Browne	1613	?1645
Thomas Campion	1596	1620
Abraham Cowley	1633	1667
Sir William Davenant	1638	1668
Sir John Davies	1596	1626
Sir John Denham	1655	1669
William Drummond	1613	1649
Phineas Fletcher	1633	1650
William Habington	1634	1654
Francis Quarles	1629	1644
George Sandys	1621	1644
Henry Vaughan	1646	1695
Edmund Waller	1664	1687
George Wither	1613	1667

Several other poets authorized one volume of poems in their middle years, notably Herrick (1648, died 1674), Lovelace (1649, died ?1657) and Marvell (1655, died 1678).

But this is a silent revolution of attitude. Apart from Milton, the poets give no reasons for the increasing respectability of print. It seems an inevitable process of change accepted as a necessity rather than a *volte-face* rationally undertaken. Undoubtedly the Civil Wars hastened the trend, because the close-knit manuscript circles were scattered by the exigencies of war; but, on the other hand, poetry like drama was a casualty of war. There was much less poetic activity, partly because poets had other things to do, and partly because the ruling authority, from 1642, was Puritan and hostile to all forms of fiction. In any case, it is best not to seek for some external social force which conditions the context of poets: social forces are agglomerates to which the poets themselves contribute, the products of a complex alignment of attitudes, symptomatic rather than causatory. And changes of attitude are difficult to date and to categorize.

We know that the writing of poetry remained a necessary social accomplishment, like skills in other arts, right through the seventeenth century. As late as Robert Walpole, statesmen sent poems to each other in their diplomatic bags, a practice which had been a habit since Henry VIII and Elizabeth. It was making poetry public which was offensive, because this turned an artist into a craftsman, and until well into the eighteenth century Grub Street was anathema. John Selden's derision is typical:

> It is ridiculous for a lord to print verses; 'tis well enough to make them to please himself, but to make them public is foolish. If a man in a private chamber twirls his band-string, or plays with a rush to please himself, it is well enough; but if he should go into Fleet Street, and sit upon a stool and twirl a band-string, or play with a rush, then all the boys in the street would laugh at him.[23]

And a hundred years later Chesterfield has the same emphasis:

> I cannot help cautioning you against giving into those (I will call them illiberal) pleasures (though music is commonly reckoned one of the liberal arts), to the degree that most of your countrymen do when they travel to Italy. If you love music, hear it; go to operas,

---

[23] *Discourse of John Selden Esq.*, edited by S. H. Reynolds (1892), pp. 135-6.

concerts, and pay fiddlers to play to you; but I insist upon your neither piping nor fiddling yourself. It puts a gentleman in a very frivolous, contemptible light. . . .[24]

In all the arts the heaviest social stigma fell upon the practitioners, those who earned a living from playing music, painting pictures, or writing poems for print: the poets seem to have won through to respectability first, and then the painters, but the distinction between *artiste* and *artist* survives to our own times to a considerable extent, particularly in music and drama, and is likely to continue to survive in any art which distinguishes between the craftsman and the creator. In Elizabethan times printed poems were inextricably linked with the 'reakhellye route of our ragged rymers', the 'rednose fiddlers' (that damning musical metaphor), the Eldertons and Tarltons and Deloneys. Those who really made no bones about seeking print, like Nashe and Greene and Munday, ran an insuperable risk through association. In the early seventeenth century it was the same: George Wither was not of mean origin or education, but his whole story of conflict with patrons and stationers is intensified by his refusal to observe courtly decorums and the consequent readiness of his adversaries to consign him to social oblivion. But while the term 'poet' was apt to have this unhappy social flavour, at the same time, after Sidney's neo-classic assertion of the *divina vis* of poetry, it carried connotations of genius and creativity almost totally opposite. Lord Chesterfield despised practitioners, but he recognized at the same time that the creative arts were valuable and, as he confessed to his son, 'I used to think myself in company as much above me, when I was with Mr. Addison and Mr. Pope, as if I had been with all the Princes in Europe.'[25] This dichotomy between the creative artists and Grub Street can be evidenced right through the seventeenth century. The kind of respect which was only given to the Sidneys and Grevilles in Elizabeth's time is gradually conceded to dedicated writers, to Milton and Dryden, and before them to Jonson and Waller, and before them to Daniel and Drayton; but it was not conceded to popular entertainers.

One can distinguish a number of strands in the complex. The preeminence of the courtiers themselves, so notable from Wyatt and Surrey through to Sidney and Greville, declines throughout the seventeenth century. There is a specific attempt at the court of Charles II to restore

[24] Letter from London, 19 April 1749.
[25] Letter from London, 9 October 1747.

this, along with other departed Stuart glories, but for all the brilliance of Rochester and his set, the amateurs by then stood little chance. Congreve and Dryden modelled their writing on the *conversation* of Rochester, but Congreve and Dryden were the *literary* leaders. Ultimately, the courtly aristocracy slipped back into the medieval pattern: they became patrons rather than practitioners, and as time went on, it must be said, less and less intelligent patrons. There is an interesting study to be made of the levels of literacy and taste among the hereditary aristocracy: certainly, the Renaissance flowering of culture seems a transient aberration from the general pattern (and even then it was confined to a minority, though an influential minority) in which the nobleman does not really need to be literate. Certainly, by the middle of the eighteenth century, to judge from the state of the universities or the public theatres, centres where the patronage of the aristocracy was still indispensable, the nobleman's personal proficiency in literary matters is at unmistakable nadir.

This left the field increasingly clear for literary aristocrats, for whom print was the necessary medium. The emergence of the literary 'squire' is also tangled with another strand, the breaking away from the songs and sonnets, the lyrical forms of the Renaissance, and the cultivation, under neo-classic influences, of forms which carried a much superior social status. The men whose ambition was epic poetry could not be classed with the fiddlers. The poets became respectable scholars. The term *scholar* has its ambiguities too. Society had long recognized the eminence of its leading thinkers, men like Bacon, Elyot, Sir Thomas More and Camden. But because of the low status and pay of the ordinary university fellow, 'poor Schollers', as Gabriel Harvey and George Wither knew, were little better regarded than fiddlers, despite the need of the age for their services as educators, controversialists and translators. The Puritan drive to assert a higher standard of public morality brought a great deal of patronage to writers of theology and works of piety, far more than that enjoyed by the authors of *belles-lettres*. The Civil Wars further stimulated the market for such scholars. But the social value of scholars declined after 1660, and by the middle of the eighteenth century university dons were as ill thought of as ever and the qualities of their scholarship were unremarkable. But the temporary association of poets with other learned writers left one permanent mark. The work of scholars needed to be printed: though they did not always seek print, there is no stigma attached to the publications of

Bacon, Sir Thomas Browne, Burton, Camden, Fuller, Hobbes, Henry More, Jeremy Taylor, Izaak Walton or any of their kind. The more poetry was seen to be the comcomitant of learnedness, the more natural was print as a medium of communication.

A third strand contributing to the respectability of print was what might be termed the 'intellectualization' of poetry, a development in response to better-educated audiences. Elizabethan taste was pretty much the same at all social levels. The same plays delighted the court, the private theatres and the public playhouses. Shakespeare and Marlowe did not have to write down for the groundlings, because the knockabout farce, and jigs and antics and brutal bloodinesses, which thrilled the butcher and baker were equally well loved in the Lords' Rooms. The different levels of reception were not so antipathetic that they interfered with an essential unity. And, by and large, the same was true with printed poems of that time: the generation brought up on doggerel broadside ballads made good sellers, not only of books of psalms and homely didactic jingles, but also of *Venus and Adonis*, *Hero and Leander*, and many a courtly anthology which had found its way into print. But this unity does not survive the reign of James.

The best index to changes in taste is provided by the theatre, where public taste observedly splits after the turn of the century, as is apparent in the establishment from 1609 of private theatres, with more expensive seats and more genteel comfort. Indeed, the story of the seventeenth century is one of decline for the public theatre and advance for the private theatre, so that after Puritan repression for the duration of the war and the Commonwealth regime, only a coterie theatre survived at the Restoration. For some time writers continued to produce plays in a form suitable for production anywhere, whether at the court or on tour in universities or country homes, or at the small private theatres, the Blackfriars and Whitefriars and Phoenix, or at the large public Globes and Fortunes and Hopes. But the dividing of the ways is seen: some writers like Tom Dekker and Philip Massinger deliberately seek out themes and plots to please the middle-class groups; others, like George Chapman and John Ford, select themes which would best be understood only in a coterie theatre. And those who try to play for all the audiences increasingly become short-tempered with lack of success. Even Ben Jonson, in later plays like *Bartholomew Fair* (1614), loses some of his poise. John Webster publishes *The White Devil* (1612) in justification of his play which had lacked 'a full and understanding Auditory', quotes Horace, Martial and Euripides in its defence, and calls the Globe 'open and black' and the audience there 'ignorant asses'. John Fletcher, trying the difficult formula of romance in *The Faithful Shepherdess* (?1609), complains that the audience seemed to expect 'a play of country hired shepherds in gray cloaks, with curtailed dogs in strings, sometimes laughing together, and sometimes killing one another', a *pot-pourri* of 'Whitsun-ales, cream, wassail, and Morris-Dances'. Francis Beaumont savagely parodies the tastes of the Citizen and his wife in *The Knight of the Burning Pestle* (1613). One recognizes the same note of learned and dedicated protest against popular taste that one finds in printed poetry from Drayton and Daniel. Nearly all the dramatists are courtly satellites, men of wit and culture, and their ambitions are no longer being met in the public playhouses.

All these strands combine to make print more acceptable, and the trend is helped on its way by publishers who are beginning to have literary, as distinct from commercial interests: Edward Blount, William Ponsonby, Simon Waterson, Humphrey Moseley. English books of *belles-lettres* begin to find their way into libraries, public and private: where Sir Thomas Bodley found English books 'idle bookes, and riffe raffe' in 1605, John Rous, Bodley's Librarian from 1620 to 1652, was the friend of Milton and the man who admitted to the shelves the Burton collection with its plays, novella, maskings and other works of imagination in the vernacular. From 1630, when the annual production of books was about four hundred and sixty, the printing presses for the first time really expanded output: by 1640 the total was nearly six hundred, and during the Civil Wars, counting pamphlets of all kinds, must have been near two thousand. In this output the writers of new works had their opportunity; and in the sixteen sixties, when the dust subsided, there was an established printed-book industry turning out nearly a hundred completely new titles each year.

At every point of this brief survey the main conclusion is that from 1600 to 1660 the chief development in the social context of poetry has been the emergence of an educated and intellectual printed-book public. Socially, the Elizabethan social structure continues virtually unchanged: London remained the magnetic metropolis, the court spread out its ramifications into the satellite circles of the great houses, the Inns of Court, the universities. Indeed, the system intensifies: perhaps there is a natural law by which all things harden, are taken to extremes, are fully exploited, before they can be replaced. Certainly, the coteries make

their mark in early seventeenth-century London and the elites assume
more and more power: already the London 'season' has begun, and
by the sixteen thirties there are parks and pleasure gardens, coterie
theatres and hackney coaches and sedan chairs, the things we tend to
associate exclusively with the later age of the squirearchy. Culture
remains centralized in 1650 as well as in 1610 and 1680. What really
alters history, and literary history, is the cumulative effect of generation
after generation produced by the *carrière ouverte*: in any year between
1600 and 1650 there were liable to be at least five thousand students at
the two universities, with hundreds more in residence in the four Inns
of Court. We can see the effect of this steady annual enlarging of
London's cultured intellectual minority in the multiplication of important groups of friends (even polymaths like Wotton and Clarendon
and Walton could not possibly belong everywhere), the multiplication
of important social centres, the proliferation of new theological groups
or sects (over eighty of them by 1650, and not really a surprising
development if one considers the overwhelmingly theological bias of
all tertiary education at the time), and not least in the printed-book
market where the intellectuals in the end became the most important
public of them all (in numbers as well as in purse-power).

   In a word, then, the social context of poetry between 1600 and 1660
becomes intellectualized. The new writers and readers are recruited into
the Renaissance courtly system with all its established structures, and
apart from the growing respectability of print, an inevitable development as we have seen, the system changes little. But the consequences
of the growth within a basically unchanged system of a serious reader-
ship, which ultimately led to the invention of new literary forms like
the novel, and new literary media like the periodicals and newspapers,
and to the establishment of a literary profession itself, are to be noted
first, in the seventeenth century, by the gradual emergence of poetry as
a national and learned art, which increasingly takes itself seriously and
draws away from its roots in popular entertainment. If dissociation may
be used as a social rather than a literary term, from the reign of James
onwards we see the schism developing, not to close for centuries and
by no means healed even in our own times, between minority and
majority taste, with all the consequences inherent upon the social
functions of literature for ages to come. This intellectualization gave us
Milton, and ultimately Dryden and Pope and their 'schools', and we
would not be without them. But it lost the saving grace of the courtly

age, the unity of the audiences, and through that unity, the universality of poetry. In the making, in the seventeenth century, we have that 'death' of poetry after Pope, of which Johnson was so painfully aware, and the creation of circumstances which were ultimately to lead to the Romantic revolt and to the conflicts of our own times.

Note

The crucial documents in the development of the English concept of metaphysical poetry are: John Dryden, 'A Discourse Concerning the Original and Progress of Satire' (a convenient modern text may be found in *Essays of John Dryden*, edited by W. P. Ker, 2 vols., Oxford, 1926); Samuel Johnson, 'Life of Cowley', in *Lives of the Poets*, edited by G. Birkbeck Hill (Oxford, 1905); H. J. C. Grierson, introduction to *Metaphysical Lyrics and Poems of the Seventeenth Century* (Oxford, 1921); T. S. Eliot, 'The Metaphysical Poets' (1921), in *Selected Essays* (1932); J. Smith, 'On Metaphysical Poetry', *Scrutiny*, II (December, 1933). Significant elaborations of the concept are to be found in G. Williamson, *The Donne Tradition* (1930); J. Bennett, *Four Metaphysical Poets* (Cambridge, 1934); H. C. White, *The Metaphysical Poets* (New York, 1936); J. B. Leishman, *The Metaphysical Poets* (Oxford, 1934); and C. Brooks, *The Well-Wrought Urn* (New York, 1947). Various aspects of metaphysical poetry are illuminated by the following works, which stand out from a large body of important scholarship: M. Praz, *Secentismo e marinismo in Inghilterra* (Florence, 1925) (English translations of the component chapters of this work may be found in Praz, *The Flaming Heart* (Garden City, 1958); L. L. Martz, *The Poetry of Meditation* (revised edition, New Haven, 1962); M. H. Nicolson, *The Breaking of the Circle* (revised edition, New York, 1960); R. Wallerstein, *Studies in Seventeenth-Century Poetic* (Madison, 1950); J. A. Mazzeo *Renaissance and Seventeenth-Century Studies* (New York, 1964); R. Ellrodt, *Les Poètes métaphysiques anglais*, 2 parts (Paris, 1960); and A. Esch, *Englische Religiöse Lyrik des 17. Jahrhunderts* (Tübingen, 1950).

For the concept of baroque literature, the following works have special importance: R. Wellek, 'The Concept of Baroque in Literary Scholarship', in *Concepts of Criticism* (New Haven, 1963); J. Rousset, *La Littérature de l'âge Baroque en France* (Paris, 1953); L. Nelson, Jr., *Baroque Lyric Poetry* (New Haven, 1961); and the essays collected in *Deutsche Barockforschung*, edited by R. Alewyn (Cologne and Berlin, 1966). The concept of mannerism is treated in widely divergent ways by E. R. Curtius, *European Literature and the Latin Middle Ages*, English translation by W. R. Trask (New York, 1953), and W. Sypher, *Four Stages of Renaissance Style* (Garden City, 1955).

Metaphysical poetry as a general European phenomenon is treated in A. Boase's pioneer studies of French literature of the Baroque period: 'Jean de Sponde, un poète inconnu', *Mesures*, 5 (1939); 'Poètes anglais et français de l'époque baroque', *Revue des sciences humaines*, new series, 55–6 (1949); and 'Then Malherbe Came', *Criterion*, 10 (1931). It is treated in a more extensive way in O. De Mourgues, *Metaphysical, Baroque and Précieux Poetry* (Oxford, 1953), and in the following studies by F. J. Warnke: 'Marino and the English Metaphysicals', *Studies in the Renaissance*, 2 (1955); 'Jan Luyken: a Dutch Metaphysical Poet', *Comparative Literature*, 10 (1958); and *European Metaphysical Poetry* (New Haven, 1961). The presence of metaphysical poetry in Spanish literature is convincingly demonstrated in two articles by E. M. Wilson: 'Spanish and English Religious poetry of the Seventeenth Century', *Journal of Ecclesiastical History*, 9 (1958); and 'A Key to Calderón's *Psalle et Sile*', *Hispanic Studies in Honor of I. Gonzalez Llubera* (Oxford, 1959).

X

Metaphysical Poetry and the European Context

FRANK J. WARNKE

★

A MID the terminological confusion that plagues English literary history, as it does that of other national cultures, the term 'metaphysical poetry' has a gratifying degree of relative clarity, a certain distinct reference to a definable concept which has taken shape in the writings of critics during the three centuries which separate us from the age of Donne and Marvell. We associate the phrase 'the metaphysical poets' with Dr. Johnson—justly enough, in view of the shrewdness with which that worthy identified the characteristics shared by Donne, Cowley and a number of other seventeenth-century figures. And yet the critical perception of some sort of important association between the poetry of these figures and speculative philosophy—'the metaphysics'—is far older than Johnson.

Dryden, for example, censures Donne for the fact that he 'affects the metaphysics . . . and perplexes the minds of the fair sex with nice speculations of philosophy.' Still earlier, during Donne's own time, William Drummond of Hawthornden in a letter to a friend clearly refers to Donne and similar poets in a condemnation of the contemporary fashion which reduces poetry to 'metaphysical ideas and scholastical quiddities' (see Wallerstein, p. 26). Both Drummond and Dryden seem to be working from principles of decorum which they feel that some seventeenth-century poets violated, and these principles, for both the late Renaissance critic and the early neo-classical one, include a more or less rigid compartmentalization of the kinds of poetry and of the kinds of diction and imagery appropriate to each. The language of speculative philosophy has its place in philosophical poetry or satire, but it is not suitable for the amorous lyric—or, presumably, for the poetry of private devotion.

The earliest perceptions of something 'metaphysical' in metaphysical poetry have thus to do with questions of diction and propriety, and they posit absolute norms from the viewpoint of which a large body of earlier seventeenth-century poetry seems aberrant. An implication which may prove worth pursuing is that in the strictures of Drummond and Dryden we find expressions of an inevitable antipathy felt by an earlier age of classicism (the Renaissance) and a later age of classicism (the Augustan age) towards a period falling between the two, a period which, in its assumptions and techniques, is non-classical, perhaps even anti-classical. Johnson, the spokesman for a more rigid classicism than Dryden's, nevertheless expands the description of metaphysical poetry in highly significant ways. To him we owe the perception of some sort of link between the learned language of the poets in question and the type of metaphor which distinguishes their practice—the conceit: 'a combination of dissimilar images, or discovery of occult resemblances in things apparently unlike. . . . The most heterogeneous ideas are yoked by violence together . . .' ('Life of Cowley'). From Johnson's time to our own, criticism has tended to focus on the question of metaphor as central to the concept of metaphysical poetry: the twentieth-century critics who have given conceptual shape to the modern revival of a taste for poetry of this sort—Grierson, Eliot, Brooks and others—have to a large degree accepted Johnson's formulation while reversing the valuation which he had placed upon the phenomenon described.

The question of precisely why a fondness for the language and concepts of metaphysics should be coupled consistently with a habit of expression through conceits requires further investigation. Eliot finds in the metaphysical poets a mechanism of sensibility which is 'constantly amalgamating disparate experience', and that critic's influential concept of a 'unified sensibility' underlying the practice of metaphysical poets and Jacobean dramatists implies at once a capacity for uniting thought and emotion and a capacity for forging unlike images or experiences into new wholes. Subsequent commentary on metaphysical poetry has suggested some bases for the distinctive sensibility expressed by it: James Smith sees the basis in 'an overwhelming concern . . . with problems either deriving from, or closely resembling in the nature of their difficulty, the problem of the Many and the One' ('On Metaphysical Poetry', *Scrutiny* II (1933), pp. 222–39); Joseph Mazzeo sees it in an implicit new poetic springing from the conception of the universe as composed, by the 'wit' of God, of universal correspondences or analogies, in the light of which everything created is potentially identifiable with everything else (*Renaissance and Seventeenth-Century Studies*, New York, 1964); Louis L. Martz sees it in the practice of formal religious meditation, which, influencing not only devotional but also secular poetry, reveals a mind disciplined in the ways of bringing into unity the memory, the analytic intellect, and the 'affections', or emotions (*The Poetry of Meditation*).

Whether or not one agrees with the polemical aspect of Eliot's essay (and few readers of the present would accept his view completely), one may readily grant that he has characterized the effect of metaphysical poetry with memorable eloquence. And whether or not one would regard such explanations as those of Martz and Mazzeo as exclusively sufficient, one would find it difficult to deny that they have made major contributions to our understanding of what metaphysical poetry is and why it elicits from us the particular reactions it does. After Martz's work, in particular, it will be impossible for any informed reader to respond to Donne, Herbert and the others in the naïve, if enthusiastic, manner of many critics of the nineteen twenties. We can no longer deceive ourselves into treating these poets as our contemporaries, but we can understand, perhaps, how they seem so profoundly sympathetic to the contemporary mind.

The insights of critics and the findings of scholars have, over the years, refined the descriptions offered by Dryden and Johnson and corrected the biases implicit in those descriptions. From their labours has emerged a concept of metaphysical poetry, generally accepted in its broad outlines, which one might phrase roughly as follows: a kind of poetry created in England during the first two thirds of the seventeenth century, distinguished by a radical use of conceited imagery, rational or argumentative structure, a specifically intellectual emphasis manifesting itself usually in a non-sensuous texture, a language—sometimes colloquial, sometimes learned—from which all traces of special poetic diction have been purged, a markedly dramatic tone, and a preoccupation, in both amorous and devotional poetry, with themes of transcendence and aspiration.

It may seem perverse, with a sound and clear conception of such poetry already an achieved fact, to attempt to point out the connections between this poetry and a broader historical pattern, a more inclusive geographical scope. Nevertheless, the attempt is necessary, for several reasons: firstly, the survival of the mistaken belief that metaphysical poetry is a 'school' and, more specifically, a 'school' composed of imitators of John Donne;[1] secondly, the belief, related to this, that metaphysical poetry is a strictly English phenomenon; thirdly, the existence of 'metaphysical' poetry in France, Germany, Spain, Holland, Italy and perhaps other continental countries; and lastly, the literary traditions and historical developments shared by England and the continent, traditions and developments which make the existence of metaphysical poetry outside England inevitable.

I shall point out a few of the more striking examples of European metaphysical poetry, and I shall try to identify metaphysical poetry in general as one stylistic manifestation of a distinct period in European literary history—a period which follows the Renaissance and precedes neo-classicism. One might as well call the period the baroque, and one might regard metaphysical poetry as one important variety of baroque literature. To employ the term *baroque*, especially in English or American literary circles, is, still, to invite controversy—not only from those who hold that the term has no place in literary studies, but also from those intent on defending the particular sense in which they use the term. Since, however, to conceive of the earlier seventeenth century as a late stage of the Renaissance is, to my mind, to endanger the possibility of a better comprehension of metaphysical poetry, and since the term baroque has already gained wide currency, its use seems indicated.

As I shall use the term, baroque will refer not to a precisely definable and analysable style but to a period, that is, to a time-span dominated by a series of norms, a selection of which conditions the style of any given writer or group of writers expressing themselves during that period.[2] Within the baroque period a number of alternative stylistic directions may be discerned: one of these is the metaphysical; another is the hectic, flamboyant, highly coloured style which is, for some commentators, the essential baroque (the term is used in this sense by De Mourgues and, with a different emphasis, by Sypher). To this latter stylistic direction I apply the term 'high baroque'. Both styles, I believe,

[1] One can understand the assumption of such a relationship in Williamson's *The Donne Tradition*, written at a time when many aspects of metaphysical poetry were still to be illuminated. It is more difficult to understand the reappearance of the assumption in such a recent work as A. Alvarez, *The School of Donne* (1961). For metaphysical poetry in England before Donne, see Martz (on Robert Southwell); see also *The Poems of William Alabaster*, edited by Helen Gardner and G. M. Story (Oxford, 1959).

[2] *Cf.* the conception of literary period in R. Wellek and A. Warren, *Theory of Literature* (New York, 1949).

can be found both in England and on the continent, and the two styles, rather than constituting exclusive choices or commitments on the part of the individual poet, show a degree of interconnection and overlap. Donne and Herbert are among the purest of metaphysical poets (although there are high baroque patches in Donne, notably the beginning of the 'Second Anniversarie'), but for a poet like Crashaw it seems to be largely a question of mood. 'The Weeper' is a horrid example of high baroque style carried to an extreme, and the 'Hymne to St. Teresa' is a notable triumph of the same style, but 'Charitas Nimia' and the letter 'To the Countess of Denbigh' are in the controlled, colloquial, intellectual manner of the metaphysicals.

Crashaw has long been considered a kind of sport in English literary history, an exotic Italian import like pasta or castrati. It is true of course that Crashaw's work was strongly influenced by Giambattista Marino, the most acclaimed of Italian baroque poets, but the latter two of the poems alluded to above are sufficient to suggest that Crashaw himself felt no essential discrepancy between the wit of Marino and the, to us, very different wit of Herbert. To assume that the native English style is metaphysical and that the continental style contemporaneous with it is high baroque is misleading—almost as misleading as to consider the metaphysical a Protestant style balanced against the high baroque as a Catholic style.

The work of the French devotional poet Jean de la Ceppède may provide a good point from which to approach a number of related questions: first, of the existence of metaphysical poetry in the continental literatures; second, of the interpenetrations of metaphysical and high baroque style; third, of the final irrelevance of the concept of influence to a consideration of metaphysical poetry as an historical phenomenon. La Ceppède's *Théorèmes Spirituels* were published in two volumes, the first in 1613, the second in 1621. The title of the work is in itself an indication of the similarity between it and the devotional verse of Donne, Herbert and Crashaw. The sonnets which make up the volumes are spiritual exercises, but they have the form of 'theorems'; that is, the religious emotions of the speaker and, presumably, of his audience are to be activated by the presentation of truths which are capable of rigorous intellectual demonstration. (For La Ceppède see De Mourgues, as well as my *European Metaphysical Poetry*.) The fusion of emotional and intellectual elements in the title of the work, at the same time that it suggests the practice of the English metaphysicals,

reminds us of Martz's observations on the technique of formal meditation and also of Eliot's aperçu concerning the unified sensibility.

Nevertheless, the *Théorèmes Spirituels* often express themselves in the
ardent sensuous imagery characteristic of the high baroque style. The
following sonnet on the suffering Christ will serve as an example:

> Voicy l'Homme, ô mes yeux, quel object deplorable
> La honte, le veiller, la faute d'aliment,
> Les douleurs, et le sang perdu si largement
> L'ont bien tant déformé qu'il n'est plus desirable
>
> Ces cheveux (l'ornement de son chef venerable)
> Sanglantez, herissez, par ce couronnement,
> Embroüillez dans ces joncs, servent indignement
> A son test ulceré d'une haye execrable.
>
> Ces yeux (tantost si beaux) rébatus, r'enfoncez,
> Ressalis, sont hélas! deux soleils éclipsez,
> Le coral de sa bouche est ores jaune-pasle.
> Les roses, et les lys de son teint sont flétris:
> Le reste de son Corps est de couleur d'Opale,
> Tant de la teste aux pieds ses membres sont meurtris.
>
> *(European Metaphysical Poetry*, p. 100)

The intensity with which the French poet dwells on the lacerated
beauty of Christ's body recalls Crashaw, as well as numerous continental poets of the baroque: it is only in the intimate address to the self
with which the poem begins, and in the subtlety with which the poet
notes the mystery of divine beauty allowing itself to be turned into
ugliness, that we note points of connection with the central traditions
of metaphysical poetry.

Elsewhere La Ceppède is considerably closer to Donne and Herbert,
as in this poem of impassioned supplication:

> Maintes fois j'ai tenté de vous suivre, ô ma vie,
> Par les sentiers connus que vous m'avez ouverts:
> Mais toujours, mais toujours, vos ennemis divers
> M'empoignant au linceul m'ont la force ravie.
>
> Ores que saintement votre Esprit me convie
> De retracer vos pas, par les pas de ces vers,
> Ce monde, ce charmeur, cet ennemi pervers,
> Me prenant au manteau, veut frustrer mon envie.

De mille vains objets il rend mon cœur épris
Dont l'amour me tient tant, et si longuement pris
Qu'à peine aurai-je temps de vous suivre au Calvaire.
Faites donc, s'il vous plaît, ô Seigneur, désormais,
Que de l'Adolescent imitant l'exemplaire,
Je quitte ces habits au monde pour jamais.
(*Anthology of French Seventeenth-Century Lyric Poetry*,
edited by O. De Mourgues, Oxford, 1966, p. 69)

The intimacy of the address to Christ is one of the results towards which meditation consciously strives, and the urgent imperative of the sestet, so suggestive, to the English-speaking reader, of Donne's *Holy Sonnets*, has the intensely dramatic quality which typifies the literary baroque. It is a metaphysical poem, and its occurrence in France at its time of publication demonstrates the inadequacy of theories which regard metaphysical poetry as an exclusively English phenomenon or as a style resulting from the influence of Donne (the date of publication of the *Théorèmes* renders untenable any suspicion of imitation of Donne by La Ceppède).

La Ceppède's devotional verse is far from being an isolated example of continental metaphysical poetry on religious subjects. The *Lágrimas de un Penitente* and other poems by Francisco de Quevedo are striking analogues in Spanish baroque literature, as the following sonnet, with its characteristic wit, will perhaps suggest:

Pues hoy pretendo ser tu monumento,
Porque me resucites del pecado,
Habítame de gracia renovado
El hombre antiguo en ciego perdimiento.

Sino retratarás tu nacimiento
En la nieve de un ánimo obstinado,
Y en corazon pesebre acompañado
De brutos apetitos, que en mi siento.

Hoy te entierras en mí, siervo villano,
Sepulcro á tanto huesped vil y estrecho,
Indigno de tu Cuerpo soberano.
Tierra te cubre en mí de tierra hecho:
La conciencia me sirve de gusano:
Marmol para cubrirte dá mi pecho.
(*European Metaphysical Poetry*, p. 268)

In this prayer before Communion, the speaker begs for spiritual renewal, pointing out to Christ that, if He does not transform the sinner's soul, He will retrace the pattern of His birth—in the snow of a cold heart, surrounded by the beasts that are the speaker's appetites. He concludes with a plea that the unworthy earth of his body be transformed into marble worthy of receiving the body of God.

Quevedo's contemporary Lope de Vega frequently fuses conceited metaphor with intimate address to the deity, as in the superb 'Pastor que con tus silvos amorosos', of which the affinities with English metaphysical poetry have been noted by E. M. Wilson:

> Pastor, que con tus silvos amorosos
> me despertaste del profundo sueño,
> tú, que hiciste cayado de esse leño,
> en que tiendes los brazos poderosos:
>
> Vuelve los ojos a mi fé piadosos,
> pues te confiesso por mi amor y dueño,
> y la palabra de seguirte empeño
> tus dulces silvos, y tus pies hermosos.
>
> Oye, pastor, que por amores mueres,
> no te espante el rigor de mis pecados,
> pues tan amigo de rendidos eres.
> Espera pues, y escucha mis cuidados,
> ¿pero cómo te digo que mi esperes,
> si estás para esperar los pies clavados?
>
> (*European Metaphysical Poetry*, p. 258)

In this example of what Martz calls 'sacred parody', Christ as shepherd is identified with the amorous shepherd of pastoral tradition—among other things, he 'dies for love'. The concluding lines typify metaphysical wit in a forceful manner: colloquially the phrase 'los pies clavados' has approximately the meaning 'rooted to the spot', but literally, of course, it means bluntly 'with feet nailed'.

Lyrics of this sort may be encountered all over western Europe from the end of the sixteenth century onward—in the *Heilighe Daghen* of the Dutch poet Constantijn Huygens, the only continental metaphysical poet influenced by Donne (see Rosalie Colie, *Some Thankfulness to Constantine*, The Hague, 1956); in some of the religious sonnets of the

Italian philosopher Tommaso Campanella; and in numerous devotional poems by the German Paul Fleming, an example of which should perhaps be cited:

> Erhöre meine Noth, du aller Noth Erhörer,
> Hilff Helffer aller Welt, hilff mir auch, der ich mir
> selb-selbst nicht helffen kan; ich suche Trost bey dir.
> Herr, du hast Rath und That. Dich preisen deine Lehrer,
> wie du es denn auch bist, für einen Glaubens-mehrer.
> Ich bin desselben Lehr. Hier steh' ich, Ich steh' hier.
> Erfülle mich mit dir und deines Geistes Zir.
> Er ist es, Er dein Geist, der rechte Glaubens-mehrer.
>
> Artzt, Ich bin kranck nach dir. Du Brunnen Israel,
> dein kräfftigs Wasser löscht den Durst der matten Seel'
> Auch dein Blut, Oster-Lam, hat meine Thür erröhtet,
> die zu dem Hertzen geht. Ich steiffe mich auff dich
> du mein Hort, du mein Felss. Belebe, Leben, mich.
> Dein Todt hat meinen Todt, Du Todes Todt, getödtet.
>
> *(European Metaphysical Poetry*, p. 180)

As Martz's arguments would imply, the consistently meditative traits of seventeenth-century religious verse may explain some of these deep-seated stylistic resemblances. But in secular poetry too one finds the metaphysical note sounded all over Europe. In a love poem of the late sixteenth century, Jean Bertaut writes such stanzas as these:

> Ne vous offensez point, belle ame de mon ame,
> De voir qu'en vous aymant j'ose plus qu'il ne faut:
> C'est bien trop haut voller, mais estant tout de flamme
> Ce n'est rien de nouveau si je m'éleve en haut.
>
> Comme l'on voit au'au ciel le feu tend et s'elance,
> Au ciel de vos beautez, je tens pareillement:
> Mais luy c'est par nature, et moy par cognoissance;
> Luy par necessité, moy volontairement.
>
> *(European Metaphysical Poetry*, p. 108)

Another French poet, Pierre Motin, mingles religious reference and profane context in a manner suggestive of the Donne of the *Songs and Sonets* and 'Elegie XIX': in one poem he pleads for a physical demonstration of his lady's favour on the theological grounds that faith without 'good works' is ineffective; elsewhere he argues that the girl, whose surname is 'La Croix', should observe the symbolism of her name by granting him mercy.

Théophile de Viau and others of the so-called *libertin* poets of France combine colloquial diction, dramatic tone and sexual realism in a way resembling that of the English metaphysicals; Huygens shows the impress of his English travels in his amorous poems as well as in his religious; and Fleming has a sequence of love lyrics in which questions of identity and the exchange of identities in the love relationship are debated with much display of intellectual subtlety in combination with dramatic immediacy (see, for example, 'Auff ihr Abwesen' and 'Uber seinen Traum', both in *European Metaphysical Poetry*, pp. 170–2).

Sometimes the continental love poets duplicate the tone of such lightly metaphysical English lyrists as Carew, Suckling and Cleveland. Hofmann von Hofmannswaldau, for example, combines amorous aggressiveness, tender jocularity, rueful playfulness and a touch of the 'metaphysical *frisson*' (the term is George Williamson's) in his 'Vergänglichkeit der Schönheit':

> Es wird der bleiche tod mit seiner kalten hand
> Dir endlich mit der zeit um deine brüste streichen,
> Der liebliche corall der lippen wird verbleichen;
> Der schultern warmer schnee wird werden kalter sand,
>
> Der augen süsser blitz, die kräffte deiner hand
> Für welchen solches fällt, die werden zeitlich weichen,
> Das haar, das itzund, kan des goldes glantz erreichen,
> Tilgt endlich tag und jahr als ein gemeines band.
>
> Der wohlgesetzte fuss, die liebliche gebärden,
> Die werden theils zu staub, theils nichts und nichtig werden,
> Denn opfert keiner mehr der gottheit deiner pracht.
> Diss und noch mehr als diss muss endlich untergehen,
> Dein hertze kan allein zu aller zeit bestehen,
> Dieweil es die natur aus diamant gemacht.
> (*European Metaphysical Poetry*, p. 188)

The historical pattern of metaphysical poetry on the continent parallels closely that of English metaphysical poetry. The work of La Ceppède, Quevedo, Huygens and Fleming, like that of Donne, Herbert and Crashaw, is based implicitly on a world-view which assumes the validity of universal correspondences or analogies which relate everything in creation to everything else, a view which assumes also a solidly hierarchical arrangement of entities in a rationally comprehensible universe (see Mazzeo and Nicolson; see also E. M. W. Tillyard, *The Elizabethan World Picture*, London and New York, 1944). The challenge to traditional cosmology presented by the new astronomy is a source of tension and dramatic conflict in the metaphysical poets, but for those mentioned above the inherited world-view is finally viable enough to be reaffirmed (see, for example, Donne's 'Anniversaries', Herbert's 'Man' and La Ceppède's 'Aux monarques vainqueurs').

By the middle years of the seventeenth century, the old world-view had become untenable in a straightforward form. The unitive impulses which lie beneath metaphysical poetry had, however, not become extinct. In England a number of expedients manifest themselves in what amounts to an unconscious re-formulation of the bases of metaphysical style. In Andrew Marvell the traditional correspondences are replaced by a radically individualistic, almost self-sufficient wit, and his poetry, without losing the cerebral quality of Donne and Herbert, directs itself towards an exploitation of external nature, a subject which had held scant interest for the earlier metaphysicals. In Henry Vaughan, also, nature becomes a principal focus—nature perceived as a set of mysterious hieroglyphics capable of transmitting an arcane wisdom beyond the reach of rational refutation or revision. In Thomas Traherne, the last of the English metaphysicals, traditional theology and the doctrines of analogy associated with it yield to an extreme reliance on individual intuition which seems almost proto-romantic in some of its thematic concerns—the world of the child, for example, or the phenomenon of wonder.

No poetry on the European continent is much like the remarkable work of Marvell, but the nature poetry of Théophile de Viau and Marc-Antoine de Saint-Amant in France shows certain resemblances, particularly in its tendency to move swiftly from vivid sensuous evocation to complex elaborations of wit. Indeed, there is some possibility that Marvell was influenced by these poets (see Wallerstein, pp. 276–7, 306–17). Vaughan's nature mysticism and his reliance on esoteric doctrine find significant analogues in the gnomic verses of Angelus Silesius and Daniel von Czepko in Germany, but his closest continental counterpart is the Dutch poet and mystic Jan Luyken, whose deeply moving devotional poetry relies as strongly as does the

English poet's on a highly personal sense of the significance of nature (see my 'Jan Luyken: a Dutch Metaphysical Poet'). Again like Vaughan —Angelus, Czepko and Luyken draw heavily on mystical philosophers like Jakob Böhme and on arcane traditions deriving from Hermeticism and from Alexandrian neoplatonism.

The characteristic attitudes of Traherne find an intensified parallel in the work of the eccentric German poet and religious leader Quirinus Kuhlmann, who, after wandering all over Europe preaching a new religion with himself as its head, was tortured and burned at the stake in Moscow in 1689. What is, in Traherne, an individualism pushed to the point of mild heterodoxy becomes, in Kuhlmann, a monomania saturated with what would be, from the point of view of any established faith of the baroque age, heresy. Neither poet is capable of the sustained achievement of Donne, Herbert, Marvell, La Ceppède, Quevedo or Fleming, but each achieves his occasional fragmentary triumphs, in which the individual sensibility, pushed to its utmost limits, catches a glimpse of that totality of being which the earlier metaphysical poets had celebrated in terms of an ordered cosmology and the ordered discipline of formal meditation.

Any assertion of a causal relationship between a literary style and the intellectual stimuli of the age which produced it is bound to remain unprovable. Nevertheless, the making of such assertions is an irresistible temptation, and one to which I shall duly succumb—although, I hope, with a certain degree of caution. Various historical 'causes' have been cited for the baroque literary styles in general and metaphysical poetry in particular. Among the most popular are the impact of the new science, especially the heliocentric astronomy of Copernicus as given support by the findings of Galileo and Kepler, and the influence of a heightened religious sensibility conditioned by the Reformation and Counter-Reformation (for the influence of science, see Nicolson; for the general religious temper, see Martz and Praz). It has also been suggested (for example, by Mazzeo) that these styles are the result of a new development in theoretical poetics, the introduction of a 'poetic of correspondences' which places radical metaphor, or conceit, at the centre of all poetic creativity, justifying the critical shift in terms of a theological conception of the created universe as metaphorical. Another suggestion attributes most baroque stylistic phenomena to an intensified concern with time and with dramatic relationships (Nelson).

It will be noted that the first two explanations are of a different order from the second two. To explain metaphysical poetry as the result of new scientific ideas or of religious sensibility is to explain literary phenomena by reference to non-literary phenomena. To explain it as the result of critical thought or technical emphasis is to explain it from within literature itself. The first approach risks to an extreme degree the inconveniences of unsupported assertion: how can we be certain that the cited extra-literary developments have *caused* the style under examination? The second approach risks not answering the question at all: are not the poetic of correspondences and the emphasis on time and dramaticality in themselves aspects of the style in question? In the latter event they are parts of the same literary development, the causes of which have yet to be ascertained.

It is, of course, possible to argue the position that metaphysical poetry (and baroque literature in general) is the result not of extra-literary stimuli but of a necessary rhythm within literary history itself —the curious systole and diastole which seem to decree that an age of classicism like the Renaissance will be followed by an age of anti-classicism (*expressionism* and *mannerism* are other terms which have been used to designate the recurrent constant: for differing uses of the term *mannerism*, see Curtius and Sypher). To uphold such a position it is not necessary to be either a mystic or a determinist. In any culture, when a certain range of artistic values has been cultivated, with an ever-increasing technical proficiency, for a considerable length of time, it is only to be expected that a point of saturation will eventually be reached and that sooner or later a sense of those values lying outside the range of the established style and clamouring for expression will lead some particularly forceful and independent poet—a Donne, a Théophile, a Marino, a Góngora—to formulate a new style to give expression to the neglected values.

No one literary style can conceivably give voice to the entire range of values accessible to literature (by 'range of values' I understand a concept embracing both theme and technique). In western literary history as a whole, two general ways of seizing experience and giving it artistic shape have recurrently crystallized themselves, and it is to the observation of their alternating epochs of domination that we owe the western concept of literary period. To the first of these modes of perception, and to the kind of style resulting from it, tradition has applied the term *classicism*; there is little agreement as to an appropriate term for the second mode and its style: one might do well to follow Curtius in using the term *mannerism*. A classical period is one dominated by aspirations towards symmetry, decorum, rationality, relative objectivity and the faithful mimesis of observed reality; a manneristic period is one dominated by impulses towards asymmetry, violation of decorum, fantasy, relative subjectivity and the imaginative distortion of observed reality. If a formulation of this sort is accepted, the baroque period takes its place as one of the major eras of European mannerism.

A theory of historical oscillation through a constant process of reaction may explain why a style change occurred in European literature in the closing years of the sixteenth century, but it does not explain why the emergent style assumed the particular conformation it did. Manneristic impulses in reaction against the classicism of the Renaissance may, it is true, account not only for some of the traits of baroque poetry but also for the poetic of correspondences developed concurrently by such theorists as Gracián in Spain and Tesauro in Italy—a poetic which, after all, sees the imaginative distortion of the universe as the poet's principal task. Similarly, the baroque preoccupation with drama, both as a genre and as a tone modifying other genres, may be seen in the context of reaction against the Renaissance emphasis on narrative. And the baroque obsession not only with the theme of time but also with other themes evoking an awareness of the illusory quality of existence makes accessible whole provinces of reality which Renaissance art, with its balance, its stability, and its assumption of the provisional or emblematic reality of the physical world, had tended to avoid.

Nevertheless, the specific content and devices of baroque art must be at least conditioned by extra-literary stimuli, and one is compelled to assume that the manneristic reaction of the late sixteen hundreds took its typical directions under the influence of new intellectual discoveries or a heightened religious sensibility or, as is most likely, of both. Metaphysical style, in this general context, reveals itself as a special, and especially intense, form of baroque art—one both related to and significantly different from high baroque poetic style. The intellectual ferment typified by the new science is present in the high baroque works, accounting to some extent for the imbalance and hectic tension which characterize them. But this ferment has proceeded further in the metaphysical works, permeating every aspect of both theme and texture. It is not so much that specific references to the new science or arguments for or against it are frequent in metaphysical poetry (Donne's 'Anniversaries', Etienne Durand's 'Stances à l'Inconstance' and several of Kuhlmann's poems are exceptional in this respect); it is rather that metaphysical poetry derives much of its essential nature from an awareness of the mutual validity of opposed truths, an awareness which issues as paradox and which is very plausibly traceable to a tension between the claims of intellectual tradition and those of intellectual innovation.

Baroque religiosity is present in high baroque poetry as symbolic description and ritualized gesture; it is present in metaphysical poetry as an intensely personal effort to establish a kind of private contact with the deity. Formal meditation, of such enormous importance to the century of the baroque (see Martz), exerts its influence in different ways on high baroque and metaphysical poets: for such poets as Crashaw, Andreas Gryphius and Joost van den Vondel it supplies a repertory of symbols; for such poets as Donne, Herbert, La Ceppède and Fleming it supplies a means of creating a self in which intellect and emotion are both fully alive and fully identified with each other.

For the high baroque poet, drama is spectacle; for the metaphysical poet, drama is essence. Crashaw's poetry, like Marino's, is theatrical in its showy impact, in its representation of reality as a shifting phantasmagoria of unstable stage sets (see Rousset for a consideration of baroque stagecraft as symbolic of baroque literature). Donne's poetry, like that of Marvell, or Théophile, or Quevedo, is theatrical in that the creation of the self as character and the purposeful playing out of the role on the stage of the poem are felt not as an avoidance of reality but as a unique experience of reality: in a world which is, like Shakespeare's, itself a stage, to select a role and play it through is a spiritual release from the role-playing of mundane existence—which is, since unchosen and unconscious, a kind of bondage.

Finally, the central baroque concern with the illusoriness of the phenomenal world issues in divergent ways for high baroque and metaphysical poets. In Góngora, Marino, Gryphius and Crashaw we find an imagery of fantasy and distortion, the deployment of which suggests an assumption that the world of sensuous experience, essentially unreal, may be toyed with at the artist's discretion: that world may be formed and re-formed into verbal artifacts which, previously non-existent, possess as much validity as what we think we perceive in what we think is nature. In the metaphysical poets we find an imagery which tends to avoid all sensuous immediacy, whether of the mimetic

Renaissance sort or of the fantastic high baroque sort. The image drawn from the world of phenomena has its importance in terms not of what it suggests to the senses but of what order of relationship or function it conveys to the analytic intellect. Thus the 'stiff twin compasses' in Donne's 'Valediction: Forbidding Mourning', so often cited as a definitive example of the metaphysical conceit, share no sensuous qualities at all with the human lovers to whom they are compared: they stand in a certain relationship to each other, and only the evocation of the relationship interests Donne.

Marvell's image of the parallel lines to which he compares his and his mistress's loves in 'A Definition of Love' operates in the same way. Elsewhere in Marvell, as in Théophile de Viau and Saint-Amant, we encounter imagery evocative of external nature, but even here, although the practice is somewhat closer to that of the high baroque poets, the poet's concern is neither with the mimesis of nature for its own sake nor with the creation of an independent sensuous phantasmagoria for its own sake, but with spiritual relationships and functions pointed to by the image from nature.

High baroque and metaphysical, as I suggested earlier, display affinities and interconnections, but they are finally separable as distinct directions, or choices, within the baroque. The choice is determined, presumably, by the personality of the individual poet or, in the case of the poets of a mixed style, by the demands of his subject or the mood of the moment. Metaphysical poetry does seem to have flourished in some countries more than in others. England, Spain and Holland possess long and rich traditions of such poetry. France, after a brief but intense flowering of metaphysical poetry early in the seventeenth century, moves into an early neo-classicism. Germany presents some fine metaphysical poems but is more typically directed towards the high baroque style. Italy, perhaps because of the extraordinary strength of its Renaissance literature, offers very little metaphysical poetry, and its high baroque, as in Marino, often strikes the reader as a kind of perverted Renaissance poetry.

The dangers of excessive schematization notoriously afflict commentators on baroque art, and the foregoing observations may well have succumbed to these dangers. One assertion can, I believe, be made with complete confidence: metaphysical poetry is an international European phenomenon.

Index